Dear Doc...

The noted authority answers your questions on drinking and drugs

Joseph A. Pursch, M.D.

CompCare Publications
2415 Annapolis Lane
Minneapolis, Minnesota 55441

Grateful acknowledgment is made for permission to reprint the following:

Page 6: From *The Times of My Life* by Betty Ford with Chris Chase. Copyright ©1979. Reprinted by permission of Harper & Row, Publishers, Inc.

Page 27: Section entitled "The Making of an Addict Athlete" originally appeared in slightly different form as "Our Stars Fall with Our Help," copyright ©1984 by The New York Times Company. Reprinted by permission.

Page 37: Section entitled "Booze at the Top: The Alcoholic Executive" originally appeared in slightly different form, under the title "The Alcoholic Leader," in *Leaders* magazine, April/May/June 1981. Reprinted by permission.

Page 47: Section entitled "Cocaine in the Boardroom" originally appeared in slightly different form in *Leaders* magazine, July/August/September 1984. Reprinted by permission.

Page 70: Reprinted from *Where Have I Been?* by Sid Caesar. Copyright ©1981 by Sid Caesar Productions, Inc. and Bill Davidson. Used by permission of Crown Publishers, Inc.

Page 122: From *Wired,* copyright ©1984 by Robert Woodward. Reprinted by permission of Simon & Schuster, Inc.

Page 184: From *My Wicked, Wicked Ways* by Errol Flynn. Copyright ©1959 by G.P. Putnam (first edition).

Page 226: From the book *W.C. Fields & Me* by Carlotta Monti and Cy Rice. Copyright ©1971 by Carlotta Monti and Cy Rice. Reprinted by permission of the publisher: Prentice-Hall, Inc., Englewood Cliffs, New Jersey 07632.

Page 262: Excerpt from *The Letters of F. Scott Fitzgerald,* edited by Andrew Turnbull and Frances Scott Fitzgerald Lanahan, is used by permission of Charles Scribner's Sons. Copyright ©1963, Frances Scott Fitzgerald Lanahan.

Parts of this book originally appeared in the *Los Angeles Times* in slightly different form. Reprinted by permission.

Pursch, Joseph A. 1929–
    Dear Doc—.

    Includes index.
1. Alcoholism.   2. Drug abuse.   3. Substance
abuse.   I. Title.   (DNLM: 1. Alcoholism—popular works.
2. Substance Abuse—popular works.   WM 270 P986d)
RC565.P87   1985   616.86   85-5896
ISBN 0-89638-083-1

Inquiries, orders, and catalog requests should be addressed to
CompCare Publications, 2415 Annapolis Lane, Minneapolis, Minnesota 55441
Call toll free 800/328-3330
(Minnesota residents 612/559-4800)

Jacket design by Susan Rinek

Contents

Introduction

They Are Often Men and Women Who Made Great Things Happen

What's a nice person like you doing with a book like this? Chances are you don't have an alcohol or drug problem yourself, but you know somebody who does. You probably want to learn more about it, or maybe even do something about it.

For me, the kind of knowledge that you may be looking for literally "happened" in 1968. At that time I was a successful psychiatrist—or so I thought. I knew there were alcoholics and drug addicts in this world, but the enormity of the problem had never dawned on me.

I was the luncheon speaker at an overseas officers' club. I was booked as the Navy's medical expert on drug abuse. My topic was "Drug Abuse Among Young Soldiers," and I was speaking to officers and senior managers. After just a few minutes into my talk, I thought that I was really "on" that day; my occasional one-liners had them practically rolling in the aisles. But then it dawned on me that maybe something else had them almost rolling in the aisles—there were lots of empty beer bottles on most of the tables, and the gin and tonic was flowing freely. I was learning what every nightclub comic knows: jokes go better with booze.

Actually, there was a more profound lesson unfolding before me. While I was "enlightening" my audience about young soldiers getting high on marijuana and LSD, the officers themselves were getting loaded on booze. Almost in a flash, the "problem" was all very clear to me—they ALL had a drug problem! The youngsters were on pot and pills, and their bosses were on booze and beer. More significantly, after my speech these officers would return to their stations to dictate messages and make decisions and then the soldiers would type those messages and carry out the decisions. In that sense, we all had a chemical dependency problem because some of the decisions made and messages sent might well affect my job, your government contract, and our national safety.

How naive and half-blind I had been all these years! I asked myself, "How can I, as a 'medical expert,' talk about drug abuse to an audience, a good percentage of whom are legally drunk?" After a moment's thought I concluded that I was in the right place, and that I was doing the right thing—it's just that the emphasis was wrong. We had a drug problem all right, but it included alcohol as well as other drugs, officers as well as enlisted men, juicers as well as dopers.

Afterward, on the way to the airport, I was visibly upset. But when I confided my disturbing thoughts to a colleague, he helped me to see the big picture. "You're picking on the military, Doc," he said. "What do you think our civilian counterparts were having for lunch today in New York, Chicago, Detroit, and D.C.? Do you think they were drinking soda pop?"

Well, after a luncheon like that, you can't go home again. From that day on it was easy for me to see the big chemical picture. Over the ensuing months I was able to consciously realize—and gradually accept—what I had suppressed over the years. I saw again in my mind's eye—only this time more clearly—the terminally ill alcoholics I had studied in medical school; the production-line drunks I had treated at Detroit Receiving Hospital as an intern; the alcoholic Navy pilots I drank with in the Mediterranean; the alcohol-impaired congressmen, admirals and ambassadors, along with the brain-damaged sergeants, generals and senators I had worked with at Bethesda Naval and Walter Reed Hospitals.

It was clear now that these people were really no different from their (prescription) drug-addicted wives and their (recreational) drug-abusing children whom I had studied at Indianapolis General, Georgetown University Medical School, and St. Elizabeth's Hospital in Washington, D.C. Nor were they different from the civilian employees I had treated in the shipyards and repair facilities in Norfolk, Mobile, and Pensacola.

Strange as it may seem, I had never really seen them as they actually were. As a hard-working doctor I had always been very busy treating "real patients," (ulcer patients, cardiac patients, etc.) doing my own ego-gratifying thing, while giving short shrift to these alcohol- and drug-abusing patients because I saw them as people with a "self-inflicted illness" who were taking up my valuable time.

All along I had missed the obvious: the humanness behind the chemicals, the covert anger behind obsequious tears, the low self-worth under "big shot" airs, the loneliness behind the busy facade. I never understood that not a single one of them had set out to become an alcoholic or to get hooked on drugs; that they were not living like this by choice; that there were puzzling things going on in their brains and guts and genes; and that they all wanted to get well as badly as I wanted to make them well—all those things had never dawned on me.

Since then I've talked with countless drunks, junkies, families, cops, and coroners. At 3:00 a.m.—in dingy clinics, drafty emergency rooms, cheap tenements, and mighty mansions—the patients and their families come closest to telling you the truth because their eyes are wild with fear, their guts are churning with guilt, and their hearts are filled with remorse. I've also sat through hundreds of meetings (AA, Al-anon, NA, OA, CA, etc.)

on four continents—meetings in which those same people continue to tell mostly the truth.

What I've learned in all those sessions is that nobody ever wants to get hooked; and that those who are addicted can recover, even if it takes a series of slips and starts. I have also had to learn that next to the drugs themselves, you and I as the "enablers" are the addicts' biggest problem because we don't understand them and because we often do them more harm than good, in spite of our best intentions.

Having had the enviable fortune of treating some of the world's richest, smartest, most glamorous and most talented people, it is also clear to me that in the beginning, addicts and alcoholics are as different from each other as the prints on their fingers; it is only in the end that they become so much alike. I've also learned that far from being weak, passive, or spineless, they are often men and women who made great things happen.

Finally, from the tangible evidence of thousands of living examples I've learned that when they want to recover, they can be their own best therapists for the most part, especially if you and I have the strength, the wisdom, and the patience to sustain them in the right kind of rehabilitating environment while they are getting a handle on their problem. If we then use good judgment and help them gradually resume their rightful place among us, they'll be free of their chemical needs, strong enough to walk in dignity, and able to bear their own responsibilities gracefully.

The issues of chemical dependency are complex enough without adding to the confusion with the limitations of the English language. So, in the chapters ahead, I have chosen to use the pronoun "he" when speaking of men and women in general— merely for reasons of simplicity and clarity. Also, many of the sections you may recognize from "Dry Doc," the syndicated column I have written for several years. Other sections are new — based on new experiences, new ideas, and new insights.

This book, then, is about people who are different from you and me in one sense only: they use chemicals when you and I use other things. Almost everything I know about them, I've learned from them; through their ups and their downs, their deaths and their recoveries, this book was also written by them.

Hopefully, this book will be a turning point for you just as that luncheon was for me.

Since I began practicing abstinence, I have become more valuable to myself and to others. I think I was always a nice enough woman—I walked, I talked, I was polite when you got my attention—but for awhile, I had been unaware of how much went on around me, and I had no particular will to live. There are a lot of people out there in the world who exist like that. I don't think they have to, I think they can change.

At first, growth is slow, it takes patience. If you expect a party with balloons and confetti and music the minute you get off the pills, the booze, whatever your poison is, you'll be disappointed. No lights flash, no siren screams. But the process of healing is interesting in itself, and peace is its reward.

With peace comes new energy; I am filled with a vitality I haven't known since I was a young girl.

The Times of My Life
Betty Ford

1

From Better Living to Bitter Living through Chemistry

You are what you eat, they say; but maybe it's closer to the truth to say that you are the way you live. An objective look at how we live shows that our use of alcohol and other mind-altering drugs has become a way of life for most—and a lifestyle disease for many. The transition from one to the other may be imperceptibly gradual. From the first experimental drink . . . to occasional drinks . . . to weekend drinks . . . to daily drinks and weekend drunks . . . that may take twenty years. Life may be more fun in the beginning but as more and more of a person's lifestyle comes to depend on the drink, it turns bad in the end: it goes from *better* living through chemistry . . . to *bitter* living through chemistry.

Generally speaking, what's true for the drink is also true for the pill, the joint, the snort, the fix, etc. The major difference is that with alcohol it might take years, and with drugs only a few months. In any case what starts as a means to an end (a social lubricant, a friendly joint, a party snort), can slowly become the end in itself. Gradually, having fun of any kind takes on a chemical hue until we can't party, swim, ski, or make love without being high. Even spectator sports lose their kick unless they begin with tailgate parties and end where the score counts less than the brew, and the sport less than the snort. Eventually, Saturday night without a chemical boost is unthinkable, and "somehow" all of one's friends turn out to be drinking buddies or drug users.

But even for casual users the chemical lifestyle can be troublesome because mind-altering drugs affect our judgment and behavior. Regardless of where we are—in the bar or in the car, on the beach or on the boat, in our home or on a trip—the most likely reason we get jailed or injured is that we were "under the influence." Studies of people who are arrested for driving under the influence (DUI) most clearly show that many people who still think of themselves as social drinkers are already hooked. As a member of the President's Commission on Drunk Driving I came to see the real substance behind the grim statistics: More than half of all DUI first offenders need treatment because they are already dependent on alcohol or drugs; and the number one cause of death for members of the Armed Forces is driving under the influence.

Not surprisingly, our drug-using lifestyle reflects itself in day-to-day problems of American industry. On Monday morning the foreman of a plant in Detroit, the head man on a ranch in Texas, the dispatcher for a fleet of city taxis, and the president of a Wall Street firm all face the same number one problem: the consequences of their employees' weekend drug abuse. The Monday-Friday syndrome, with absenteeism, hangovers, and poor quality workmanship, is our chemical fallout. You have to hope your new car wasn't assembled on a Monday. And on Wall Street the expression "morning trader" has acquired a new meaning—it refers to somebody you don't deal with after lunch because his judgment is shot.

Thus, what starts as fun and games, the beautiful life, or the high life turns for many into a lifestyle disease. It goes from "This is the life!" to "This is life?" to "Life on the rocks," and "Life is the pits!"

The American Way of Drinking

When I take a medical history (which always includes a discussion of the patient's drinking style), many a patient is amazed at his actual intake of alcohol. To him, his drinking had always seemed average or normal. Now he feels that drinking kind of "sneaks up" on him. He suddenly realizes that many times in the past he drank when he had no personal need or intention of having a drink; that he often drank just because circumstance, custom, or another person's suggestion somehow manufactured the reason for drinking.

How do I help such a patient gain this insight? Simply by discussing with him the American way of drinking, and then helping him compare it to his own way of drinking. Let's each of us look at our own lifestyle and see just where, what, and why we drink.

For many of us, it's almost as if alcohol has become a staple of life. Like sugar and salt, we use it daily. From a psychological standpoint, we use it to control almost any shift in our emotions. We use it to assuage psychic pain, loneliness, feeling "ill-at-ease"; we also use it to celebrate and to mourn. Pharmacologically, we use it as a stimulant, anti-depressant, sedative, analgesic, tranquilizer, aphrodisiac, and (especially if it didn't work as an aphrodisiac) as a soporific.

We use it when we feel good, when we feel bad, to pick us up, to calm us down, as an eye-opener, and as a nightcap. At cocktail parties we use it to say hello, to break the ice, to get in step, to unwind, as a socializer, and a friendship maker. At dinner parties we use it as an appetizer, as a main beverage (beer or wine), as an after-dinner drink, and as "more of the same" during the late-evening socializing. Before we leave the party we have "one for the road" to sustain us as we drive home toward that nightcap, all to be followed in the morning by a Bloody Mary or "some hair of the dog."

Executives talk business while having martinis, and the salesman buys a round when he lands a contract. And if his pitch falls flat and the clients depart, he gulps a double to control his frustration.

In sports we drink at the clubhouse, at the golf shack, on the beach, during the hunt, and at the races. We drink cold beer at baseball games because it's hot in those bleachers; and we drink Irish coffee at football games because it's cold in those bleachers. World Series winners shower in champagne before the press and TV, while the losers get stoned in some unnamed hotel.

We drink when we hear good news, when we hear bad news, when we go off to war, to celebrate peace, to commemorate a birth or mourn a death. We drink at birthdays, reunions, Christmas, Halloween, and New Year's Eve. Drinking goes with courting ("Candy is dandy but liquor is quicker," said Ogden Nash), with engagements, marriages, anniversaries, and nowadays even with divorces.

Now let's go back to the patient in my office. When he sits down with pen and paper and does some hard addition of drinks he's had, it becomes clear to what extent drinking has become part of his life.

"Holy Perrier!" he is apt to say. "Why have I been drinking so much?" And after talking about it some more, I urge him to make the following resolution: "Since heavy drinking is not good for anybody, from now on I will drink alcohol only when I personally feel that I want to—not when others want me to, or when the occasion calls for it. That way, only I will be responsible for how much I drink. From now on, the invitation, 'What would you like to drink?' will literally mean *drink* and that will include soft drinks, coffee, fruit juices, etc."

As the result of such self-analysis, many of my non-alcoholic patients and friends have dramatically reduced their intake and are happy about it. They report that their sleep is improved, they are more alert, their sex life is better, they lose weight more easily, they save money, and they actually find time to smell the roses. In short, they savor life more because in the past their other senses were mildly, but almost continually, numbed by booze.

But there are still plenty of folks who haven't got the word yet. It seems as if the Pentagon, the Hill, the board room, suburbia, and the inner city—all can't do without booze. *The twin pillars of America are protocol and alcohol: Without protocol we don't know what to do—without alcohol we don't know how to do it.*

Relief Drinking Spells Trouble

From the amoeba to the genius, we all want to avoid stress. "Relief is just a swallow away" is a sign of our times, and alcohol is the most frequently swallowed relief provider. It's no surprise that relief drinking is an early sign of alcoholism.

When drinking makes you feel good, that's called social drinking. But when you drink to get relief—that's no longer social drinking. That's called medicinal or self-treatment drinking. It's time for you to see if a pattern is evolving.

Let's look at a typical case.

At first, good ol' Charlie has one martini with the boys after work at the Let's Relax Saloon. Groans of "Wow, what a day!" and "Boy, am I glad this day's over!" slowly give way to soft lights, sea stories, and back-slapping camaraderie. Social drinkers all. *But for some, a silent voice in the brain whispers, "How do you spell relief? B-O-O-Z-E."*

Months or years later, Charlie starts having an extra martini to steel himself for the rush-hour drive. And while his wife Betsy gets dinner, they have a martini together because it helps them to "communicate."

Eventually, even with a couple of drinks under his belt, Charlie still feels tense when he walks in the house. Betsy—harried-looking, one hand on her forehead, the other clutching her apron—says, "Oh, I'm so glad you're home. The washing machine broke down. Richie fell and had to have stitches, and my mother just called, and . . ."

Charlie, now really tense, cuts her off. "Don't talk to me until I've had a drink," as he heads for the liquor cabinet.

Shaken by the bad news, he settles in the family room and gulps his martini.

I'm sure Charlie thinks he is "just having a social drink." But he has, in effect, written a prescription for himself. Here is what the prescription says:

Patient's name: Good ol' Charlie.

Drug: Martini.

Dose: One double.

Directions: To be taken at once.

While Charlie is having his "social drink," Betsy withdraws to the kitchen. Without even thinking, she opens a kitchen cabinet, pulls out a vial of pills and takes a Valium. Thus, while Charlie is taking martinis, Betsy is taking Valium. You might say it's valtini time in suburbia.

Twenty minutes later she peeks into the family room. She can see that Charlie's medicine has taken hold. He's slouched on the sofa, one leg over the armrest with his loafer dangling from his foot, his collar open, necktie knot at halfmast. The TV is on, but he's not really watching. Even his facial muscles are relaxed. The transformation is complete. Relief was just a double away.

"Rough day, Charlie?" she asks soothingly.

"Nah, just the usual. But I'm okay now." He sounds much calmer. "And what's this about the dryer breaking down?"

"It's not the dryer, Charlie. It's the washing machine." She's still a little flustered.

But Charlie smiles broadly. "Washing machine, dryer, what's the difference? I'm gonna get a raise next month, remember?"

And with an expansive wave of the hand he says, "Buy a new one."

Betsy can sense that he is in the right frame of mind to settle complex issues, so she presses on sweetly, "Also, my mother called."

Charlie, taking another sip, is downright friendly. "Oh, yes," he says, "that's what you said when I walked in the house. And how is that dear lady?"

"Well," Betsy says cautiously, "she's arriving tomorrow night for a visit."

Charlie sits up ramrod straight. He realizes that he made a mistake on that prescription.

It should have read:

Patient's name: Good ol' Charlie.

Drug: Martini.

Dose: One double.

Directions: To be taken at once *and every 20 minutes for relief*.

For relief drinkers, a regular martini remedies things like office stress or rush-hour traffic; and a double takes care of a broken washing machine or stitches in your kid's face. But a mother-in-law visit calls for a higher dose of medication.

As Charlie heads for the liquor cabinet again, he growls, "Don't say another word until I pour another drink." And Betsy withdraws to the kitchen.

Charlie and Betsy both know that relief is just a few swallows away. What they don't seem to realize is that Charlie needs more and more swallows for less and less stress. It is high time for them to look at social drinking versus relief drinking.

Drinking Buddies Are Hazardous to Your Health

When an alcoholic is drinking, his buddies can be his worst enemies. That was certainly true for Bob. I saw Bob in consultation because on his third post-operative day as a surgical patient he was found drunk in his hospital bed. His doctor thought that Bob might have a "drinking problem."

"What's your reaction to that?" I asked Bob when I saw him in consultation.

"I only had a couple of drinks with my buddies," he said defensively. "They just happened to have some booze along when they came to visit. They meant no harm. After all, they're my best friends." He looked annoyed. "If you're gonna call me an alcoholic—I'm not gonna talk to you."

"Bob, I can't call you anything because I've never seen you before. Your wife Helen told me some things on the phone, but without talking to you, I can't really say anything."

"That's better," he said.

"Tell me about your drinking and your friends. At what age did you start?"

"I was 16. A friend kept bugging me to try it. I finally did. It was fun. A year later I started 'serious drinking' with an older buddy."

"What does serious drinking mean?"

"That's when the guys set out to get drunk, usually on Friday night." He suddenly looked up and decided to check his enthusiasm. "But we always did it on purpose. We knew what we were doing."

"When did it get to be a problem?"

"What do you mean—a problem?" he asked defensively.

"Helen says you insulted your boss once."

"Nah, she's exaggerating. Besides, I didn't mean it. Later my friends said, 'Relax, Bob. When you told the boss to stuff it, that wasn't you talking—that was whiskey talking.' Besides, I didn't even remember doing it."

"Do you often forget things like that?"

"Oh, maybe a few times." He looked up suspiciously. "What would that mean, anyhow?"

"It's called 'blackouts'—it means the brain is . . . ."

"Couldn't be serious," he interrupted, obviously not wanting to hear any more. "That happens to my buddies, too."

"Did you ever get hurt while you were drinking?"

"I broke my ankle once—I stole second base at a company picnic."

"Were you drinking?" I asked.

"Sure. It was a hot day, you know. But the guy on second blocked the base—that's really why I got hurt. My buddies said so."

"How much were you drinking?"

"Oh, maybe two six-packs. Couldn't have been much. I still remember the pain."

"Have you ever gone on the wagon?" I asked.

His face lit up. Here was a chance to show me that he was not an alcoholic. "Lots of times, Doc. I can quit any time I want to. A year ago Helen was bugging me, so I quit for thirty days—no problem."

"Did any of your friends stop drinking?"

"Last year Alex quit. We were surprised. We didn't expect that from him, but then we figured he probably got religion. Later I saw him once by accident. I was surprised. He wasn't religious at all. He said he had gotten treatment for a drinking problem. Didn't miss the booze, he said. He looked real good—made me wonder about myself for a minute."

"How is Alex now?"

"He still works at the plant; I hear he got promoted. Somehow I don't see him much."

I let Bob think for a while. "Have any of your drinking buddies died?"

"Last year we lost Herman. He was on our bowling team. But it's not what you think, Doc. It was a liver problem from the war."

"Bob, liver damage means it's time to get treatment so you can quit drinking. That'll give the liver a chance to heal. Now, if Herman . . ."

Bob held up a hand to slow me down. "In a case like that— maybe you're right, Doc. Herm might still be around if he could have quit."

"Bob, your tests show that you have liver damage, too."

"You mean the booze is gettin' to me? You know, Doc, lately my hangovers are worse. I told my buddies about it. They said, 'Just cut back for a while.' " He seemed thoughtful.

"Bob, sometimes your best friends are least likely to help, especially if they have the same problem. I remember Carlotta Monti talking about W.C. Fields and his friends. In her book, *W.C. Fields and Me,* she said, 'During his sickness, I kept arguing with his friends, begging them not to bring him liquor. With the medication he was taking, it was both torturous and dangerous for him to drink. Despite my precautions, they still smuggled in the bottles.' "

"Boy, they were friends right to the end, weren't they?" He was staring out the window, subdued.

"We're out of time, Bob. For your interview tomorrow I want Helen to be here with us; and Alex from the plant, ask him to come, too."

"Can't say that I'm crazy about that idea, Doc. Can I ask some of my drinkin' buddies to join us?"

I shrugged. "Sure, but I don't think they'll accept."

"Why wouldn't they, Doc?"

"Why does bologna shun the grinder?"

The Myth of the Happy Alcoholic

The happy alcoholic is a myth. He may appear happy to those of us who know him only casually, but if you're living with an alcoholic on a day-to-day basis, you know that his predominant mood is anger.

Generally speaking, all human beings know anger. We feel it, we hang onto it, and we vent it when we're fed up or provoked. But for alcoholics, anger is a more important issue. They learn to use it as a tool for emotional self-preservation.

Early in the disease, when they still have enough awareness so that they are conscious of situations and feelings which lead to *anger* drinking episodes, they learn to use anger to justify—in advance—the drinking they are about to do. In that way, they can later prove that they drank because they were provoked, that they were actually driven to drink by somebody else's action or behavior, and that they are therefore not alcoholic.

Take, for example, a functional alcoholic like Happy Hour Harry. After a hard day at the office, he feels tired and frustrated. On his way home, he decides to stop at his favorite attitude-adjustment clinic for just a couple of social drinks. In no time at all, he "just happens to strike up a conversation with two fascinating strangers."

He knows he should be going home right now. But the thought of squalling kids who need attention, broken toys that need fixing, and a harried wife who needs a partner—none of these can possibly compete with the soothing ambiance of the bar, the pleasure of swapping lies with sophisticated strangers, and a chance to spill maudlin confidences with "long-lost friends." (Actually, the long-lost friends he's talking to right now at the bar are people he'd never heard of until twenty minutes ago.)

In short—and through a mental process that only alcoholics seem to understand—Harry "knows" in a pre-conscious sense that he's going to get drunk again tonight. But since he is a decent sort of guy, he first has to justify it to himself, to his wife, and to his friends.

So he casually saunters over to the pay phone to call his wife.

"Liz, I'm tied up with some clients here." Heaving the weary businessman's sigh, he goes on, "You and the kids go ahead and eat . . ." He sounds almost self-pitying. "I'll be along shortly, as soon as I can get rid of these people."

He hopes he's pulling it off, but his wife has been playing this game almost as long as he has. Like spouses of souses everywhere, she too knows that Harry is going to get drunk again tonight. But just like Harry, she too, is powerless to change it.

"Harry," she begs, "*please* don't come home drunk again tonight. P-U-L-L-E-E-A-S-E don't do it, Harry."

By now Harry is into his act so well that he's beginning to feel downright indignant. "Liz," he says, feigning surprise, "I can't believe this is happening. Here I am, trying to scratch out a living for you people, and you talk to me like this!"

There is silence on the other end. By now Harry has steamed himself up enough so he actually feels white-lightning anger. "Lemme tell you something, Liz. Just for that—tonight I *am* gonna stay out, and maybe I will get drunk!"

He slams the receiver down. He is filled with justification, and he is devoid of guilt. Now he can rejoin his "long-lost friends" at the bar and get drunk in peace.

Once again, anger saved the day.

The Myth of the Sudden Alcoholic

Rarely will you ever find a senior citizen alcoholic who never touched a drop of alcohol until he or she was 40 or 50 years of age. The majority of them have been problem drinkers all along, even though nobody ever considered them to be alcoholic.

A most interesting, successful, and tragic type is the man who was endowed with an unusually healthy constitution which, for many years, enabled him to abuse his body and psyche by alcohol excess and workaholism. As a general rule his friends and colleagues tolerated him—even idolized him—because he "worked hard and played hard." Actually, his life was tenuously balanced on work and booze. Take away work—through retirement, layoff, or illness—and you have an "instant alcoholic" because all he has left is booze.

An example of such a case is a man whom we shall call Ray. He began drinking in his late teens. As a pilot in the Armed Forces, he was happiest at Happy Hour. He learned to drink abusively, but he always got away with it because he was a real party boy. "The best pilot we have—when he's sober." He got drunk frequently and into fist fights occasionally. His brawls got him at least one injury and several complaining girlfriends.

In civilian life as a salesman he drank heavily, especially on trips away from home, but he was always on the job and had no hangovers. He was admired and envied for his strong constitution. He could really hold his booze.

His wife complained from time to time, and some of his behavior raised a company eyebrow here and there, but as a top salesman at the office and a good provider at home, his drinking was looked upon as something that "goes with the territory."

When he became a vice president, he cut back on his drinking and focused more on working. And later, as president of the company, he was known throughout the industry as a bona fide workaholic and a heavy social drinker.

Outwardly a great success, he was in fact leading a very narrow life because work and booze were his only defenses. When his wife had a scare with cancer, and when his 26-year-old son was murdered, he briefly compensated by drinking too much for several months, but "who wouldn't drink at a time like this," people said.

Minor disappointments, like his daughter becoming a hippie, he handled by working harder and by repairing his injured self-esteem with more plaques for his den and more honors for the company.

Six months after retirement he was "suddenly" noticed to be a chronic alcoholic because he was drinking around the clock and neglecting himself. He was arrested for sleeping in his car by the side of the freeway. He also had high blood pressure, liver damage, early diabetes, and evidence of alcohol poisoning of his bone marrow. Ray was obviously going to die if he didn't stop drinking.

At this stage of his illness his wife came to see me with the question, "How can I get him to stop?" My answer was that she alone probably couldn't. I suggested that we hold a pre-intervention meeting without Ray's knowledge—a meeting which should include family members, but also the company doctor and the chairman of the board, both of whom Ray held in high esteem.

When this group shared with one another current impressions and past observations of Ray's functioning, they realized that Ray was sicker than any of them had thought. I was able to help them understand that he had actually been an alcoholic for the last 25 years, but had been able to function because of his robust constitution, his talent for talking his way out of trouble, his skill as a salesman and as a manager, his family's willingness to put up with his drinking, and his workaholism that benefited the company, even when he was president. At this point Ray was unable to help himself—but they could help him to help himself.

The next morning all of us met with Ray in an intervention setting. He was flabbergasted and confused, but he was still able to comprehend what we were telling him. Touched by the love and concern of his friends and family, he became tearful and accepted their recommendation to go for rehabilitation.

In the alcohol treatment unit of the hospital, his physical problems were carefully assessed. At the same time he was introduced to permanent abstinence.

In family treatment his wife and daughter learned how to support him emotionally without, at the same time, "enabling" his alcoholism any further. He was taken to Alcoholics Anonymous meetings where he met some recovering alcoholics who were also executives and professional men. Gradually he replaced part of his workaholism with hobbies and sports activities which he had discontinued over the years because drinking and working had become the mainstays of his life.

Ray, the sudden alcoholic, had gone from drinking and working to living and loving. The same people who had helped him stay sick had finally helped him get well.

Could You Pass a Drunk-Driving Test?

Alcohol and drugs cause all kinds of accidents, but probably the most outrageous are those involving drinking and driving—not only because of the number of people involved, and the fact that so often the innocent victims are the ones who die, but most regrettably because the accidents are avoidable. "If only," cries the perpetrator of the crime, "I hadn't had that one more for the road, those three children would be alive today!"

Have you ever thought that you could drive as well after a couple of drinks as you can sober? Or that the drunk-driving laws are too conservative?

Many seemingly reasonable people feel that way.

Spurred on by my recent appointment to President Reagan's Commission on Drunk Driving, I decided to put the idea to the test myself. How well could I drive under the new regulations?

My friend, Paul McAvoy, arranged for me to take the test of a drinking driver's first offender's course. A recovering alcoholic with 10 years' sobriety, Paul teaches such a course in Orange County, California.

"The program is very simple," Paul explained. "You first take the obstacle driving test when your BAC is 0. Then you drink to a blood-alcohol level of .10 and repeat the test."

That should be no problem, I thought. I am 52 years old, 5 feet 11 inches tall, and weigh 150 lbs. I have run a marathon, I am a psychiatrist with a busy practice, and I am a social drinker.

My lab partner in this drunk-driving experiment turned out to be Sylvia, 22, weight 120 lbs., height 5 feet 2 inches. A month ago she was arrested for drunk driving. She had been drinking when her boyfriend accused her of flirting with his boss. In a fit of anger she had left the party and totalled her car when her blood-alcohol level was .22.

We began the experiment by taking the drive-sober test through an obstacle course in the fairgrounds parking lot. Sylvia knocked down 13 rubber cones, and I knocked down 24. Next we sat down at the bar with soft lights, potato chips, pretzels and all. Under the watchful eye of a video camera, Chuck the bartender, a reporter, and my friend Paul, Sylvia and I started to get in shape for the real test. She drank red wine and I drank Scotch.

At the outset, the reporter's notes described me as cool, dignified, confident; Sylvia as shy, self-conscious, and reticent. Sylvia said she was nervous because I was a psychiatrist.

After about three drinks I had to start forcing myself to drink. I sensed a lack of control. "I'm not as sharp as I like to be," I said to the bartender, according to the reporter's notes.

Sylvia, on the other hand, was getting really loose. Giggling, she said, "I feel more and more in charge of myself." But she was also showing a change in personality. She became maudlin and described the troubles she had had with pot smoking; she relived the fight that had led to her accident and complained that she had been "falsely accused" of flirting by her boyfriend. Reliving this, she was momentarily down, but then she bubbled again. "I feel so good—this is the first time I ever talked to a real psychiatrist."

I remember wanting to quit the experiment at that point. Drinking was becoming a real effort. I had to "pump those drinks" to make my BAC go up, but Sylvia was becoming even more effervescent.

Walking to the breathalyzer, I found it necessary to put a little broad base into my walk (walking with feet wider apart) because I sensed a slight unsteadiness. Back at the bar I felt insecure. I was aware that the sharp edge was gone.

By contrast, Sylvia was becoming very friendly, comfortable, and happy with herself. She said, "Drinking like this makes me more trusting. The guys get better looking."

At the end of two hours Sylvia had had five drinks and I had six. On the finger-to-nose test, I missed my nose consistently. Walking to the rear, I really walked broad-based, a regular sailor-on-the-rolling-deck or wino-walk. I could tell I was impaired, but I was determined to hide it.

I asked Sylvia how she would do on the driving test now that she was drunk. She laughed. "I'm a little high," she said, "but I'm not drunk. I'll probably drive better than before because I now feel relaxed and confident."

Her BAC was .10—mine was .07. On the driving test she ran over the obstacles with impunity, knocking over 20 cones (13 when she was sober); and she created a new lane where there was none before.

I started out driving carefully and slowly to compensate for my relative lack of control and to do as well as possible. But without consciously intending to, I suddenly sped up, squealing tires during the turns in an effort to avoid hitting the pylons. I crunched 35 as opposed to 24 while sober.

A startling fact is that if I had been arrested driving on a highway at that point, I actually would not have been legally drunk because my BAC was only .07.

What did we learn from this experiment? Regardless of how well you think you'll do, regardless of whether you slow down or speed up to compensate for the effects of drinking—you'll do worse. It's clear to me that drinking and driving are unsafe at any speed.

Alcohol, Drugs, and Sports

To clinicians who treat alcohol and drug problems on a daily basis, the present controversy surrounding drugs in professional sports is like a flashback to the World War II Pentagon mentality.

Today it's hard to believe that as recently as 1965 the Secretary of Defense, with a straight face, was able to reassure the Congress that "alcoholism is incompatible with the discipline and stringent lifestyle which is required of the professional soldier." At that time alcohol- and drug-abusing servicemen were called weak sob sisters, and their stories were said to be exaggerated. "Anyway," the brass party line said, "nobody poured the booze down their throats. They have a self-inflicted illness; and they should be kicked out of the armed services because they're a disgrace to the uniform."

Clearly, the brass wanted this problem to go away because it conflicted with the image of the general, the soldier, the man. Because of this attitude and because alcohol and drug addiction were treated as a disciplinary problem resulting in dismissal without retirement of any offender, it is not surprising that in 1965 there were no "real alcoholics" or drug-abusers in the Navy, for example.

But by 1970, that same Navy was treating 20,000 new cases of alcoholism per year. Why? Because the brass had learned that if you treat these chemical casualties as patients who have an illness (rather than as characters who have a bad habit), and if you hold each of them personally responsible for maintaining his recovery, you end up saving lives, building morale, and improving the operational readiness of the fleet. By 1980, the Navy under this new system had treated thousands of such cases successfully, among them 8 admirals, 285 department officers and hundreds of pilots.

In recent months the rush of personal stories by recovering alcoholic or addicted athletes in all of our news media makes it clear that there is, in fact, an alcohol/drug problem in organized sports today. Not surprisingly, the reaction from interested parties shows that in terms of attitudes, the modern sports world is just beginning to come out of the Stone Age.

Today's sports world—equivalent of the 1965 Navy booze and drug dilemma—is a chorus of angry owners, sullen coaches, immature players, down-the-line agents, an overprotective players' association, and disappointed fans. Those few players who have dared to tell the truth about their own alcohol or drug involvement—or the extent of the problem as they know it to exist in the sports world generally—are attacked as crybabies and weaklings. Their stories are dismissed or said to be exaggerated. "Nobody stuck a needle in their arms," the critics cry. "They should be kicked out because they are a disgrace to the sports world."

What's wrong with this attitude? It doesn't make things go away, that's what's wrong with it. Where there is smoke, there's pot! We all know there is a problem. I have personally known and treated drug- or alcohol-dependent military men from corporals to admirals; and I have treated athletes from stars to rookies. Among the former are Congressional Medal of Honor winners, astronauts, and other men who made history; and the latter include Cy Young Award and Heisman Trophy winners, Super Bowl and World Series stars, and Hall of Famers. There have even been some managers, coaches, and owners who have succumbed to the grape or got hooked on the snort. I see very little difference between soldiers and athletes, heroes or stars.

Much like the Navy of the '60s, in today's sports world we see denials, evasions, charges, countercharges and subpoenas. These won't change anything. *Shoving cocaine up your nose is like sticking your head in the sand: you feel changed but nothing else is changed.*

One of the things wrong with the present system is that the owner treats the player as a write-off or a depreciation, much like a business treats a computer. But the owner knows that it's not cost-effective because the player burns out before his time unless he can be traded. Unfortunately, trades don't solve the problem either. I know of such a trade that was consummated between two teams. Before long it was clear that in return for their bonus baby on bourbon they got a superstar on cocaine. Each team had hoped that the change of scene would change the player. Naturally, it didn't.

The player's agent zealously guards the addicted player's rights by keeping the feds and the owners off his back, even as the player spends a fortune on taxis and limos because he's lost his driver's license due to alcoholism. Unfortunately, this cover-up is only enabling the player to get sicker and ease him into early retirement, degrading invalidism, or premature death.

The business manager uses every possible form of denial to keep his athlete client in demand as a comedic star of beer commercials even after the athlete has become a national joke as an amateur saloon boxer. Not surprisingly, Mr. Manager feels ambivalent while collecting his fee because he is beginning to see that even 25 percent of nothing is nothing, and that he may be getting nothing from this player in the future.

All the factions of the sports industry (owners, agents, athletes, etc.) need education so that they can understand how mind-altering chemicals impair functioning by affecting the player's judgment, behavior, performance, and health. Even aside from moral or role model considerations, it is not enough to say, "What a player does on his own time is his own business."

A ditch-digger can booze it up on Friday night and perhaps perform acceptably on Saturday morning, but a freebasing pitcher will likely be throwing balls, not strikes.

The sports teams need to learn how to do interventions so that those members of the team who already have a chemical problem can be helped into treatment. Very few actually volunteer for rehabilitation. Finally, the whole sports industry and each individual team needs to learn how to accept a rehabilitated player back to his job openly and how to make him responsible for his own recovery.

Our biggest problem is our heritage, our prejudice that alcohol or drug dependence is a weakness, and that it is a hopeless condition to treat. When you have personally seen an athlete fumble his way from the front page into rehabilitation, then get his stuff together and his self-esteem up and return to the starting line-up again—functioning better than ever—then you know that treatment of addicted athletes can be highly successful.

But to make this possible, we have to to become honest and change our own attitudes. If we want to keep our stars as heroes, we have to treat them as people—not property.

The Making of an Addict Athlete

On the lecture circuit I always get questions about athletes who "went wrong" through alcohol, drugs, or unlawful behavior. "How could it happen?" the audience demands. "Who is to blame?" the media wants to know.

After treating many such athletes, I have come to the conclusion that we are all to blame: parents, teachers, coaches, doctors, lawyers, the community, the news media, the fans—and, of course, the athlete himself. We are his enablers; we didn't cause him to go wrong, but we did make it possible. To understand how that happens, let's look at a composite story of such an athlete.

Roy is the oldest child from a large family that is poor, God-fearing, and strict. When he is 10, his father gives him the whipping of his life because on his way home from school Roy cut across the mayor's lawn.

At age 12, he is trying out for Pop Warner football or Little League baseball. As he throws a long pass or bats one over the fence, the old codgers in the bleachers squint, and wheeze, and holler, "What's his name? Hey, kid! Let's see you do that again."

Whew! Roy's a little surprised himself. He has no idea how he did that, but they give him the ball—and he does it again, with congenital ease. Nobody knows it just yet, but at that moment a star is born; the hooting and shouting in the bleachers is but a prophetic whisper to the mounting roars of his major league future.

From that day on, Roy is different. He becomes his home-town's natural resource. On Saturday nights they come in droves from surrounding towns to cheer his rifle arm, his deadly eye, his sprinting stride. More importantly, on a psychological level something insidious is beginning to happen to both Roy and to the world around him. As his value to the sport grows, his responsibility to society diminishes. We expect more and more from Roy the Star—and less and less from Roy the Young Man.

A year later, while horsing around with the guys, he acciden-tally whips the ball through the front room of the mayor's house. (Three years ago his father almost killed him for stepping on the mayor's lawn; today that same mayor gloats to his neighbors who are gathering on the lawn: "That ball went clear through the house—and out the kitchen window. My wife is saving the ball 'cause someday that boy will pitch a World Series or quarterback the Super Bowl.") Roy stands to the side, anticipating punish-ment. Scared, then puzzled, he blinks and wonders. Something is different now. And as the neighbors smile and crowd around the mayor's wife—she's holding high the souvenir ball—bashful Roy walks away, but with the earliest hint of a swagger.

Others, too, judge Roy by new standards. At home he gets away with talking back; in school he gets good grades even when he cuts classes; and his third drunk-driving charge is covered up. Every girl in town wants to date him. And when he gets rough with a cheerleader at 2 o'clock in the morning, the coach smooths things over with the girl's father.

Slowly, something withers and dies inside of Roy. (The something called "social conscience" is what's dying.) Why? Because nobody levels with him anymore. He lies, and we act like it's the truth; he bends a rule, and we rationalize it for him; he loses his temper, and we blame some provocation. The emotionally healthy part of him still reaches out for limits, but his testing behaviors find no social guidelines or legal restraints.

The message from his role models—us—is clear: There is nothing he can't have if he grabs for it; right and wrong are different when you are a star. If you draw cheers on Friday night, social fumbles don't count the rest of the week. In a couple of seasons bashful Roy becomes a spoiled child, then a strutting, sociopathic star.

He leaves his hometown as a professional athlete with a "clean record" (including 12 overlooked traffic tickets). Emotionally immature, he is 20—going on 12. In the big city, he plays for television audiences, coast to coast headlines, and megabucks, but nothing else changes. When after a drunken brawl, he runs his car through a plate-glass window, the store is glad to get the publicity, the cops ignore his boozy breath, and the mayor hugs him at a Boy Scout banquet that same night. Roy is courted by businessmen, and by countless women. Politicians pose with him, talk-show hosts flatter him, and hangers-on drink or do drugs with him. Everybody wants to be seen with him—but nobody wants to be honest with him. (The rare person who does confront him gets cut from his good graces.)

The people around him seek fame by association. He thinks they're phony. He feels used and lonely, but he can't articulate his feelings or deal with his problems except by losing his temper or shouting, "No comment." Even the letters from Mom sound obsequious. (Is it because he bought the family a new house?)

The money in his contract increases, his game becomes more skillful, his behavior more shameful. "Is there anything I can't do?" he silently wonders. He has public license to let it all hang out at times "to cope with the pressure." But the private guilt he feels over the public things he does makes him feel worse. Behind the playboy facade is a person in pain.

Fortunately—or so it seems—he discovers "better living through chemistry." On a daily basis, he has learned (from his role models) that the best fix for a pulled groin, a guilty conscience, or slumping spirits is a pill, a drink, or a snootful of star dust. Unfortunately, once the drugging or drinking begins, it doesn't always remain social—for some, it becomes a disease. For the star, this is particularly dangerous because we pretend that we don't know he's doing it—even when we know he's overdoing it— as long as he can move that ball and tote that score.

To maintain his growing celebrity and medicate his inner pain, he drinks and snorts and deals and pops until he goes over the line with unacceptable social behavior, organic malfunction, or deteriorating athletic performance. With midnight paranoia, breakfast diarrhea, tremors at lunch, daytime drapes drawn, phones off the hook (could the line be tapped?), his life is now unmanageable. It's *bitter* living through chemistry. He is sick! Though he's unable to say it, he's begging to be treated. Instead, he ends up getting traded.

He goes from team to team, from Big Town to Boom Town— where he finally goes bust. At age 32, when he's hooked on booze, dealing cocaine, or guilty of manslaughter, that's when

Little League mothers, big-city sportswriters, and network anchor persons ask: "How could it happen? Who is to blame?"

Indignant, we act as if it all happened this week; and we're angry because he did it to himself, by himself.

Actually, he didn't. When he became a star—we became terrible role models. Except for athletic performance, we made no demands. We fudged on setting limits and we gave him no guidelines. Eventually Roy became as bad a role model for us as we were for him. Having developed no internal restraints at all, he has become anti-social and expects to live above the law, because that's where we put him.

Intelligent medical management calls for testing and evaluation of any athlete at the first symptom and for proper treatment, ongoing reevaluation, and monitoring once the diagnosis is made.

Characteristic elements of the addictive or antisocial life are immaturity and impulsiveness, which get Roy into trouble, and lying and rationalizing, which get Roy out of trouble as long as the world around him permits it.

Rehabilitation, therefore, is a process of "growing up" in clinical settings where therapeutic role models (counselors, therapists, probation officers, and so on) finally do what Roy's enablers failed to do. In the process Roy learns to play by the rules—on and off the field: to pay for liberties he takes, cars he wrecks, and loans he makes; to apologize for feelings he hurts; to compensate for reputations he destroys, and to accept punishment for laws he breaks. It may take months—or years—of clinical "growing up," depending on how young he was when we enabled him to stop growing, and how sick he has become—physically, mentally, and chemically.

Over the long haul a man is the sum of all of the moments of his life. The stumbling jock is a reflection of all the role models he has encountered; and we are the moments, the milestones on his long road of self-destruction. Before he can be a good role model for our children, we have to finally put him through the school of life we spared him from.

If the fallen star is a crybaby, it's largely because we didn't allow him to cry when we should have. That's why we have to baby-sit him—therapeutically, one day at a time, one deed at a time—until he's grown up.

Every Manager Has a Drinking Problem

On a recent flight I ended up sitting next to a man who had what I call a second-hand alcohol problem. As I was buckling my seatbelt I noticed him eyeing me. He was trying to figure out if I would be worth talking to or whether he should forthwith dig into his workaholic briefcase. "Well," he said by way of small talk, "at least the flight is starting out on time. My name is Jack. I'm in sales. How about yourself?"

So far he looked less than interested in pursuing a lengthy conversation, but when I said, "I'm a psychiatrist. I specialize in treating alcoholics," he became downright enthusiastic.

"No kidding?" He shoved his briefcase back under the seat and plunged right into the conversation. "Hey, listen, Doc, you won't mind if I ask you a question, since . . . heh, heh, heh . . . neither of us can go anywhere for a couple of hours. I know this fellow . . . ah, ah . . . I mean I have this friend—well, actually, it's really my partner—we own a small business. He might have a drinking problem, but how can I be sure?"

"What makes you suspicious?"

"Well, he's always cutting down on his drinking, always trying to prove he doesn't have a problem."

"Sounds like an early stage drinking problem."

"Really? How can you say that?"

"Well, think of your Aunt Erma or Uncle Alfred. Has either of them ever cut down on drinking?"

"Hmmm, I guess not. Now that you mention it, I've never thought of cutting down myself. I see what you mean. Anyway, at first Bob—that's my partner—he went on the wagon, but only for Lent. Then, not too long after that, he went on the wagon to lose weight. The funny thing is, he's never had a weight problem. Then he started to confide in me more and more. By now, I'm practically his personal shrink. It turns out his wife complains a lot about his drinking. He says she complains just like his ex-wife did."

"Sounds like maybe Bob can't control his drinking," I suggested. "Has anybody else complained about it?"

"Well, his bartender gets irritated. Sometimes Bob is already lit when he comes to the bar, and after a few drinks, Bob gets silly or feisty, and this causes arguments and upsets other customers."

"How did Bob react to the bartender's complaint? Did he switch bars?" I ask.

"No, but he switched to drinking beer only. But that only gives us a new problem. We used to never know which drink made Bob crazy—now we don't know which beer will tip him over."

"What does his doctor say?"

"The doctor says it's affecting Bob's liver." My travel companion was beginning to look worried. "Gee whiz, Doc, it's making me nervous just talking about it like this. This is your way of teaching your patients, heh?"

"Well, yes, humor helps. But tell me, how is this 'cutting down' affecting his job performance? You're his boss, you should know."

Jack was lost in thought. He was startled when the stewardess banged the cocktail cart into the armrest of his seat. He glanced at me uneasily and waved her on. "No, no drinks right now," then turned back to me. "Well, actually, Bob never drinks at work. He's never been drunk in the office." Jack was doing his best to look calm but he was obviously getting more and more irritated. "But it's this constant cutting down. We all talk about it all the time—not in front of him, of course. But it seems like Bob is either on the wagon, just coming off the wagon, or planning to cut down again.''

"Look, Jack, let's put this all together: it seems like Bob is either tapering off, tapering on, or on the wagon. The drinking is bothering his family, his friends, and you, his boss. His game of playing beer roulette is causing personality changes, which annoy the bartender, and liver damage, which worries the doctor. Also, Bob is preoccupied with drinking because he's always thinking about drinking or thinking about not drinking.''

"Doc, I guess you're saying that there is definitely a drinking problem?''

"Definitely. Bob and you definitely have a drinking problem.''

"What do you mean, Bob and I, Doc?'' Jack said sharply. He was leaning slightly away from me, his eyes a shade less friendly.

"Look, Jack,'' I said reassuringly, "you are a businessman with a drinking problem. Bob is your drinking problem. Bob can't control his alcohol, and you can't control his drinking. He's preoccupied with his drinking, and you are preoccupied with the consequences of his drinking. He can't drink without creating problems, and he can't cut down without creating problems, and you know it.''

Jack made a face that said, "Boy, of all the people on this plane, and I had to sit next to this one.''

"Doc, you've hit me with a two-by-four,'' he finally said. "I guess I can't really argue with you. But what can I do about it?''

"For openers, you can get some information and help from any alcohol treatment center in your city so that you can eventually do an intervention on Bob. You see, Bob needs your help to get him to take a look at his life. Also you can go to some AA and Al-anon meetings to learn more about it yourself. They're listed in your phone book, they're anonymous, and they're for people who are close to a problem drinker.''

Jack slumped in his seat mulling the situation over when the smiling stewardess and her medicine cart came by again.

"Sure you won't change your minds, gentlemen?"

"Yes," I said. "I think I'll have a Scotch and soda."

Jack looked incredulous. "Doc, you mean after all this, you're gonna have a drink?"

"Sure," I said. "The problem is not what, when, where, or why you drink. It's what your drinking does to your family, your health, or your boss—that's what makes it a disease."

"Well, in that case, I'll have the same," Jack smiled happily; and lowering his voice to the stewardess he added, "Since you passed us by the first time around, make mine a double."

Every Customer Has a Drug Problem

It's Monday morning at the Boozemobile Plant. Bob, the assembly-line foreman, is scratching his head because Leroy is absent again. Lately this happens every Monday and most Fridays, too. The problem is that Leroy drinks too much. In a way it's a good thing that he's absent because when he's hung over, Leroy is nothing but an administrative problem: he's impossible to work with, he makes too many mistakes, and he has to be sent to the plant nurse, anyway.

"Henry," the foreman calls out, "I need you to fill in for Leroy today. I don't know why he isn't here. Must be sick again."

Henry looks pained. He doesn't like being taken off his own job, especially for Leroy. Everybody knows that Leroy is probably sleeping off a bender and that the foreman won't do anything because of the paperwork and union trouble.

But Henry is a nice guy. He hates to make a scene, so he just grumbles. Calm on the outside and with a knot in his stomach, he vents his anger by doing a poor job. As each trunk lock assembly rolls by, he bangs it hard with his rubber mallet instead of tapping it gently into place.

Two weeks later, in another part of the country, Betsy Brown is having a super day. Today she starts on her Hawaiian vacation. Although it's snowing, she arrives at the airport 30 minutes early. She finds a parking spot close to the terminal. Everything is going just perfect until—"Oh, my God—I can't unlock the trunk of my new Boozemobile! Something's wrong with the lock. I can't believe this is happening. My luggage, handbag, traveler's checks, airline tickets, hotel vouchers—it's all in the trunk. What have I done to deserve this?"

Betsy has just become a victim of the Monday-Friday syndrome. Every day, especially on Mondays and Fridays, thousands of Americans do poor work because they abused their brains with alcohol or drugs the night before. Psychological impairment from this abuse, although hard to document, is real. A top-notch salesperson insults customers; the affable manager is irritable; the efficient secretary is scattered; a master craftsman becomes careless; and a talented executive has to be prematurely "retired." More easily documented signs are absenteeism, sickness, accidents, and grievance proceedings.

The way to change the situation is through an Employee Assistance Program (EAP), which trains supervisors and medical personnel to refer troubled employees for help instead of covering for them, or eventually firing them. In 1980, General Motors Corporation's EAP showed that treatment of drug- and alcohol-abusing employees reduced sickness and accident benefits by 35 percent, grievance proceedings by 50 percent, and absenteeism by 40 percent.

But that won't happen on a nationwide scale until all managers and labor leaders learn that a handout is not a helping hand; and until health care deliverers stop "retiring" such patients—with phony diagnoses—in order to avoid union-management problems.

Booze at the Top: The Alcoholic Executive

Doctor, I, uh, have a personal problem which will require discreet handling. I am the president of a large corporation. The problem is our chairman of the board, who is the founder and father of our operation. Several of us on the board of directors, as well as some of his friends, are worried to death—we are at our wits' end. Everything we've tried has done no good. We are afraid and embarrassed to talk to him personally. We think he may have alcoholism. What can we do?

Sound farfetched? In 1982 alcoholism in industry cost over 60 billion dollars annually. The alcoholic executive contributes an inordinate share to the cost because of his high salary, the costly consequences of his marginal decisions, and the not infrequent six-figure retirement with which he is prematurely shunted off into invalidism.

The tragedy of a brilliant executive who is sliding from mahogany row to skid row is avoidable. He can be diagnosed, rehabilitated, and restored to his potential if somebody can help his peers understand what his problem is, and if his peers are willing to do what is necessary to get him into treatment. I know this works because I have treated many such patients who are back on mahogany row.

Who is he? How do we recognize what is happening to him? And how do we help him?

First, who is he? He's usually the firstborn or only child who did well in school and in athletics, did a brief stint in the armed forces, and was a comer in your organization. He's usually one of two personality types and has a certain style of operating.

He might be Jack Armstrong, the all-American businessman: energetic, intuitive, charismatic, with seemingly boundless, infectious optimism. His ability to see clearly through confusing corporate interplays enables him to consummate daring deals with otherwise hesitant souls or pull off a merger among traditionally diverse factions.

His counterpart, Malcolm W. Harrison III, is more on the reasonable, unflappable, tactful side with conservative aims, manners, and dress—a quiet, dignified style. He's a stickler for details with an encyclopedic mind. His advice is concrete, cautious, always backed up by reams of data, and clear for anyone to grasp because he gathers and makes understandable all the necessary information.

While Jack and Malcolm seem like opposite sides of a coin—flamboyant vs. somber; intuitive vs. analytic; daring vs. cautious; and optimistic vs. conservative—they have much in common. They both have talent which quickly becomes obvious; their superiors, through unconscious identification, help them rise in the corporate structure; and they both enjoy the power and ego gratification of knowing that they are able to make affairs move, albeit by different routes.

They work much harder than their less successful peers, and they have considerable stress from internal turmoil which is not suspected by anyone except their psychiatrists and their wives. Their existence on mahogany row is a month-to-month struggle to stay on top and move ahead. It might be envisioned as a dynamic, but tenuously balanced, equilibrium which brings them closer and closer to chronic fatigue and exhaustion. It is then that alcohol use, previously at social levels, becomes an important self-treatment for chronic fatigue and exhaustion.

Unfortunately, heavy drinking has negative effects on all of us, in the following areas of our functioning, and in this order:

- judgment
- behavior
- performance
- health

Over a period of one to five years of heavy drinking, Jack becomes hypomanic and impulsive with a dozen unrealistic schemes, with frequent absenteeism, accidents, and occasional incidents where his behavior is "unbecoming a company officer." And Malcolm becomes depressed, seclusive, psychosomatically ill, with impotence, constipation, migraines, and inability to make decisions.

With Jack and Malcolm's judgment impaired, their behavior becomes increasingly more bizarre and public, at times throwing a bad light on the corporate image. Naturally, their performances are also impaired. In the final stages, they both come late to work with hangovers, wearing tinted glasses, chewing breath mints, and walking in a cloud of shaving lotion. They have become chronic alcoholics.

Unfortunately, both Jack and Malcolm have mentors who pegged them as promising years ago and now feel they made a mistake. Also, each has loyal assistants and secretaries who cover up for them, and the corporate philosophy makes this possible because "we owe them something for years of brilliant service." And since everybody knows that all companies have employees like Jack or Malcolm at one time or another, the problems become more tolerable, although increasingly more expensive.

A temporary solution, while the company holds out hope that the alcoholic will come to his senses and pull himself together, is not to involve him in any important decisions. Or there may be an ineffective Dutch-uncle talk by the CEO about "a need to cut down." ("Can't you see what this is doing to your family? Take a month off; or see the company doctor to get yourself straightened out.")

The corporate medical director, because of personal career interests, may diplomatically sidestep the issue and send the alcoholic to a psychiatrist. The psychiatrist then prescribes tranquilizers to help the patient *cut down*. In that way the company ends up with a drunk who smells better—but functions no better.

All the while, the alcoholic becomes more isolated at work and at home, unable to do anything except get sicker. When he finally does the unpardonable—and every company has its own standard for what that is—he will be prematurely retired. Actually, he is being invalided because in six to twenty-four months after retirement, he will be dead of drinking, accident, or suicide—all of which mean *alcoholism*.

What, then, is the nature of the problem? Jack and Malcolm are alcoholics, and since they are executives, they are victims of the VIP Syndrome. Had they been fork lift operators, they would have been rehabilitated through the Employee Assistance Program of the company. But since they are VIPs, they were treated inadequately and prejudicially by not being treated at all. As a matter of fact, the higher an alcoholic's rank in our society, the less likely it is he will even be diagnosed, let alone treated for his disease.

What should have been done? Like any other alcoholic, the alcoholic executive's chances for recovery are best if he enters rehabilitation as a result of an intervention. The people who can do that most effectively are peers, loved ones, and bosses.

The first step is usually taken by someone (the boss, a peer, a subordinate, or a loved one) who can no longer stand by and watch the talented executive destroy himself. The problem should then be presented to an expert or a specialist in the field of substance abuse. The next step is to 1) gather objective data (facts) to show how the alcoholic's drinking has affected his job performance and 2) subjective data (feelings) to show him how his drinking is affecting those who love him, care about him, and depend on him.

From the trained consultant, the novice interveners—the boss, the wife, a friend, the corporate legal counsel, and the corporate medical director—will quickly learn the disease concept of this illness. They will lose their fear that "if we get tough with him, we will lose him." It will become clear that treatment is the only hopeful solution and the only humane, loving, and responsible thing to do.

The participants in the intervention first must come to agree that he has an illness for which he needs help; that he will go for treatment immediately to a facility designated by the group; that the family will be involved to whatever degree is advisable; that the treatment will be paid for through the company's program; and that upon completion of treatment, he will have his old job back if he recovers and maintains sobriety. These resolutions are then presented to the alcoholic.

Proper interventions almost always lead to immediate entry into rehabilitation and to between 80 and 90 percent successful rehabilitation. During my Navy practice, I saw 8 admirals and 285 medical department officers recover from alcoholism and return to the same jobs they held while they were malfunctioning as drinking alcoholics. The same is true in my civilian practice where I see VIPs from the world of business, academia, the law, sports, entertainment, and politics.

Sometimes an employer will ask, "How can we put him back on the job now that he is diagnosed as an alcoholic?" Or "How can we trust an alcoholic?" I always tell them about the several hundred alcoholic pilots whom I have seen in recovery. People ask me if I get nervous when flying with a recovered alcoholic pilot. My answer is always "Oh, yes! But what really makes me nervous is the realization that if I had taken this flight six weeks ago, I would have been flying with a *hungover* alcoholic pilot."

The Three-Martini Lunch

It's silly for the Congress and the IRS to argue about whether the three-martini lunch should be deductible. Of course it's deductible. It always will be. I see evidence for it every day. Listen to a conversation with one of my patients and judge for yourself.

His name is Harry. He is 52, an executive. His wife sent him to me. "Doctor," he said nervously, "she worries because I drink martinis at lunch. I say there is nothing wrong with that. I drink with colleagues, we talk business, and it's deductible."

"Tell me, Harry, how many martinis do you have for lunch?"

"What do you mean, 'how many'? I have one while we order lunch. Sometimes I have another one."

"Sometimes?"

"You're starting to sound like my wife. All right—I usually have two."

"Do you ever have doubles?"

"Well," he said reluctantly, "sometimes I start with a double, especially if I had a tough morning."

I looked him straight in the eye. "Harry, are you a three-martini lunch drinker?"

Harry sighed, avoiding my glance. "I guess that's closer to being accurate."

Since I have never seen a martini-lunch drinker who was a teetotaler the rest of the day, I probe further. "What do you drink right after work?"

"Well, I usually have one at Joe's Bar with the boys. After a rough day," he added.

"One?"

"Usually. Sometimes I have two."

"Do you drink on the commuter train?"

"Only if I run into people I know—you know, social drinking."

"How often is that?"

"All right!" Harry's voice was sharp. "I usually have one on the train. What do you want me to do—be unsociable?"

I tried to soothe him back down. "Harry, to figure out if you have a problem, we have to be honest. Now tell me, what do you drink when you get home?"

"I have a martini with Helen before dinner." He smiled patronizingly. "She drinks white wine, so I keep her company."

"What do you drink during dinner?"

"I told you already—she is a white wine freak, so we split a bottle of wine, Helen and me."

"You split it evenly?"

"Well, I usually have most of it."

"What do you have for a nightcap?"

"A brandy, but only if I'm real edgy."

I glanced at my tally sheet. "Harry, you have eight drinks and the better part of a bottle of wine each weekday."

He is pale and sweating. "I never added it up like this. I guess I'm hittin' it pretty hard. Any damage from that?"

"The lab tests will tell us. Anyway, I agree with your wife— you're drinking too much. I want to see you next Monday. Oh, ask Helen to come along."

Since three-martini lunch drinkers don't abstain on weekends, I know that his total intake is even higher, and that means damage to one or more of the following: stomach, liver, brain, bone marrow, heart, or pancreas.

Actuarial tables tell us more about drinking than IRS loopholes do. They tell us that heavy drinkers die 12 years before their time. So, if you're like Harry, make no mistake about it. The three-martini lunch always has been, and always will be deductible—maybe not from your taxes, but always from your life.

Successful Addicts Also Die

This morning you argued again with your alcoholic. The argument was about his drinking. You came away relieved when he finally said, "I couldn't possibly be an alcoholic because I'm too successful . . . ." But now you wonder if he maybe tricked you again.

Your confusion is understandable. Clinical experience shows that success and alcoholism often go hand in hand right to the very end, especially if the alcoholic is rich, powerful, famous, or talented. At first his heavy drinking or drug use may even help his reputation. "He works hard and he plays hard" people say about him. And "even after a three-martini lunch, he still drives a shrewd bargain."

Even after he's gotten pretty sick, the boozing tycoon may continue to do well financially. The reason is that he managed to hire the right people—loyal professionals—who continue to do their jobs conscientiously and thereby make him financially successful for months or years. Similarly, a drug-dependent or alcoholic former athlete who has a "recognizable face" remains successful as long as his image is marketable. His past glories give him a shot at becoming a sportscaster, writing books (with ghosts), selling fluff to fans, posing with macho merchandise, or doing public relations work.

In much the same way, a drug-addicted artist keeps making money from royalties and residuals while he snorts away his ability to produce new things. Last year's TV sitcoms, reruns of old movies, and re-releases of hit songs keep his image alive in the public view while his body is dying in Malibu.

Many addicts don't live long enough to die on the down-slope. Among well-known alcoholics and addicts who died at their peak—usually by accident or overdose—are Oscar-winning movie greats, platinum-disc rock stars, Hall of Fame athletes, million-aire philanthropists, politicians of all parties, and artists of all persuasions.

If you're living with such an alcoholic or addict, you need to ask yourself some questions. Has he produced anything new lately? Does his business run itself? Does he live on rerun royalties? When he says "I don't need a job," ask yourself if he could get a job. In other words, is he unemployed . . . or is he unemployable?

The bottom line? Success doesn't help alcoholics. The reason you and he fought this morning is not because he got drunk. You fought because he got drunk *again*.

The bad news is that he tricked you again because you believed him again.

The good news is that you're becoming aware of the repetitive nature of his problem; that it will happen again and again—unless he undergoes positive change.

The tough news? There will be no positive change in any of this unless you start it. To make it happen, the part of you that's beginning to catch on will need education so that you can more clearly see behind his alcoholic rationalizations; and the gullible, dependent, non-assertive part of you that's been going along with his sickness will need counseling to help you start those positive changes.

The real bottom line? If you don't change—he won't change. He'll just end up as another successful, dead alcoholic.

Cocaine for the Workaholic

In 1885, Freud wrote, "I take very small doses of cocaine regularly . . . " He used it to abolish fatigue. By 1890, he and other doctors stopped its use because they saw it was addictive.

Why is coke addictive? Because, in just a few minutes it gives you confidence and euphoria, makes you feel like a big shot, and gives you a burst of energy, without at the same time slurring your speech or scrambling your thoughts. (It may even speed up your thoughts.) It seems tailor-made for the overachieving workaholic who feels driven to get to the top.

Melvin was such a guy. He was a New York writer, a nice guy, a hard worker, and a recreational user. "After a hard day's work, a line or two at parties gives me quick energy, a feeling of being on top and clever ideas literally spark from my tired brain." At one such party he arrived tired, but after snorting himself "up" recreationally, he started dazzling a Hollywood producer. "Melvin," the movie mogul was saying, "I'm absolutely mesmerized! We need your ideas in my new picture. I want you to fly to the Coast and talk to my director."

"This could be my big break," Mel thought. The next day he worked through lunch, then left New York at five and landed in Hollywood at 9 p.m. Surprised that the meeting scheduled for tomorrow was going on right now, he asked to be driven to the studio instead of the hotel.

"Mel, you're bushed," his escort said. "For your body it's midnight. Why don't you see the director tomorrow when you're fresh."

"Nonsense. Let's go to the studio," Mel urged, thinking to himself, "Sure, I'm tired. Wasn't I tired when I dazzled the producer? Coke always picks me up at parties; why not use it for work just this once?"

Well, coke always delivers—in the beginning at least. He amazed the director and the writers. For them it was evening, but Mel sparkled like it was morning.

For Mel, that meeting was a chemical turning point. More and more he used cocaine for work on the set—and for fun on the town. He became known as the star writer: full of ideas, tireless, always "on." But clinically he was no longer a recreational user. Three months later, the film in the can, he came to see me. "Doctor, now that you've heard my story, could I be headed for trouble?"

"Yes, Mel, you're well on your way because cocaine makes you more than you actually are. You see, when you landed in Hollywood at 9 p.m., your brain was tired, your body spent. But coke helped you deny your limitations. Actually, you were a set-up for addiction because you are an overachieving workaholic; you have inordinate ambitions—but you are only human.''

Mel looked angry. "I used it only to make a better picture," he hissed defensively. "I'm not a junkie!" He looked troubled, lost in thought. After a few minutes he added with a hint of insight, "But I do want to see you again next week to talk some more."

Like many a salesman, actor, politician, or entrepreneur I have seen, Mel was a coke-addicted workaholic. Coke had become his success fuel.

In therapy, he will learn that to be mature you have to accept yourself as you are. If you need seven drinks to be sociable, you're not a party boy—you're a boozer; and if you need cocaine to be brilliant, you're not an egghead—you're a cokehead. Even Freud had to come to terms with that.

Cocaine in the Boardroom: It's a Killer

Perhaps from the beginning of time, and certainly before Sir Thomas More described a place called Utopia in 1516, people have used various drugs to inspire the feelings of carefree well-being or euphoria. These drugs have created different sensations or "highs" with different adverse side effects. However, today clinicians, scientists, and a growing number of everyday users are becoming increasingly aware that coke is the most potent euphoric drug known to man; pushers and dealers know its enormous potential for abuse and addiction (the cocaine trade would rank number 7 in *Fortune*'s 500). Coroners (they always have the final word) know that cocaine's nickname is killer.

Over the past decade, cocaine has gradually become the drug of choice for entertainers, athletes, those in the fast lane, and spoiled rich kids. What is less well known is that it is quickly supplanting alcohol as the most dangerous occupational hazard in executive suites. Why is this happening?

By giving the brain's pleasure centers a euphoric jolt, cocaine seductively reinforces the very qualities of which CEOs and other leaders are made: drive, self-confidence, assertiveness, can-do optimism, and a sense of power and well-being. Coke elevates your mood, inclines you toward gregariousness, gives you a cool feeling of omnipotence, energizes the body, and heightens sexual awareness. It may even speed up your thinking and make you more intensely aware of what's going on around you. Coke, in short, is the most potent and pleasurable stimulant we know.

What makes it especially dangerous is the prevailing wisdom characterizing cocaine as nonaddictive; many casual users will affably tell you that unlike opiates, alcohol, or amphetamines, cocaine not only makes you feel good, but you can't get hooked on it because it's not physically addicting. That, however, is only half-fact and terribly naive at that.

Cocaine is the most dangerous drug on the scene today simply because while it is (probably) not physically addicting in the clinical sense, it is *psychologically* the most addictive drug we know. To understand what that means, consider the experience of Randall (a pseudonym), a CEO and typical coke user we treated some time ago. In his mid-40s, Randall was a fast-track success story who had become the head of a large corporation. Conservative in dress and political outlook, he was personable, articulate, well-groomed, and able to appreciate the younger ideas of his assistants. With his Palm Beach suntan and Newport Beach backhand, Randall was the last person anyone would suspect of having a drug problem. Randall in fact had no history of drug problems at all.

For over twenty years he had no trouble handling his alcohol, and the only other mind-altering substance he ever sampled was a little marijuana during his college days. Also, like many other

CEOs, he had always considered drug users weak-willed, unstable people.

Then one day he and his new sweetheart, Kate, attended a party where he was somewhat taken aback when he spied the younger crowd passing around lines of cocaine. In order to maintain his reputation as a flexible leader and because he knew that cocaine is not addicting, he decided to go along and try some. He clumsily snorted two lines (thought it was a bit untidy and tasted bitter) and looked up, embarrassed. His friends, however, complimented him on being a modern Renaissance man, able to run a large corporation yet still be himself and have fun with totally different people in a totally different setting.

In less than five minutes he was feeling the positive effects of the coke; even though he had felt very tired when he arrived at the party, he was now feeling his best. If anything, he was even better than his best. He felt clever, energized, and witty—even brilliant.

Over the next few weeks he attended several more parties with his new friends and his new drug. Soon he decided that coke might actually be better than alcohol, with all of the good feelings and none of the bad—no slurring, stumbling or hangovers. Before long he was buying his own small supply, not from sleazy dealers, mind you, but from respectable people—people like himself. Much as drinking increases in alcoholics, his new-found habit grew from occasional party use to weekend fun, then to a private toot on Wednesday nights to overcome the midweek slump, and eventually to daily use. At the same time, more and more of his friends "coincidentally" turned out to be coke users. And when Kate wondered whether he might be using too much, he reassured her that he was still able to take it or leave it.

In less than a year he started to suffer more and more from crashing—the let-down and depression that began to follow the euphoria. He was alarmed when he realized that the only way to fix the apathy, blues and depression was to use more coke. He vaguely remembered someone saying, "Every time I use a line of coke I'm a new man. The only trouble is, the first thing the new man wants is another line of coke." Randall's drug bill was now $600 a week.

In almost all cases the disease progresses insidiously by going through three stages: *compulsion*, *loss of control*, and *using in spite of the consequences*.

Compulsion means you will use coke whenever it's available. If a friend drops by your house unexpectedly, and just happens to have some coke, you face a dilemma: are you going to snort? If your answer is a reflex "yes," you have cause for worry. A truly recreational user will be able to think the situation over, then decide to use or not; he will decide to snort when he wants to have fun, and only if getting high fits in with his plans for the rest of the day.

Compulsion, on the other hand, means that you will use it simply because it's available. That is a problem—it means that cocaine has begun to run your life. From now on it will more and more often screw up your whole day—you run into some coke in the morning and can't say no, even though you had already planned a very busy afternoon.

Loss of control is worse than compulsion—when you run into some coke you don't just do a couple of lines but you keep on using until either you or the coke is exhausted . . . and then you frantically try to find more. At this stage coke isn't just changing your day, it's taking you out of action for several days. Like your alcoholic uncle who binges with booze, you go on binges with coke. Loss of control also means that you set out to snort one line to get it on with your lover but end up on a coke run; you have very little sex and your lover is furious. Social drinkers drink a little and make love; and alcoholics drink a lot and pass out.

Using in spite of consequences means that you are no longer able to weigh the risks—you may have been arrested or you're on probation, yet you still do it. Recovering from hepatitis? You still do coke by injection. A case of bronchitis? You still freebase (and aggravate your cough). Behind on your rent? You still shell out $150 for a gram. You're getting in the hole deeper, and you know it. But you don't care because coke has become your life's obsession.

As Randall's need for larger quantities of cocaine increased and he became aware of possible legal problems, he would eventually have other people buy the cocaine for him—to deny to himself and others that he had reached the point of tolerance, i.e., needing more and more cocaine just to keep going. (Several prominent patients I have treated asked two or three trusted subordinates or servants to buy the cocaine so that the addicts themselves are never apprehended with cocaine in their possession.) This usually means that such trusted buyers eventually make this kind of service worth their while by selling the cocaine at a considerable markup to the users because they are in effect taking the chance that the addict is avoiding—chances of being apprehended with sizeable amounts of cocaine in their car, in their luggage while going through the turnstiles of international airports, etc. Naturally, this escalates the cost that sooner or later becomes a noticeable drain to all but a very few cocaine addicts. This often leads to selling cocaine to offset the addict's own use or getting into one or two sizeable buys involving international sources, running into hundreds of thousands of dollars. This makes Randall, the respectable pillar of the community, the businessman, the philanthropist, into an international dope smuggler and criminal by association and financial affiliation.

What started out as fun and feeling on top winds up as a frenzied flight from pain, paranoia, and death. The irony is that as the user gets sicker, he is less and less able to see it. The real magic of the powder is that every noseful tells you that you don't really have a problem.

Halting the Fight

A new addict (or a close caring person) is sometimes able to effect a positive change and get help if the following are kept in mind. To find out if there is a problem:

1. Ask somebody who knows you well to evaluate your use pattern objectively, but be sure that this person is not into drugs himself. (If there is nobody you can trust, chances are you're already addicted and paranoid.)

2. Consult a drug or alcohol clinic. If you're skittish, you can give a phony name, but do tell the truth about your habit. (The consultation will cost you less than you spend on a gram of cocaine.)

3. Go to some Cocaine Anonymous meetings. If there aren't any where you live, go to some Alcoholics Anonymous meetings. They are free, and you will see and hear yourself in the stories of others—in the compulsions, obsessions, and other characteristics of addiction that are the basis of your disease.

Finally, if you're still not convinced you're addicted, just stop using cocaine and see how you feel. Chances are you'll end up asking the same question that my patients ask time and again: "If cocaine isn't addicting, how come I can't stop using it or thinking about it?"

Bumper Sticker Chemistry

Wearing your heart on your sleeve or flaunting your causes on bumper stickers is typically American. Anything from "Save the Whales" to "Ban the Nukes," we stick on cars. But now something new has happened in bumper slogans: the chemical people (alcohol and drug addicts) have joined America's graffiti on wheels.

You see their slogans on every road, but you don't get their message. The reason they seem to speak in an "in" language is because they've gone public with a private conflict. By baring their souls on their bumpers, they share their sobriety, philosophy, and need for kindred spirits who no longer need chemical spirits. To help you understand their language, here are some of their mottos and their meanings.

"One Day at a Time" means that the bearer has learned to conquer his addiction in the only way anyone can conquer anything: one day at a time. (Not to drink ever again sounds too tough, but one day at a time you can do it.) "Easy Does It" means to quit being so intense, to stop pushing the noodle, not to worry so much, and not be so uptight. "Live and Let Live" means to stop trying to control everybody and everything; things won't stay the way you arrange them anyway.

How do you become a recovering person? Well, you "Choose No Booze"; you "Try Hugs—Not Jugs," because "It's Not Okay to Use." And what do you get if you take this advice? You get "Reality—What a Concept!" You become "Clean and Serene" so that you can "Do It Sober."

But there are pitfalls, especially in early recovery. HALT is a warning. It means not to get too Hungry, Angry, Lonely, or Tired, because that's when you're apt to slip (drink or use).

Some stickers intend to poke fun, but inadvertently tell more than they mean to, especially if you study the driver of the car too. I recently saw a bumper sticker that gave me a scare: "I Brake for Hallucinations." The car was a flashy sports model. At the light I pulled alongside and studied the driver. He was what in the good old days we called "hip, slick, and cool"—shirt unbuttoned to his navel, gold chains around his neck, a Haight-Ashbury cast to his darting eyes, fingers dancing on the steering wheel. Probably a cocaine dealer, I thought. I rolled my window down. "What is the meaning of your sticker?" I asked, smiling.

He was startled. He shot me a paranoid glance. "If you don't know it—you don't have it," he sneered and roared off.

Aha! I thought. This guy's not only a cocaine dealer, he's also a user. How different his response was from the reaction you get when you acknowledge a recovering person's sticker—a smile, a wave, a thumbs up. Just in case, I decided to give him a wide berth.

A week later I saw a sticker which showed that even cocaine addicts can recover. The car was clean, but an older model; the driver obviously a sober, recovering cocaine addict. With humor and insight, his bumper quip focused on the one conflict that brings all cocaine addicts to their knees (unless the coroner sees them on their backs first). The message was right on the money, or right on the nose, you might say. It read simply: "My Other Car Went Up My Nose."

Out of the Mouths of Babes: A Christmas Parable

Out of the mouths of babes comes the truth. Why? Because small children are psychologically naive. Instead of saying the right things—they say the things that are right. Their innocent statements are right on—but only when they're made by somebody else's child, and when their meaning doesn't pertain to us.

Why should we feel that way? Because we know that up to a certain age, everything our babe knows, he has learned from us. Therefore, whenever he is "spontaneous," he is bound to reflect our family attitudes and lifestyle.

Not too many years ago I came upon a Christmas story that makes the point well.

Halloween had come and gone, and casting week for the school Christmas play was over. All the good parts had been assigned and rehearsals were about to begin when the ambitious drama teacher decided that Johnnie, the school principal's young-est son, should also have a part in the play. But since Johnnie was only three years old and unable to read, the drama teacher decided to give him the part of the innkeeper; that way he would have only a few words of dialogue which he should be able to memorize. "Besides," the crafty dramatist thought, "Johnnie is such a cute little boy, he will probably steal the show anyway, and the principal will be pleased."

For three weeks they ran the play, scene by scene over and over again. With extra special care, the manger scene was rehearsed like this.

Joseph is played by Leroy Jenkins, age 9. Stiff-legged in his paper costume, he knocks on the door of the inn.

The door opens and Johnnie, the innkeeper, looks up expectantly.

Joseph (in stilted monotone): "My wife Mary is with child. Is there room at the inn?"

Johnnie (impish, bright-eyed and bushy-tailed): "No, there is no room at the inn."

End of scene.

Simple enough, thought the drama teacher. Nothing can go wrong.

During the rehearsal Johnnie proved more than competent for the brief part. The teacher was pleased to discover that there was a big ham in little Johnnie, but she had a nagging worry because once or twice a little frown puckered his forehead. Was he becoming aware of the insignificance of his part? Was he thinking that compared to the other kids, he hardly had any lines at all? Maybe so. During one rehearsal he tried to add a line of his own, but the nervous director held him strictly to the script.

The night of the big play finally arrived. The halls were decked with holly. The mistletoe over the library door was a welcome attraction for the older teenagers who did the ushering. With curtain time approaching, the audience was buzzing.

In the front row, looking cool but feeling nervous, were the proud parents of the thespians. In their midst, sitting like a conspicuous patriarch and making small talk with the local minister at his side, sat the school principal himself. He was justly proud but outwardly modest, bowing to compliments from all sides about his Johnnie being the youngest of the players.

With ooh's and ahh's from the excited audience, the curtain finally rose: the set designers from the arts and crafts department had outdone themselves; the inn and the manager looked downright Biblical in electric moonlight. The Johnsons nervously spotted their boy Alfred tending his cardboard camel; and the Gonzales girl, her throat dry with nervous tension, did her best to stroll nonchalantly through the paper trees, using the same gait she had seen on brides going up to the altar.

All went well—more or less. Finally, the manger scene was upon them. Joseph, walking carefully in his paper costume, approached the inn. He peered overhead at the spotlight moon, then knocked on the door.

The door opened and Johnnie the innkeeper looked up expectantly. (Hiding behind the paper wall, the drama teacher stood by just in case Johnnie might need a cue.)

Out in the audience the principal was thinking, "Ah, what a natural born actor my Johnnie is," and the drama teacher was silently praying, "With only one line, what could possibly go wrong?"

Joseph (in stilted monotone): "My wife Mary is with child. Is there room at the inn?"

Johnnie, eager to play his part well, but also aching to have more than just one line, was suddenly inspired with an ad-lib of his own.

"No," he said, "there is no room at the inn." Then pausing for dramatic effect, he added, "But come on in and have a drink anyway."

Out of the mouths of babes . . . .

Dear Doc...

Question: Our son is 23 years old. Every day after work, he has to have at least one beer in order to "relax," and on weekends he seems to enjoy wandering around the house always with a can of beer in his hand. Is this a dependency problem on alcohol?

Answer: You raise a hotly debated point, namely, how much drinking is alcoholic dependence. Your son is showing a sign which most alcoholics can recall happening to them early in their alcoholism, namely, psychological dependence. That's also known as chemical drinking or "relief" drinking, which is just another way of saying "drinking to relax." It's no different from having to have tranquilizers on a daily basis.

The reason this is debatable is that many people seem to be able to do it for a lifetime without becoming overtly alcoholic in the sense of getting drunk, suffering social and legal damage, etc.

Daily reliance on alcohol in any amount is not a good idea. Tell your son about your concern. Ask him to stop drinking for two months to see how it affects him. He might realize that he needs to find some non-chemical ways of relaxing. The time to make those changes is when you're young.

Q: My husband gets drunk and causes scenes that hurt his business (he and my brother own a small company). When I tell him about his drinking behavior, he gets mad and calls me a nag. I think he's an alcoholic. But sometimes he quits altogether for two weeks and says that proves that he is a social drinker because he "can take it or leave it." What do you think?

A: Social drinkers can take it *and* leave it. They can drink some— and then leave the rest, that is, switch to a non-alcoholic drink or go home. Problem drinkers, on the other hand, gradually lose that option. If they want to be safe, they have to make an all or nothing choice, i.e., take it *or* leave it (not drink at all).

Actually, your husband is a moderately far advanced alcoholic because his drinking affects his work. Talk to your brother about doing an intervention on your husband because unless your husband gets help, he will almost certainly get worse, and so will their business.

Q: Do you have any literature on the "heavy social drinker?" My husband says that he is really a heavy social drinker and not an alcoholic.

A: The world's literature is full of information on the heavy social drinker: It is found in the index under "alcoholism."

Clinically, the expression "heavy social drinker" is a euphemism for alcoholic. People who are truly social drinkers don't drink heavily because heavy drinking makes a person asocial (boring, emotionally absent, sleepy), unsocial (repetitive, forgetful, confused), or anti-social (abrasive, impulsive, hostile, combative).

I know a recovering alcoholic physician who for years was known as a heavy social drinker. Every time somebody said, "I think I'll have a drink," he would say, "So shall I" (which he pronounced "social I"), as he knocked back another double. Usually, a short while later he would be so "social" that nobody would want to socialize with him for the rest of the evening.

Q: How much alcohol is considered acceptable? By that, I mean, how many ounces per day—not how many drinks.

A: What is considered "acceptable" depends on who asks the question. The only definition to achieve international recognition was "Dr. Anstie's limit." Anstie (a 19th-century physician) said that three ounces of whiskey or less per day was normal.

Today, many people consider that kind of drinking to be heavy drinking. I give my patients a more practical definition: Normal drinking—or drinking that is not harmful—is drinking less than the amount which causes psychosocial, medical, or job problems. People can easily fool themselves and others about how much they drink; but it's more difficult to fool others in the long run about observable effects of the drinking. Something that causes a problem—is a problem.

So, you have to figure out what kind of drinking effects or drinking consequences are "acceptable" to you.

Q: Last week my boss said my job might be in danger if I don't change my drinking pattern. He was even implying I might be an alcoholic. I have always felt that anyone who can work, jog and drink (I jog five miles three times a week) can't possibly be an alcoholic. Is jogging good insurance against alcoholism?

A: Jogging is good exercise and an excellent conditioner for cardiopulmonary fitness, but it is no guarantee against alcoholism. As a matter of fact, jogging can be used as a defense against realizing your alcoholism. I have treated many alcoholics who were runners, including some Boston Marathoners. As a psychiatrist, I learned from them during their treatment that for several years they were—in a preconscious way—aware that they were using their jogging as a defense against fully realizing their alcoholism. And later, when their disease was becoming obvious, they could talk about their jogging exploits and thereby prevent others from making snide remarks or expressing honest concern about the drinking problem.

Whether or not you are alcoholic depends not on your running but on your drinking. Talk to your boss, your family, your friends, and your doctor about the effect your drinking has on your life. Also, read the article entitled "One More for the Road" in the June, 1980, issue of *Runner's World*. If you have a drinking problem and you go through rehabilitation and manage to remain abstinent, you will find that not only your running time, but also the physical and mental enjoyment you get from running will improve tremendously.

Q: My husband is 70 years old. We've been married for 40 years. Last summer he was arrested for drunk driving. Over the years, we both felt he drank too much at times, but now we both agree he had a drinking problem because he had a complete blackout. He didn't remember being arrested or even driving.

He hasn't touched a drop since. He goes to Alcoholics Anonymous and I go to Al-anon. It has helped a lot, but now he says that when one year is up he might try to drink wine only. I'm running scared. What can I do?

A: People who get drunk and drive and have blackouts at any age are usually alcoholics. When they do it at age 70, it is suicidal and homicidal because they already have diminished brain and reflex capacity simply because of their age.

Keep going to Al-anon and urge him to keep up with Alcoholics Anonymous. Have a joint family discussion with your children and grandchildren. Show him your love and your family resolve. There might even be some shedding of tears—and that's good. Many 70-year-olds quit comfortably after such an emotional meeting.

Q: I've just had my third drunk-driving conviction in three years. Only one of them involved an accident. I am 45 and a professional person. I have never had trouble with the law except for

DWIs. I have an excellent work record, and I'm respected as a community leader.

My DWIs were all related to excessive drinking after extreme disappointments of the work day. I see them as extremely immature behavior on my part. Am I an alcoholic, and what can I do?

A: Three drunk-driving convictions even in five years is a serious sign of a drinking problem. The good news is that you don't sound like an immature personality at all. If anything, you're probably too much the other way. You sound like an ideal treatment case. Find a good treatment program in your area and learn better ways of dealing with your disappointments at work.

Q: My 60-year-old father is starting a drunk-driving diversion course because of his second driving-under-the-influence charge. Frankly, he is such a sick alcoholic that I don't see how he's going to understand what they're teaching him. With my help, he took one of those multiple-choice alcoholism tests and scored very high. He has all the symptoms except a history of delusions and hallucinations.

The problem is he doesn't think he needs help. He doesn't want help. He says he can quit any time he wants to (but he somehow doesn't seem to want to), and all the while he keeps on drinking and destroying himself. How can I help him? I feel responsible for him because I am responsible for him.

A: All the negatives that you are citing in order to demonstrate his unwillingness to go to treatment are the same ones I see in almost every alcoholic patient I treat. Take it from me, there are few, if any, real volunteers in alcohol treatment hospitals.

Arrange for a professional intervention through an alcohol treatment center. Give him all your love and support—but insist that he gets treatment. If your sincerest efforts fail to get him into treatment, at least make sure that he no longer drives a car. You may even have to have him arrested if he does drink and drive. This may sound frightening or cruel to you, but it might be the most loving and responsible thing you can do for him. It would also get his attention.

Q: In your answer to the lady whose son was arrested for drunk driving, you said the worst thing that could happen to a young man guilty of drunk driving is for a lawyer to get him off on a legal technicality. That may be true, but I think what's even worse is to let a drunk driver keep on driving and probably *kill* other people. I've had three friends killed by drunk drivers. When will people care enough to stop drunk drivers?

A: My answer was aimed at the type of lawyer who repeatedly gets drunk drivers off on legal technicalities even when the lawyer knows that the client has alcoholism. Nevertheless, your point is well taken. Letting a drunken person drive is potentially deadly for him and other people.

"When will people care enough to stop drunk drivers?" you ask. The answer is simple to state, but difficult to make into a reality. The best way to stop a drunk driver is to see that he doesn't get behind the wheel of a car in the first place. Only you and I, that is, the people who know him, can do that. (Lawyers and even policemen get into the act much too late.)

In order to pull that off, we have to be willing to do something about the situation right then and there, such as driving our drunken friend home, paying for a taxi, or letting him sleep it off on our couch; and be willing to take his anger and rejection (which he will have forgotten by the next morning, anyway). Unfortunately, many people don't get to this stage until they have personal cause for righteous anger, as you have.

Q: The President's Drunk Driving Commission has recommended that the minimum drinking age be raised to 21 in all states. I was gratified to hear that. I was dismayed, however, when I read that

President Reagan opposed this recommendation. How can the President not be aware of the seriousness of this problem, and how can he stand in the way of a report by his own commission?

A: Your letter suggests that your sentiments are genuine, but your information is a little off the mark. The Presidential Commission on Drunk Driving made a recommendation to the Congress to withhold federal funds for highway construction from those states that failed to establish a minimum drinking age of 21. A White House spokesman was quoted as saying that the Administration does not support a *federal law* setting a minimum drinking age of 21. However, there is no doubt about President Reagan's sincerity as a human being when he speaks personally on this problem. "Drunk driving is a national menace, a national tragedy, and a national disgrace," President Reagan said. "It is my fervent hope that this report will receive the attention it deserves, and that it will speed the adoption of whatever measures are appropriate to remove this hazard from our national life."

Those of us who met with President Reagan on two occasions to present to him the findings of this commission were convinced of his sincerity and his awareness on a personal level of how serious a national problem drunk driving really is.

Q: I was stopped for "driving under the influence." I know that I didn't have any more drinks than I usually do, and I certainly didn't feel drunk. I passed almost all the roadside tests, except I made one little mistake, which is why the police insisted on doing a blood test. The test showed my blood-alcohol concentration to be .25. As I was leaving the police station, I heard one policeman say to another that I was probably an alcoholic. I realized that my blood-alcohol level was above normal, but I also knew that I didn't act drunk. What I want to know is how could that policeman call me an alcoholic?

A: The blood-alcohol concentration at which most states will draw the limit for driving under the influence is .10. The fact that you appeared to be normal, that you were able to walk, were able to drive your car and pass "almost" all the roadside tests even though your brain was operating under a blood-alcohol concentration of .25, all these facts indicate that you have a tremendous tolerance for alcohol, and that is a cardinal sign of alcohol addiction. A helpful analogy would be this: a half a grain of morphine puts a normal person flat on his back, but a heroin addict can take two grains of morphine, drive his car, and not appear loaded. But when you test him, you'll find out that he is loaded.

Think about it this way. If we gave your Aunt Betsy enough alcohol so that her blood-alcohol level would be .25, she would be in an intensive care unit because her ability to breathe would be compromised, to say nothing of her ability to maneuver an automobile in city traffic. Policemen generally assume that somebody with a blood-alcohol level of .10 or .12 could be a "social drinker" who has had "one too many." Your very high blood-alcohol level, combined with seemingly normal functioning, clinically makes you an alcoholic. This is what the policeman was alluding to.

Q: Our 22-year-old son was arrested for drunk driving. According to police reports he was visibly drunk at the scene. He also had a positive breath machine test. Since he is still in college and dependent on us financially, he asked me to find him a lawyer who "can get me off so I won't lose time from my studies."

I am well-known in this community. I have a good reputation and could easily find such a lawyer. However, my wife thinks I should let him take the local drunk-driving diversion course and accept his punishment. Although we are both sure that he's not an alcoholic, we can't agree on what to do.

A: Your wife is definitely on the right track. If the facts are as you state them, then your son is guilty of drunk driving. It means that he was drunk—and he was driving. It also means that he needs to learn how alcohol affects the brain, the body and driving performance.

The worst thing you can do for a young man guilty of drunk driving is to get him off on a legal technicality. That will only reinforce his denial.

Have your son take the drunk-driving course. If he's not an alcoholic, the knowledge he gains from the course will enable him to modify his drinking. As a result, he will never again have a drunk-driving problem. If, on the other hand, he is an early alcoholic, getting him off now will reinforce his denial and contribute to his eventual death. Time and again I see middle-aged chronic alcoholics with severe, terminal physical complications of alcoholism. What they all have in common is that 10 or 15 years earlier, they had had several drunk-driving episodes which they were able to minimize or deny while they continued drinking and getting sicker. The culprit in such a case was usually a well-meaning cop who drove "the kid" home, an opportunistic lawyer who "got him off," or a politically savvy judge who slapped him on the wrist.

The cop, the lawyer, and the judge were all serving their own interests—at the expense of their young client. Are you about to do the same? Are you tempted to preserve your good reputation in the community at the expense of your son?

Q: I am writing in regard to a friend who is in a prison in Alaska. He is 35 years old, a college graduate with an IQ of 130, and has been a chronic alcoholic for years. He is serving time for first-degree murder. He remembers nothing of the incident during which he shot his friend. His blood-alcohol level at that time was 0.40 percent.

He wants to improve himself and is taking correspondence courses. What can he do about his alcoholism?

A: Your friend is undoubtedly alcoholic as attested to by his blackouts and by the fact that he was even able to stand up with a blood-alcohol level of 0.40. (Normal people usually die of alcohol poisoning if their blood-alcohol level gets that high.)

Your friend can start taking correspondence courses on alcoholism and drug addiction. More importantly, he should get some counseling and insist on attending AA meetings. There are Alcoholics Anonymous groups in almost every prison, with some 30,000 members of AA attending them. (These are prisoners who joined AA after they got into prison.) The recidivism rate for ex-convicts who are members of AA is extrememly low. Also, attending AA meetings and growing emotionally in the program of recovery will increase his chances for parole.

More importantly, he will have to learn how not to drink if he's ever going to live a normal life and stay out of prison. If there is no AA group in his prison, have him write to Alcoholics Anonymous, General Service Office, Post Office Box 459, Grand Central Station, New York NY 10163. If he writes to them about his problem, they will see that an AA meeting is started.

Q: I am 23 years old and doing a two-year sentence in prison for a crime I committed while I was drunk.

One night when I was real drunk, a friend and I broke into a restaurant and I was arrested. I remember nothing about the break-in. Is it normal not to remember what you are doing when you drink? I drank for about 13 hours that day. What can I do to help myself? I don't want to come back to this prison.

A: No, it is not normal not to remember what you are doing when you're drinking alcohol. What you had is called an alcoholic blackout. It happens to alcoholics quite often, and many of them, like you, end up in jail.

You have already begun to help yourself by acknowledging that you have a problem. Ask your prison authorities to involve you in counseling. Also, ask them about attending Alcoholics Anonymous meetings. In almost every prison there are such meetings conducted by visiting AA members from nearby communities on a regular basis. Learning to live the AA way of life while you're in prison is your best guarantee for not having to return to prison again.

Q: I had my first drink of alcohol as a combat soldier in Vietnam. After becoming a civilian I continued to drink more. In the last eight years I've had seven arrests for assault and battery in connection with excessive drinking and flashbacks to my Vietnam days. I've also lost two families, a business, and several hundred thousand dollars of assets during my drinking binges.

At present, I am serving a 15-year sentence for bank robbery, which I committed while having a flashback and while I was drunk. I think I wanted to commit suicide, but I didn't have the guts to do it. I was hoping the cops would do it for me.

What can I do to understand my past and to change my life?

A: You sound like a chronic alcoholic of the binge-drinker variety. The drinking has to stop and your alcoholism has to be treated before you can have a normal life. You may also have other psychological problems for which you may need additional therapy.

Ask the prison authorities for an opportunity to get counseling. Also, start attending Alcoholics Anonymous meetings. They are free and available in all federal correctional institutions. I know many recovering alcoholics who found AA and treatment while in prison. Today they are happy, serene, financially secure, loving family members, and productive people.

Q: I am a 52-year-old woman and newly appointed as an executive of my company. Lately I drink at home to "relax" because if I started showing anger or signs of frustration on the job I would be committing political suicide. I can't afford to be seen as "too emotional."

How do recovered, alcoholic executives handle job pressures? What do they do when their emotions tell them to scream or throw things, but their knowledge of corporate politics tells them to smile and keep a stiff upper lip?

A: Your drinking is pathological because you are using alcohol to fix your emotions and a frustrating life situation. Recovered alcoholics have learned to stay within their limitations, that is, they no longer feel compelled to do other people's work as well as their own; and they have learned how to maintain a balance between work, family life, and hobbies. Most of all, they have a spiritual sense of why they are in this world, which most of them got through their friends and their sponsor in Alcoholics Anonymous. When life's pressures mount, these are the things they turn to, with much better results than the alcohol they formerly turned to.

Q: I have been drinking for 25 years. I'm desperate. I want to stop drinking. It has ruined my life. I still have a job, but I lose about one day a week from work due to terrible hangovers. I have also lost my fiancee because of it. I have tried the AA program. Is there anything else I can do?

A: You are a middle- to late-stage alcoholic with family, work, and health problems due to drinking. Ask your foreman or the medical department of your plant to refer you to the Employee Assistance Program. Since AA alone has not worked for you, you need a rehabilitation program where you will also learn how to use AA as a support system after the hospital treatment is completed.

Q: I am a successful workaholic lawyer and a Type A personality. I am neat, I am punctual. I can sniff out problems, and I continually overachieve in anything I do. Unfortunately, I am also becoming an alcoholic. Are Type A personalities treatable?

A: They are among the best treatment cases precisely because of the traits you have. Through modern treatment methods, you will learn to use your personality assets in the pursuit of sobriety. You will also learn how to remain productive and at the same time be good to yourself and sniff the roses.

I remembered the booze after each rehearsal, after each show—a relaxant, I felt, to ease the tension. My feelings of guilt, my gnawing self-doubts that I was worthy of the adulation, produced a constant fear that the gift would be taken away as suddenly and as mysteriously as it had been bestowed on me. A fifth of Scotch at a time soon became two fifths. Then came the barbiturates and the tranquilizers the doctors gave me to wean me from the booze—except that I took the pills by the handful and washed them down with booze. God, the vomiting, the fits of mindless violence that overcame me—ripping sinks out of walls, trying to throw Mel Brooks out of an eighteenth-story window...and the paranoia. Everyone was out to destroy me.

Where Have I Been?
Sid Caesar

2

Is It Booze, Drugs, or Mental Illness? The Answer Is Yes!

Most alcoholics or drug addicts at one time or another fear that they are losing their minds. As a matter of fact, if you have known people who have such problems, you too, may at times consider them mentally ill. The reason is that mental symptoms and behavioral problems are the most common manifestations of chemical dependency. Indeed, these people are likely to consult psychiatrists or end up in a mental hospital for varying periods of time.

Why should this be? Are chemically dependent people for the most part mentally ill? The answer is No! And the explanation is very simple. The reason they appear mentally ill is because excessive doses of mind-altering drugs—including recreational drugs, alcohol, and even prescription drugs—produce distressing mental symptoms even in normal people. Such varied symptoms as anxiety, depression, insomnia, poor impulse control, personality change, sexual dysfunction, paranoia, delusions, illusions, hallucinations, amnesia, and even suicidal, homicidal, or genocidal ideations can all be caused by alcohol or drug abuse.

The good news is that these symptoms almost always disappear soon after a person becomes clean and sober, i.e., free of mind-altering drugs and alcohol. The people of AA have known this for a long time, and clinicians who work in rehabilitation hospitals find this out very quickly.

The bad news is that physicians and psychotherapists *in general* don't know this. What's even worse, they feel that alcohol or drug abuse is a sign of an underlying mental disorder. Thus when a chemically dependent person seeks help from a medical professional, chances are nine out of ten that he or she will get a diagnosis of anxiety, depression, or worse, along with a prescription for tranquilizers even though the symptoms were caused by drugs in the first place. And since most physicians don't know anything about cross-tolerance or sedativism, the patient will in due time become addicted to more than one substance (or poly-addicted), usually to alcohol *and* whatever tranquilizers were prescribed.

Actually, the dependent person—let's say he's a friend of yours—now has a multiple monkey on his back. He may drink less, but he will obviously be "out of it" because of the combined effects of booze and drugs. Meanwhile, the therapist and he will set out on a therapeutic search for the underlying mental problem. The goal of this approach seems to be that your friend will be able to return to social drinking or recreational drug use as soon as his underlying mental problem is solved. Meanwhile, your friend will be allowed to drink and smoke pot "reasonably" to help him bear the strain of his problems.

Naturally, your friend will love this arrangement for obvious reasons, but nothing positive will happen. The therapy will go on with ups and downs until the patient quits going to the sessions, goes broke, or dies from an overdose; or until the therapist finally realizes that treating a patient psychologically while he's still using drugs is about as effective as sending a sick jelly fish to an orthopedic surgeon.

As an intelligent person you've had some doubts about this case all along. Even before your friend got into therapy, your basic question was "Is he on something, or is he mentally ill?"

The answer to both questions is "Yes"—he is on something, and it makes him mentally ill. Before any real progress can be made, the therapist and your friend and you have to accept the idea that in almost all cases the booze or drugs produced the symptoms— instead of the other way around.

Most successful therapists have learned this the hard way. When I began insisting that my patients go through rehab and stay clean and dry for at least six months before I would look at them again psychiatrically, they began telling me how and why they had lost respect for previous therapists. One of my patients said, "When my doctor told me to cut down, I couldn't believe it! I already knew that it can't be done, but how come he didn't know? It made me wonder about his competence in other areas. The only thing for me to do was to keep on drinking and keep on lying."

Chemically dependent people are no more mentally ill than the rest of us. If anything, they have basically healthier ego defense mechanisms. Those few who after six to twelve months of abstinence and emotional growth still need intensive psychotherapy become tremendously rewarding patients because their brains are clear. As a result, they bring into therapy the same intellectual and emotional resources which they formerly shared with their bartenders and their drinking buddies.

However, it will probably be up to you to get your friend or loved one to that point by getting him into a drug-free treatment track to begin with. Left to their own devices, substance abusers will always prefer treatment which allow them to use "at least a little something," and they will continue to get high on something.

Dependency, Denial, and Depression

The three "D's" of alcoholism are *dependency*, *denial*, and *depression*. The drinking problem begins with *dependency*.

People in general start drinking in a variety of settings and for similar reasons. But if you are an alcoholic, you gradually become emotionally dependent on some of the things that go with drinking.

The *dependency* is usually tied to the good feelings that come with the drinking scene—for example, the camaraderie of the saloon for the lonely; the storytelling ability for the tongue-tied; the opportunity of being a big shot for those who otherwise feel inferior; a way to be casual for those who are rigid; and a means of feeling sexy for those who are frigid.

As the drinking habit gets worse, it causes problems with your personal relationships, the law, your health, or your boss. Sooner or later, snide or sincere remarks tell you that you need to change your drinking pattern. But when you try to cut down or go on the wagon, you come face to face with your emotional dependency which is fulfilled by the alcohol and/or the drinking scene.

Now you're in a bind—cutting down makes you uncomfortable, but drinking at your present rate complicates your life. You have to either do something about the problem—or deny that you have a problem.

Predictably, *denial* (denying that you have a problem) is the more usual reaction. Therefore those people who have been hinting at your problem will have to change their tune, or you'll have to get them out of your life. Family members who can't learn to live with your problem as it is will find themselves abandoned or divorced. Friends who complain will be traded in for drinking buddies so that eventually you can honestly say, "Everybody I know drinks as I do." Birds of a feather drink together.

To deny the meaning of your drunken-driving episodes, you have a number of options: start driving extra carefully; have other people drive you; take cabs; move next door to your favorite watering hole; or switch to drinking only at home.

To deny health problems you try vitamins, exercise binges, health fads, or nerve pills; or you stop going to doctors altogether. (Many of my alcoholic patients had no physical or dental exam for years in order to keep their problem secret.) You may also get a new doctor—maybe one who drinks as much as you do.

To deny your problem at work, you become an intermittent overachiever. You volunteer for brief, unpleasant or inconvenient tasks that nobody at the office wants to do. That way you accumulate brownie points which you can later use as trading stamps for troubled times. For example, when you're hung over and run your fork lift into a stack of oil drums, the foreman will probably get the boss off your back by saying, "Let's not be too tough on Charlie. Remember, he worked through the Fourth of July weekend when we were in a bind." You may also switch to a new line of work where heavy drinking is a part of the work scene.

Depression, the third "D" of alcoholism, sets in when the dependency finally has to be faced. It happens when the denial no longer works because the drinker's environment stops cooperating. The family and maybe even some drinking buddies are no longer willing to go along. Sometimes there is a troublesome legal problem, for example, a hit-and-run driving accident, or you were arrested for exhibitionism. (Actually, you were drunk and innocently urinated between cars in a parking lot at midnight.)

In the area of health problems the denial stops working when the drinking puts you in the hospital because of high blood pressure, hepatitis, cirrhosis, etc.

At the office, denial stops working when the boss can no longer afford the actual or potential consequences of your drinking. That's when you hit the bottom line: because of your marginal judgment, decreasing performance, increasing absenteeism, or inflated expense account, you are fired or retired. If you

are lucky and your employer cares about you, he will order you
into treatment for alcoholism.

For most chemically dependent people, there is a natural
progression from an occasional chemical fix to outright daily
dependency on chemical panaceas. Regardless of what biochemical or hereditary aspects of alcoholism might be, using *denial*
instead of accepting the reality of one's *dependency* seems to
make sense at first; and *depression,* the third "D," is an
unavoidable way station on the road back to reality and sanity.
That's why alcoholics who are depressed in the early phase of
their rehabilitation usually have a good prognosis for recovery.

If your loved one is now in treatment for alcoholism and has
been delighted about the whole process from the first moment on,
it means that he needs more confrontation and evaluation. He's
either psychotic and doesn't realize what's going on, or he's
immature and has a lot of growing up to do. In short, he is still
using denial, because he's not yet facing the reality of his
problem. To give up such a universal problem fixer as booze is
downright depressing.

Drinking and Depression: Cause and Effect

Drinking and depression are as American as Scotch and soda or
apple pie and ice cream. Brooding Bogart boozing in Rick's bar
in the movie *Casablanca,* a mother turning to the bottle in the
"empty-nest syndrome," and the recently retired workaholic
drinking himself to death—they are all bread-and-butter Ameri-
cana. It's pretty obvious, you say. They drink like that because
they're depressed—that's just common sense.

Well, sometimes common sense is nonsense. The clinical fact is
that if they drink like that, no wonder they're depressed. The
medical literature shows that even in normal people, heavy

drinking can cause all the symptoms that are classically seen in depression. Among them are insomnia, appetite disturbance, sexual problems, lethargy, apathy, anxiety, depression, suspiciousness, paranoia, and suicidal ideas. Also, the effectiveness of every drug prescribed for anything is altered in the presence of heavy drinking.

When a heavy drinker with depression comes to see me, I use a very direct approach. I tell the patient, "Look, you say you're drinking because you're depressed? That no longer makes any sense. The drinking has obviously not helped you. In fact, you're getting more depressed. The reason is that heavy drinking makes your symptoms worse and gives you new problems.

"It may be true that you started drinking because you were depressed; *but now you're depressed because you're drinking.* I want you to stop drinking until we get your problems cleared up."

What will the reaction be when the doctor explains these things to the drinker? Well, that depends on the drinker's personality and on the type of drinking problem he has. If the patient is a social drinker, he will take the doctor's advice seriously. He stops drinking, and almost immediately his problems get better, and in about four weeks the results are dramatic. Why? Because the prescribed drugs he had been taking and the other treatments he was getting for whatever problems he had are finally starting to do what they were designed to do.

If, on the other hand, the patient is a problem drinker, his reaction to the doctor's advice will not be favorable. Even though the doctor and he may have had good rapport in the past, the patient will suddenly develop serious doubts about the doctor's judgment. Why? Because he doesn't like the advice he got. He may try to stop drinking temporarily to please the doctor. But when he realizes that he has become dependent on alcohol, he'll get even more depressed and he'll drink even more. He'll probably also start to hide his drinking because he feels guilty.

Naturally, he won't feel better, and his problems won't get any better.

If the patient is an alcoholic, there will be no question in his mind about the quality of his doctor's judgment: he will conclude at once that any doctor who gives that kind of advice is clearly incompetent. To solve his problem he will stop seeing his doctor altogether and at the same time increase his visits to the bartender. In his spare time he will go doctor-shopping until he finds one who is willing to start a whole new cycle of tests and pills to study and treat the depression. He will stay with the new treatment and gladly suffer any number of tests—provided the doctor continues to condone heavy social drinking as "understandable under the circumstances."

The worst thing that can happen to the depressed drinker is to find a psychotherapist who is willing to make an interim diagnosis of "symptomatic drinking." The working assumption is that the doctor and the patient will set out on a search to find the underlying cause of the depression. This is a doomed project because no matter what the therapist says or thinks, the patient will interpret his remarks to mean that the drinking is due to depression, and that a series of treatment sessions and a variety of pills will eventually lead him back to the point where he will not only feel better, but can also become a social drinker again.

The situation is much worse if the therapist ignores the patient's drinking altogether. The danger here is that the patient will take this to mean that heavy drinking is necessary for him as a coping device until the depression has been cured.

Meanwhile, the effects of alcohol on the body and on the medications that the patient is taking continue to aggravate all the symptoms and dig the black hole deeper. The doctor is reluctant to insist on abstinence, and the patient continues to "have just a few." They are both hoping that only a slight amount of the patient's depression is due to the effects of alcohol; that moderate drinking won't make it much worse.

This line of reasoning is both false and dangerous. It is very much like wondering how much of your headache is innate, and how much is caused by your banging your head against the wall.

The first order of business is to stop banging your head against the wall. If you can't do that, you are probably a head-bangaholic. No depression is so slight or so deep that drinking won't make it worse. The patient who treats himself has a fool for a doctor; and so is the depressed patient who drinks has John Barleycorn for a doctor. In either case, the prognosis is poor.

Cutting Down? Maybe It's Time to Cut It Out!

"Cutting down" on drinking is the problem drinker's way of attempting to prove that he is still in control of his drinking.

Let's talk about John and Mary. John's drinking was all fun and games—until he started to get drunk even on those occasions when he intended not to get drunk. At that point they both agreed that John should cut down. It was surprisingly easy—for about a month, but after that, as he occasionally got drunk again, he had to start using rationalizations in order to explain away his problem.

"I know it was your birthday," he would argue defensively the next morning. "The reason I got drunk is because I didn't eat. I came to the party straight from work and drank on an empty stomach." At other times he would argue, "Mary, don't get on me about last night. You know it wasn't my fault. It was Jack's fault. He always makes the drinks too strong." Or, "My hay fever made me more susceptible."

As he got sicker, he also found more face-saving reasons for cutting down or for going on the wagon: there was Lent; a New Year's resolution; his upcoming annual physical; or laughingly, "just a bet with the guys at the office."

The actual reasons for cutting down were really the complaints he was getting about the consequences of his drinking—complaints, which, by the way, he would have to discredit by his rationalizations. For example, his loving, but complaining wife Mary was dismissed as "a nut when it came to drinking"; and complaints from his daughter were brushed aside as "sophomoric ideas" about drinking and smoking that she gets from her liberal, pinko-commie health science teacher.

He became more concerned when a flight attendant refused to serve him more drinks and when his boss made a comment about hangovers. Finally, one morning he could not remember what had happened at a party the night before. The look of horror on his wife's face made him cry out, "I am going to stop drinking for 60 days to prove to you once and for all that I don't have a problem."

The next week was awful. Lunch without drinking was easy—he simply went on a no-lunch diet. But facing Mary after a day's work and starting dinner without having had cocktails was difficult. (He thought of Hemingway who, early one afternoon, told his butler, "Bring in the drinks, for God's sake! Somewhere in the world it must be 5 o'clock!")

The "Tonight Show" with ginger ale wasn't funny; and he had a hard time falling asleep without a nightcap.

After a particularly bad night of tossing and turning (caused by the interrupted sleep of the abstaining heavy drinker) and an early morning argument with Mary, he showed up at the office looking terrible. A colleague took one look at him and said, "John, if I looked like that when I'm not drinking—I'd drink."

But by the fourth week of not drinking, something positive seemed to have happened: John looked and felt better than he had for years. His eyes were clear, the athletic spring in his step was back, and Mary noticed that he was feeling his oats again. And after sixty days on the wagon he announced with pride and relief, "Mary, this should prove for once and for all that I don't have a problem. To celebrate the occasion I'm going to have a double Scotch and then go to sleep.''

The next morning he awoke at ten o'clock—very hungover and unable to remember what had happened the night before. As he blinked the world into focus, he saw Mary standing at the foot of the bed, taller than he had ever seen her. With that hurt look on her face, she was saying: "John, last night you set out to have a drink. On your third double when I said something about it, you got mad. You hit me, and you stormed into the bedroom. By three o'clock in the morning, you had drunk a quart of Scotch.

"This morning I didn't wake you; and I didn't call your boss. I'm through covering up for you. You definitely have a drinking problem."

In the alcoholic's life, this is the point in time when he can start his recovery because the people who are close to him have come to realize that he has lost control. If they now get honest with him, his chances for recovery are excellent. Unfortunately, what usually happens is that the people who can help him the most, namely wives, friends, and bosses, are more apt to abandon him by divorce, estrangement, or premature (or forced) retirement. They do this because they want to avoid the pain of confronting him. It is in this way that all of us—drinkers, spouses, friends, bosses, and even doctors—perpetuate the drinker's problem—and our own problem.

Reward Drinking May Be an Early Sign

Alcoholic drinks are something many people give or receive as a reward. Buying drinks for a sports hero, toasting a celebrity, treating an old friend to a drink, or giving somebody a case of booze for Christmas are all part of our culture.

If you drink normally and have no problem with alcohol, you would say, "That's all part of social drinking. A drink or two is enjoyed by two or more people because it breaks the ice, facilitates conversation, renews a friendship, commemorates an event, etc.'' And most people would agree with you.

However, when you start buying drinks for yourself because you ''deserve'' a drink (you did a good job today); or you're toasting yourself in the barroom mirror; or you're celebrating something—but you're the only one present at the celebration, then you might be entering a phase called ''reward drinking,'' which is often an early sign of a drinking problem.

The transition from social drinking to reward drinking is gradual and insidious. It happens every day even to some of the smartest, richest, and most beautiful people.

Let's look at this transitional drinking stage in more detail because, like a chest X-ray, it could save your life.

Remember the time you were still a non-drinker because you were a child? You had never tasted booze in your life, and you didn't know what you were missing. But you were more than a little curious about drinking because the big people were doing it. And then one day, you tried it: behind the barn, or after a homecoming dance, or as a seventeen-year-old sailor on shore leave in Hong Kong.

The hows, whys and wherefores don't matter. Whether you loved it instantly or hated it doesn't matter. I have known alcoholics who were drinking champions right off the bat, and I know other alcoholics who required years of practice before they could hold their booze.

The significant point is that sooner or later you liked what alcohol did for you. You say that you drank because you liked the taste, because it made company more enjoyable, because it was a custom, or because of a hundred other things. Chances are you drank because of the good feelings you got from alcohol.

Maybe that's when you first discovered Friday night Happy Hour: the warm, chummy atmosphere, and the guys talking at the end of a hard week. You rewarded them by treating them to a drink, and they rewarded you by treating you to a drink.

That worked fine until you discovered that Wednesday was Happy Hour too. Soon, you were rewarding yourself twice a week for the same week. You probably didn't notice that some of your co-workers seemed to get enough "reward" with one or two drinks on Friday, while you had progressed to a double dose. Why didn't you notice? Because you had begun to select your friends on the basis of how much they drank.

It happened one Friday night when you and Bob were at Happy Hour. You wanted to reward him with another drink, which, of course, meant that he would have to buy a round in return. Suddenly, to your utter amazement, he left his beer half finished and went off to a PTA meeting. To you, that was downright weird. It gave you an eye-opening insight into your friend, Bob. It made you feel depressed.

Covertly angry, you picked up your drink and you moved to the other end of the bar where you met some regulars—guys who held their own Happy Hour daily. Almost instantly you felt more comfortable, especially when they agreed with you that Bob must be a weird guy. Even though they didn't dwell on it, a part of you made a decision never to drink with Bob again.

And soon thereafter you could honestly say that "everybody I know drinks a lot." As a matter of fact, a year later you heard that Bob had been transferred to another plant six months ago; and you'd never noticed that he was gone. You didn't know people like Bob anymore.

About the same time you came to realize that mowing your lawn could actually be fun. (Formerly, your wife had a hard time to get you to acknowledge that you even had a lawn.) But then you discovered that if you parked a cold can of beer on the front step, and if you slowed down with every other pass of the mower

and took another swig of beer, it somehow made your lawn-
mower work better.

And then one Saturday morning you heard your neighbor say
to his wife, "Hey, look, Martha, there's Charlie mowing his lawn
again. Look how he's sweating. No wonder he's having a beer.
When a man works that hard, he deserves a beer." And thus, you
became a devout lawn mower.

So much so that if it rained on a Saturday morning, you'd be
pacing in your living room, at times staring out the window,
furious because your lawn had to go uncut. What was really
frustrating you was that you had to come up with some other
bona fide reason for having a couple of beers at 9 o'clock in the
morning. Maybe that's how you got so interested in working with
your tools in the garage where you just had to have a beer
because it was hot and stuffy in there without an air conditioner.

Gradual and insidious, isn't it? For that reason I recommend
that every year or so the smart social drinker should give himself
a test: See how happy you can be without Happy Hour. Does
your gasohol mower still work when you drink lemonade? Does
everybody know you drink a lot?

Well, as the old saying goes, birds of a feather drink together.

Alcohol and Memory Loss

"I don't remember doing that" is a classical refrain in the lives of
drunkards and alcoholics. It's a type of memory loss caused by
alcohol effects in the brain and is usually a sign of alcoholism.
Better known as an alcoholic blackout, the experience can be
puzzling, embarrassing, litigious or costly, depending on whether
you are the alcoholic, his family, his lawyer, or his boss.

The blackout is not the same as fainting, passing out, sleeping
it off, drinking yourself into a stupor, or having a seizure. Rather,
it is a circumscribed period of amnesia: The drinker seemed to be
his usual drinking self (dancing, talking on a phone, bowling,

borrowing or lending money, driving a car, etc.) but the next morning he had no memory of what he said or did.

Business deals, surgical operations, murders, and marriages have been performed or committed by people in blackouts. Blackouts may cover a span of minutes, hours, or days. Sid Caesar in his recent book *Where Have I Been?* describes how, at the height of his alcoholic drinking, he traveled with his wife to Australia, filmed an entire motion picture, and returned to the United States. To this day he does not remember the trip, Australia, or the movie.

With rare exceptions, blackouts occur during heavy drinking, and are due to a failure of short-term memory formation. Basically, the normal brain knows three types of memory: immediate memory (ability to remember events for up to one minute); remote memory (you remember what the weather was like on your wedding day—unless you got married in a blackout); and short-term memory, which is in between.

The theory is that alcohol in the brain interferes with the formation or storage of short-term memory. Regardless of future findings, the facts are that the person in a blackout does well from minute to minute while drinking, but later has no memory of what transpired.

About 70 percent of alcoholics have blackouts. Some have them from their first drinking experience on, while others develop them after years of drinking. Non-alcoholics can also have blackouts, but they usually have only one or two such episodes because they cut down on their drinking and avoid further blackouts. Alcoholics, on the other hand, consider blackouts the price you pay for drinking. They rationalize that "everybody has that problem once in a while," partly because most of their friends are also blackout drinkers, and also because they don't want to—or can't—cut down on their drinking.

Blackouts happen most frequently when the drinker gulps large amounts of alcohol rapidly, when he's very fatigued, when he mixes other drugs with the alcohol (especially sedatives, tranquilizers or marijuana), or if he has a history of head injuries (especially boxers or other contact-sport athletes).

Blackouts are the dread of alcoholics on the morning after. A clinical example is Charlie. He peeks out of his living room window and heaves a sigh of relief because his car is parked in the driveway. But he remains uneasy because he can't remember how he got home.

"Have I harmed or killed anyone?" he wonders. Wearing slippers and a robe, he circles the car in ankle-deep snow and casually inspects the bumpers. "Whew—at least I didn't hit anything." Next he goes through his wallet. "Boy—80 bucks gone! I hope I had a good time. I sure paid for it." Then he telephones you. "Wow!" he says, "That was some party we had last night, eh?" hoping that you will tell him what exactly did happen.

If he is blessed with a nagging wife, he is spared the search. All he has to do is walk into the kitchen and groan and listen to a detailed tirade.

A different type of alcoholic, for example the "Aunt Betsy" type of alcoholic, usually has a different pattern. She telephones you at 8 p.m. She sounds a bit slurred, but otherwise fine as she tells you about a particular event. The next morning she calls you again and casually describes the same event without any awareness that she told you the same story last night. She also has bruises on her thigh and can't remember falling down.

If you have blackouts, you know about it by now. To figure out if your loved one has blackouts, just test your memory against his—on the morning after—but be sure you do it a number of times, because even chronic alcoholics don't have blackouts every time they drink.

How do you avoid having blackouts? Here are some guidelines. Don't drink rapidly; don't drink heavily—especially when you're tired; don't mix alcohol and other drugs; and don't drink at all if you've had a head injury. Also, don't drink to "forget," because even with booze you can't forget the things you already remember.

Resentment and the Chronic Drinker

An early sign of a drinking problem is chronic resentment—with flashes of anger. When John Doe begins to suspect that he has a drinking problem, he is angered by anything (people, places, or situations) that reminds him of the fact that he is losing control over his drinking. More and more he is annoyed by any casual reference to his drinking. As he gets sicker, his anger flares when others tell jokes about drunks, or even when the subject of drinking comes up in ordinary conversation. At the office, in full view of his co-workers, he angrily slams a newspaper on his desk. When somebody asks what is going on, he yells at the top of his voice, "Here's a story about another one of those phony celebrities coming out of the closet with a drinking problem. I'll bet you there is really something else behind it. It couldn't be alcoholism."

His social life begins to change. He starts avoiding certain restaurants even though he likes the food there. The reason he no longer wants to go there is because they don't serve alcohol. For the same reason, he adamantly refuses to go to Disneyland.

Anger also causes him to start avoiding old friends. "The Snyders are getting to be a bore," he tells his wife Mary. "Let's not get together with them anymore."

Mary is puzzled. The Snyders have always been among their best friends. What she doesn't know is that Rick Snyder quit drinking recently.

John's anger also causes him to avoid non-drinking situations such as Little League games. But one day when his son is pitching in the play-offs, Mary pressures him to go. Before leaving the house, he has a number of stiff drinks because he knows there won't be any booze at the ballpark. While settling down in the bleachers, he gets into an argument with another spectator; and five minutes later he is in a shoving match with the homeplate umpire. Amid cat-calls from the bleachers, Mary finally gets him out of there by making him realize that his son's team is not yet playing—they are still warming up on the next field.

John is momentarily puzzled, then angrily flings his coke into the bushes and stalks off to go home and get a drink. "Ever since they banned beer from this park, it just isn't any fun to come here," he growls as he guns his car out of the parking lot.

John is angry because people, places, and things repeatedly remind him that he has a drinking problem. He is always thinking about drinking—or thinking about not drinking. From time to time, to prove to himself that he doesn't have a problem, he commits himself to self-enforced abstinence known as "white-knuckle sobriety" or being on the wagon. At such times his anger becomes even more distressing. But, since alcohol is a good solvent for anger, he falls off the wagon again.

Such a miserable dry period is a good time to have a consultation at a treatment center for his "drinking problem." Besides that, the biggest favor you could do him is to offer to go with him to Alcoholics Anonymous meetings where he will be guaranteed anonymity and non-involvement until he chooses otherwise. Seeing and hearing all those "alcoholics" exuding warmth and serenity—without even a hint of anger in the house—could become a turning point in his life.

And if he angrily storms out of the AA meeting, you have lost nothing. As a matter of fact, his reaction will only confirm the diagnosis: normal people don't get angry at Alcoholics Anonymous meetings.

"I'm an Alcoholic" Means What?

A prime reason for the alcoholic's reluctance to admit to his disease is his fear of the stigma.

Webster defines *stigma* as (1) a distinguishing mark burned or cut into the flesh, as of a slave or criminal; (2) something that detracts from the character or reputation of a person, group, etc.; a mark of disgrace or reproach; (3) a mark indicating that something is not considered normal or standard.

Today the most prevalent stigmatized disease in the world is alcoholism. It stigmatizes the alcoholic, his family, and his employer. The connotation of shameful, unacceptable or other-wise degrading things that it carries in many people's minds prevents many alcoholics from accepting their disease and seeking help. In that way the stigma of alcoholism has undoubtedly been responsible for the deaths of more alcoholics than the physiologi-cally destructive nature of the disease itself.

(Stigma is also responsible for the miserable lives which many non-drinking alcoholics lead. Most of us know people like that either professionally or socially. These are people who quit drinking alcohol because it was destroying them, but they were nevertheless unable to accept the idea that they had alcoholism. Unfortunately, many such people don't really live—they exist. They are chemically "dry": tense, bitter, depressed, and angry. They are "white-knuckling it" through life one miserable day at a time by using will power and by contemptuously looking down on "those alcoholics.")

Many a sensitive, genteel and otherwise noble soul in the depths of alcoholic anguish has asked me, "Doctor, what would I be admitting to if I said I am an alcoholic? I just can't do that to myself, nor can I do it to the people who love me and care about me." At such times the best thing I can do is to tell the patient of the definition that I once heard an alcoholic give about his disease at an Alcoholics Anonymous meeting. Here is what he said:

"When I say I'm an alcoholic, I make a simple admission, and here is what it is: I admit that I cannot take a drink safely; and that is all I admit. By that I don't admit to being depraved, psychotic, neurotic, wishy-washy, weak-willed, of little learning, unemployed, unemployable, from a poor background, a broken home, or to any of the other opprobrious and terrible things that are often associated with the word *alcoholic*. I simply admit that I cannot take a drink safely."

As definitions go, this one is brilliant. It concisely defines the problem and at the same time points out the first step which is necessary in its solution. What this fellow is saying is that an alcoholic is an *unpredictable drinker*, and that the first step in the solution of the problem is to admit that the problem exists and to stop drinking altogether.

Scientific evidence more and more clearly points to the alcoholic as being a person who, through a combination of genetic, physiological, psychological, and social forces reacts to alcohol differently than other people do. Much like a penicillin allergy which can come on after the very first exposure to the drug or after years of intermittent therapeutically successful use, alcoholism may be evident after the first drink or after years of seemingly normal drinking. An undeniable sign that the worm has turned is when drinking becomes *unpredictable*.

The choices open to an alcoholic are these: (1) he can yield to the stigma and destroy himself by drinking in spite of negative consequences; (2) he can quit drinking (without admitting to a problem) and go on existing in haughty, miserable, white-knuckling denial; or (3) he can defeat the stigma by accepting his disease and getting whatever help he needs to get on with his life.

Incidentally, the man who gave the above definition had his last drink in 1969. Since then he has become happy, healthy, wealthy, and wise, though not necessarily in that order.

The "Problem Drinker"

A frequently misdiagnosed type of alcoholism is exemplified by people who are often called "problem drinkers" because they seem to drink alcoholically when they have problems. They are not physically addicted to alcohol and show no loss of control. They can take it or leave it and at times drink normally.

But they also use alcohol to relieve emotional or physical pain. They then drink at unacceptable times, in unacceptable places, in excessive amounts. It may cause them to miss work, spend more money than they can afford, and create problems with friends and family, but for the most part they continue to function. Often their denial is reinforced by professionals—especially psychiatrists—who diagnose them as "symptomatic alcoholics." The implication is that the drinking is symptomatic of an underlying disorder.

An example of such a patient was John. In recent months he seemed to have no alcohol problems at all. But then he came home from work one day and heard his wife say, "John, I've just been to the doctor. I need a cervical biopsy to make sure I don't have cancer of the cervix. I'm going into the hospital tomorrow morning."

John grew silent. What if she really has cancer? She could die; he would be left with the children. He got so nervous he decided to have a drink to settle his nerves. Three hours later he was drunk and passed out.

The next afternoon, in order to brace himself to visit his wife in the hospital, he had several drinks. When he arrived at the hospital he was frightened, impatient, and angry. When the nurse asked him to have a seat in the waiting room, he caused a scene, and hospital security had to escort him off the premises because he was drunk. His wife was embarrassed and angry because his "drinking problem had come back again."

On his way home John was ashamed and angry at himself. He stopped in a bar for a couple of drinks to settle his nerves. An hour later he was picked up for drunken driving. When he was released from jail at 1 a.m., he had partially sobered up. But when he got home and his neighbor asked him if he was all right, John was so insulting that the neighbor decided never to speak to him again. To help himself go to sleep, John had several more drinks.

The next morning he slept right through the alarm clock and missed work. His foreman, angry because John was not on the job, told the plant manager, "Fire him or lay him off." And when a couple of John's fellow workers pointed out that John had "real problems" (namely, his wife's possible cancer), the foreman did not want to hear any of it. "Don't tell me about his problems. Everybody has problems, but he gets drunk when he has problems, and then I have problems. I have run out of patience—John has done this before."

(What the foreman was alluding to was that six months ago when John's daughter got pregnant by a hippie, John got so upset that he went on a three-week bender to help him forget his troubles.)

Meanwhile, John's wife was still in the hospital recuperating from her biopsy. When her doctor came into her room, he had good news. "Mrs. Smith," he smiled happily, "you don't have cancer. As a matter of fact, you didn't even need the biopsy. The computer made a slight error. That suspicious cancer smear was actually of a woman named Smythe. So, you are perfectly clear and ready to go home."

Relieved of her cancer fear, Mrs. Smith suddenly realized she had another real-life problem, namely her husband's drinking problem. She made several phone calls, got a cab, and instead of going home, decided to move in with her mother. She would finally get the divorce that everybody had been urging her to get for some time. Why? Because John's drinking problem had repeatedly caused problems for both of them. He was unwilling or unable to change, and she was no longer willing to live with the problem.

In the final analysis, John is an alcoholic. His drinking has repeatedly caused family problems (talk of divorce), social problems (arguments with friends and neighbors), legal problems (drunk-driving arrest), and job problems (fired). The practical and humane way to look at it is that if drinking causes this many problems for the drinker and other people around him, then he should quit, even if he is not an alcoholic. And if he can't quit, he obviously is an alcoholic—and somebody who cares about him should see that he gets some help. The late Professor Jellinek put it succinctly: "Alcohol plus damage equals alcoholism." And Father Joseph C. Martin says, "Something that causes a problem *is* a problem."

Marijuana *Is* Addicting

Former National Institute on Drug Abuse director Dr. Robert DuPont calls marijuana the "single biggest new health threat to our nation."

To understand what he means, let's leave marijuana for a minute and talk about drug addiction in general. Addiction can be physical or psychological. You are physically addicted to a drug if you get withdrawal symptoms (insomnia, shakes, convulsions, or D.T.'s) when you don't take the drug; and you are psychologically addicted if the stuff makes you feel so good that you would consider driving through a blizzard to get some when the supply runs low.

For many years, medical academicians have insisted that physical addiction is the only true addiction, and that psychological addiction is only a bad habit. That kind of ivory-tower nonsense is dangerous to society. Those of us in the clinical trenches who treat the chemical casualties in everyday life know that the *opposite* is true. In clinical practice, physical withdrawal symptoms are usually cleared up in one to six weeks. What causes patients to return to drugs or drink is the psychological addiction that has become their lifestyle.

For example, after his withdrawal symptoms are gone, a certain patient can't say no to his pals at the saloon or the club because he feels more loved and appreciated by them than he does at home; another patient may feel that he can't be a salesman and not drink with his customers; and a woman may find herself going back to pills not because her body needs them but because the kids drive her mad.

Now, let's look at marijuana again. What makes pot so dangerous is that the experts call it non-addicting simply because a pot smoker who is off marijuana seems to have no physical withdrawal symptoms. Instead, scientists, doctors, and other experts should point out that pot produces psychological addiction, that is, a compulsion to use it even after it has clearly become a legal, health, or economic hazard for the user.

I treat many patients who are 30 years old and hooked on grass. They can't stop even though they want to. For example, a man's fiancee won't marry him unless he quits. A woman says pot saps her drive and slows her work on her master's thesis. A young executive knows that pot smoking threatens his job—his boss privately told him, "Executives in this company don't smoke grass." An auto mechanic who is on parole knows that getting busted would mean jail. The dry alcoholic teacher says pot always leads him back to booze and other drugs, and then he has to start all over again. All of these people want to cut down or stop—but they can't.

During their teens, they argued in favor of pot the same way their parents defended booze: they enjoyed it, everybody was doing it, and they could quit anytime they wanted to. They even felt smug because they thought they had discovered a "safe" drug. Unlike alcohol, marijuana wasn't addicting, according to health experts.

Today, these patients know that they were addicted to grass by age 20 because they were willing to take risks with it—like carrying it through airline checks in foreign countries even though they knew that being arrested would mean jail for a long time. Also, naively perhaps, they are angry because the system— parents, schools, and the scientific community—looked the other way when they were using pot.

Today, these patients have their own simple, realistic definition of addiction. They say to me, "Listen, Doc, I don't want to hear any more experts defining addiction. When you get to the point where Friday night without pot is a bummer, then you're hooked. All I want to do is get off the stuff—and stay off—so I can get on with my life."

If you have any doubts about yourself, why not give yourself the Friday-night bummer test.

Is He an Alcoholic or a Psychopath?

It was time for morning report at the alcohol treatment unit. "Elwood is a model patient," the student nurse bubbled. "He's been here only three days, and already he's made more progress than other alcoholics who've been here three weeks. I just love him!"

"Let's wait and see," the chief therapist cautioned.

The next day, Elwood's uncle signed him out of the hospital; two days later Elwood was gone—with uncle's car. And a month later, uncle's secretary found out that she was pregnant. Meanwhile, Elwood was on the East Coast, managing an old Army buddy's political campaign . . . and the story goes on.

Actually, Elwood was not an alcoholic. He was a sociopath or a psychopath (a con artist), a person who breaks social rules

without feeling shame or guilt. Why are these two personalities—
the alcoholic and the sociopathic—often misdiagnosed in the
minds of not only lay people but also professionals? Because a
sociopath has no conscience, and alcohol sedates conscience in
anyone, reducing inhibitions and guilt. Thus any drunk can be
pegged either alcoholic or sociopathic depending on his behavior
while he is drunk. However, although the two may look alike
when they're drunk, they're different when they're sober because
they have different characters. The distinction is crucial because
with treatment, most alcoholics recover—but sociopaths rarely
change. Let's compare Jack the alcoholic and Elwood the
sociopath.

Jack, the alcoholic, has middle-class values: empathy for
others; and shame, guilt, and remorse over his social transgres-
sions. Some would say he's so conventional that he's boring.

Elwood the sociopath, on the other hand, is made of more
glittering stuff: charming, bright, energetic, and articulate. But
under this facade he is bad news: self-centered, pleasure-loving,
and manipulative, with a quick sense for other people's vulnera-
bilities. Deep inside he is emotionally cold because he can't
identify with the feelings of others. He may be a romantic lover
or a charismatic leader, but he has no staying power: he gets
bored quickly and moves on to new scenes. He's like a Fourth of
July sparkler—burning at both ends—and you are left holding the
middle. For the moment, you get fantastic light, but you'll end up
being burned.

Elwood drinks to have a good time or to get others drunk so
he can get what he wants, in business or pleasure. "Candy is
dandy but liquor is quicker," he grins infectiously.

If a judge, a wife, or a boss gets him into treatment, he'll play
the game: he feigns remorse when it's expected; he sheds
crocodile tears in group therapy; and he makes a pass at a
nurse—all in the same hour. He tells his wife, "I'm a new man"
and then spends hours phoning still-hopeful entries in his "little

black book"; he plots grand business deals with future partners, but writes phony checks to weary creditors.

In the hospital, while Jack the alcoholic is anxious, depressed, and guilt-ridden, scheming Elwood is comfortable because he knows that he'll soon be gone. When doctors pin Elwood down, he gets himself sprung from the hospital by family, friends or lawyers right into the open arms of other guilt-prone relatives or excitement-starved patsies who need him to spark excitement into their boring lives.

Elwood's crippling defect is his lack of social conscience. "Individual rights" and other legal sanctions are tailor-made to help him avoid treatment or punishment. Add to this his radar sense for people who'll bail him out because "He's so brilliant—if he could only see it," and you have a lifelong script for never-ending maladjustment.

If you know somebody like this, ask yourself the following question: When was the last time he was in trouble without drinking or using drugs? If the answer is "never," it means you've got a Jack—an alcoholic. It also means you should do an intervention and get him treated for his alcoholism.

If, on the other hand, the person you know is bad news—on *or* off the stuff—then you've got an Elwood. Release him with love. Cut him loose. It may sound cruel, but it isn't, because Elwood becomes treatable only when he runs out of gullible relatives, trust funds, and creditors.

Drunks Are Hard to Love—or Hate

Many people agonize over the dilemma, "Is our loved one an alcoholic, i.e., a sick person, or is he just a bad person?" This question often comes up because the most heartbreaking part about loving either an alcoholic or a sociopath is the person's bad behavior.

The problem is that this person is usually one of the brightest, most interesting people you know. Among men, this kind of person's behavior arouses admiration, envy, and vicarious wish-fulfillment ("I wish I could get away with the things he does"). Women, on the other hand, perceive this kind of person as clever, romantic, and lovingly ruthless ("He's trouble—but he's fun to be around").

Unfortunately, this kind of person also arouses other feelings. Men often see him as a protege, so "developing his potential" becomes their challenge. In women, on the other hand, he provokes a chronic stimulation of their mothering instinct. In a way, everybody wants to make him into "the good person he really is."

But, because he stimulates the best and the worst of our most deeply buried urges—and at the same time makes our lives fascinating and miserable—we end up confused. Our emotions about this kind of person go up and down, hot and cold, loving and hateful, but we never come to a final decision about him.

If you live with such a problem, you may need professional help for yourself because you can't see the forest for the trees, or the behavior for the disease. I've had many letters and calls in response to a column entitled, "Not Enough Character to Be a Drunk," in which I dealt with the problem of how to tell the difference between a sociopath and an alcoholic/addict. Here is a typical letter.

"Dear Doctor: Your article on 'Elwood the Sociopath' changed my life because it described my 25-year-old son perfectly. My husband and I now know that our son is not an alcoholic or a drug addict. His 'game' was drugs and alcohol. Over the years my husband and I had many painful, heartbreaking times with our charming, intelligent, handsome, lying, scheming, scamming 'Elwood.' At the same time, we were being drained financially with 'loans,' lawyer's fees, and many other problems.

"My husband was able to 'let go' of our son some time ago, but I could not. As the mother, I was always protecting, forgiving, or 'understanding.' I finally had to get help for myself.

"With the help of outpatient psychotherapy and especially by learning Transactional Analysis, I slowly began to see the situation as it was. Your column came at precisely the right moment for me. It helped me to see that I have been harming my son by bailing him out, and that I was also harming the rest of our family by my overprotective actions on his behalf. The column also helped me to understand why our friends had given us such contradictory advice about our son. The reason is that a number of our friends are doing the same kind of 'enabling' with their own children, some of whom are in their 30s and, just like our 'Elwood,' have handsome, charming, winning ways.

"My husband and I finally concluded that if our 25-year-old son cannot support himself financially, control himself emotionally, or accept help professionally (even at our expense), the best way we can help him is to no longer support him financially or provide other cop-outs for him.

"It was a very hard decision for me to make—even with professional help; but I'm glad I made it. My husband and I both feel relieved. Since we stopped giving our son money, we've not heard from him. We used to be on an emotional seesaw. Now we are sadder but wiser, and therefore more helpful. We still love him. We hope and pray that one day he will seek help and turn his life around."

Releasing with love—as taught by Al-anon—is the only humane answer to this kind of dilemma. If your loved one is an alcoholic, chances are very good that in treatment he will find help and become the kind of person you always knew he could be. But if he's a sociopath, the chances are not so good. It will take longer for him to change, even if he does find help. In either case, you must do your part first. By getting help for yourself, you may also start him on the right road.

Dear Doc...

Question: Our 16-year-old son is currently in juvenile detention while waiting for an opening in a treatment center. Your column on "Elwood the Sociopath" reminded us very much of our boy. We have four children, and he's the only one who is like that. He has been a chronic drug user and alcohol abuser since he was 12.

The reason he is in juvenile detention is that he was guilty of several petty thefts and one sizable burglary (the burglary involved our own house, and police investigations revealed that it was an inside job arranged by our son). He admitted that the things that were stolen in the various episodes were all turned into drug money for himself and his friends.

He has already spent one year in a psychiatric hospital, but it didn't seem to change the way he wants to live. He is a very bright boy, and we now wonder if he is a sociopath.

Answer: If you and your husband are willing to provide additional history, the diagnosis of sociopathic can easily be made. Your sketchy letter suggests that he is a chemically dependent adolescent who meets some of the criteria for the diagnosis of sociopathy, namely, repeated conflicts with legal authorities, lack of guilt feelings when hurting others, and a hedonistic (pleasure-seeking) view of life.

However, in the face of even moderate abuse of mood-altering (and therefore behavior-altering) drugs, it is not possible to make a diagnosis of sociopathy until a professional attempt has been made to treat the alcohol and drug abuse in a facility which specializes in that kind of treatment.

The reason for the diagnostic dilemma is that antisocial or sociopathic behavior often is a result of alcoholism or drug addiction. Most psychiatrists today agree that treatment of such a patient is not effective if it is done in a strictly psychiatric hospital.

Q: The letter from the couple about their sociopathic son was an answer to my prayer. I've been struggling to find an explanation for my brother's incredible exploitation of our late parents and their finances.

You've captured so utterly the feelings of people who become dupes of a sociopath. The families and victims are both fascinated and afraid to act. They are repeatedly subjected to violent explosions of temper, followed by tears and pleadings, and always, always, by insidious appeals to their own deepest need for feeling important, helpful, and wanted. I regret it is too late for my parents to benefit from this information.

A: It may be too late for your parents, but at least you have learned. Your new understanding is helping you, and it is helping your brother because you will no longer kill him with kindness. Also, you now know that you cannot trust him with your investments until he has gone through treatment and demonstrates significant change in his judgment and behavior.

Q: Your column about the sociopath came on like a floodlight in the dark confusion of my life. It explains both my uncle's manipulative behavior as well as his exploitation of our family fortune. (I am the only other heir.)

The first lawyer I consulted accused me of being paranoid because my uncle's "business" ventures sounded too fantastic to be believed—he was involved in stocks, raising horses in Saudi Arabia, and selling swampland in Florida. The second attorney was equally disbelieving until—by sheer coincidence—one of his other clients came in with the same complaints as I had. The other client's charges involved—of all people—my uncle. Interestingly, there are two other people who were also taken by my uncle, but they still swear by him. (For what it's worth, one of them is my uncle's drinking buddy.)

I have discussed the whole case with a therapist. Combining the information from your column and the opinion of my therapist, it is now clear to me that my uncle is not an alcoholic. He is a sociopath who abuses alcohol, and also abuses other people.

A: Sociopaths love to mix business with booze because alcohol loosens the customer's judgment too. As I have said before, "Candy is dandy but liquor is quicker" applies to commerce as well as it does to romance.

Q: The letters from parents of sociopathic children sound like I have written them. Our 25-year-old son fits the description exactly. His problem became noticeable when he entered puberty. By the time he was 15 it was quite obvious; and it has steadily gotten worse over the past 10 years.

When he was 18, he moved out of our house because he resented being "controlled" by me, and especially by my husband. Nevertheless, when I look back now, even though our son at the time said that he wanted independence, he remained "dependent" on us by insisting that we keep fixing his "incidents" such as financial indebtedness, trouble with the law, etc.

About a year ago my husband died. But for at least four years before that, he was able to see the light. Although he had joined me in our many vain attempts to help our son (by bailing him out time and again), my husband eventually warned me by saying, "If our son is determined to go down the drain—we can't stop him, but we do have a choice as to whether or not he takes us with him."

During the last year of his life my husband also said, "If anything ever happens to me, you had better learn to turn a deaf ear and say no, because if you don't—our son will bankrupt you."

I now realize my husband was right.

A: It's time you stop berating yourself. It is often the husband or father who first sees the light and is able to put a corrective foot down in the argument. The reason is that women are raised to be nurturing and mothering. Now that you are a widow, try living by your husband's advice, and at the same time help your son to grow up by no longer making excuses for his behavior.

At this point it makes no difference whether your son is really alcoholic or sociopathic. At age 25—with no other diagnosable illness—he will have to undergo some personality changes in order to eventually gain self-respect and be happy and productive. If you continue to be unable to say no, talk to a counselor about *your* problem and focus the therapy on that particular issue.

Q: The letters about sociopaths and alcoholics all ring true—but, alas, too late. Our 45-year-old son is no longer drinking, and he is also no longer acting like the sociopath he seemed to be. Nine years ago we got him into alcohol and drug treatment, and that seemed to make the difference.

My husband was able to sort out the issues more clearly before I was able to see what was going on. What finally opened my eyes was reading a book called *The Mask of Sanity* by Hervey Cleckley, M.D. (Mosby). It dealt with a number of case histories that impressed me because most of them sounded just like our son. But my husband insisted that our son had to get rid of the alcohol problem first.

A: Dr. Cleckley's book is the classic on sociopaths. Although it was written many years ago, it offers valuable insights. But today we know that it is risky to make a final diagnosis of behavioral or mental conditions when a patient is using a brain-altering substance. Another more recent book is *Psychopaths* by Alan Harrington (Simon and Schuster).

Q: I have a friend who is well-educated, gentle, and well-mannered during the day. But when the cocktail hour hits, he undergoes a complete change of personality: he becomes uncouth and sometimes violent.

His drinking has caused embarrassment and fear in our home when he is visiting, and it has cost him many clients in his business.

He claims that his drinking personality is his real personality, but I find this hard to believe because his anger is usually unjustified. What does this personality change mean? Is this a mental condition or is alcohol responsible?

A: A frequent symptom of alcoholic drinking is a change in personality. Your friend is "gentle and well-mannered" when he is not drinking. That means that he is capable of normal mental functioning and that he's not mentally ill.

The fact that his personality change occurs only when he is drinking and has led to alienation of family, friends, and clients means that he has a serious drinking problem for which he needs help.

Talk with his wife or other responsible members of his family about it in a loving, helpful manner. Many times the alcoholic's family members believe that nobody else has noticed how sick their loved one really is. Very likely, they'll be grateful to you for having been honest and helpful.

To say that his "drinking personality is the real one" is like saying that the surgical patient who was cursing while he was being anesthetized is revealing his real personality. A drugged brain produces drugged behavior.

Q: My husband is an "intellectual" alcoholic. He denies that he has a problem. He is never physically abusive, but often abuses me verbally. He drinks three or four double vodkas every night.

He drinks a double in two or three tosses. He says drinking makes him feel "less nervous and mellows things out." Actually, it makes him more aggressive and verbally abusive. Is he an alcoholic?

A: Among the early stages of alcoholism are gulping drinks instead of sipping them and undergoing visible personality changes in connection with drinking. His statement indicates that he uses alcohol as a tranquilizer. Both of you need counseling before the situation becomes worse.

Q: I have lived with an alcoholic for several years, but now he's very bad. He throws things and damages furniture and clothes in the house. It's affecting my nerves badly. I am thinking of moving out. Your column is always about the suffering alcoholic. Well, the lover or wife is under strain, too. How can I deal with this problem?

A: You are angry and no one can blame you. You are also in love with an alcoholic who is becoming progressively sicker. Your live-in doesn't really want to be like this. He has a sickness and is obviously asking for help in his own sick way. As for lovers and wives suffering with the alcoholic—you couldn't be more correct. This is a family disease, a partner's disease.

Get your friend to a physician but go along with him so that you can give additional history to the doctor. Your friend will probably need in-patient treatment. But you also need treatment because you are the kind of personality (loving, supporting, suffering) that is compatible with an alcoholically drinking partner.

Don't let anyone prescribe tranquilizers to "help your nerves." What you need is Al-anon and counseling so that you can understand yourself and your friend better.

Q: My husband can drink two six-packs and be the life of the party but sometimes even one six-pack makes him crazy, like sideswiping cars, almost beating his uncle to death, and abusing me. He is a lot of fun, though. He says life without booze is boring. Do you think he has a problem?

A: You both do. He is an unpredictable drinker—he can never predict what's going to happen when he drinks. But he keeps on drinking because he probably can't party, talk to friends, or watch a football game unless he's high, which means that he's psychologically addicted.

Your problem is that while he's hooked on booze, you are hooked on how interesting your life is when he is drunk. He says life without booze would be boring. Your letter suggests that your life would be boring, too, if he didn't drink.

You should both get counseling while he is off booze.

Q: I admit that I'm a problem drinker simply because when I drink I have problems, usually with other people or with the law, e.g., assault and battery. When I don't drink or when I drink moderately (which happens less and less often), I am a nice person; I never fight or hurt anybody.

In an effort to find out why I drink like this, I've taken several college courses, and I have read a number of books about alcoholism. I feel that if I could figure out why I drink the way I do, I would no longer have this problem. Is there anything you can suggest that I can read or study?

A: If knowledge about alcoholism could prevent the disease, there would be no alcoholic doctors, certainly no alcoholic pathologists, or coroners. The most effective thing I can tell you is that you drink the way you do because you are an alcoholic. If you were not, you would drink differently.

Even God can't change the past; but you can influence your future by doing something about your present. Make a commitment to yourself that you're going to attend at least twenty

Alcoholics Anonymous meetings. If that does not seem acceptable to you, then enter an alcoholism treatment program. College and books teach you how to make a living. AA and rehabilitation teach you how to live your life.

Q: Your advice to the woman who thought she had a drinking problem because she "drank alone to forget about the workday and relax" made me curious. You told her to stop drinking for a month to see if she has a problem.

Several of my friends said it would be idiotic, stupid, unenlightening, etc., to follow your advice. They all admitted that they drink alone at a certain time every day and that they "need that drink to relax."

Additional random sampling among more of my friends just got me more of the same kind of answers. Are my friends kidding themselves? To me, your advice seemed practical because the woman in your column had begun to question her own drinking.

A: Your random sample is not really random for society in general because only 30 percent of the people drink like your friends do, and 30 percent of the people don't drink at all. Your friends' comments reveal more than a take-it-or-leave-it feeling about alcohol: your friends have psychological addiction. When you "need" alcohol on a daily basis, you are dependent or hooked. Hopefully, your study will cause some of them to question their lifestyle.

Q: I am 28 years old and I work as a secretary in my husband's office. Three months ago, I started seeing a psychiatrist because of insomnia and nervousness. I see him once a week, and I take Valium in the daytime and Dalmane to sleep. On the advice of a girlfriend, I started to have a highball before bedtime. It worked very well, but now I want to have two or three highballs for sleep; and I'm starting to think about wanting a highball to stimulate my appetite before dinner. My father was an alcoholic, and I'm afraid of having inherited his problem.

When I mentioned to my psychiatrist that I'm developing a drinking problem, he brushed the subject aside, saying that we will eventually deal with whatever that might be. The frown on his face made me think he was uncomfortable with the whole idea. He quickly moved on to another subject. Do you think I have a problem?

A: Yes, you have at least one problem. As a matter of fact, you may have two problems. The first problem is that you are showing signs of a growing psychological and physical dependence on sedatives and alcohol. Your second problem is that you may have the wrong psychiatrist.

What you're describing is an alarming development. Mention this immediately to your psychiatrist and insist on discussing it now, not later. Also, talk to him about discontinuing Valium and Dalmane as soon as possible. If your psychiatrist minimizes your drinking again, it means that he is uncomfortable about it for any one of a variety of reasons.

None of these reasons, however, should stop you from getting a therapist who can deal with your growing alcohol and drug dependency which is a much more immediate and potentially fatal problem than the insomnia and nervousness for which you came to therapy in the first place. Many physicians are not aware of early signs of psychological dependence and have been trained to wait for cirrhosis, pancreatitis, or other "organic" signs of alcohol damage. This may be a time when you, as a patient, have to exercise your own judgment.

Q: I used to tell my husband, "Come home to do your drinking." Now that he's had four drunken-driving arrests, I have said, "No more drinking ever!"

He travels on business. When I ask if he kept sober on a trip, he snaps, "Drop it! I don't drink and don't want to talk about it.'' When he is home and "dry," he is up-tight and sharp with me and the children. I am still worried. How can I believe he is really not drinking?

A: Your husband sounds like a decent, stubborn, proud man who feels better when he drinks. Many alcoholics are like that. You can't be sure he is not drinking. You'd have to watch him every second—24 hours a day.

I see two possibilities: (1) He is not drinking at all—and feels miserable because he misses it; or (2) he is drinking on trips—and feels guilty about it.

Regardless of the drinking status, the quality of your life is even worse than it was before. Obviously, your husband is a man who can't quit drinking and at the same time live comfortably without some kind of help. That is evidenced by the fact that he snarls or snaps, but doesn't communicate. Start some counseling with someone acceptable to your husband (psychologist, minister, psychiatrist, etc.) in order to deal with his anger about drinking or not drinking. And if your husband won't participate, then start going to Al-anon and get treatment yourself because you are living with a dry drunk.

Q: I am only 12 years old, but I understand things, and would like to know what I can do because I'm worried for my brother.

He is 22 and has a drinking and drug problem. I found pot and little pipes in his car along with two different kinds of pills. Sometimes he sleeps during the day, all stoned out in bed, and is gone during the night. He drinks a lot and he can't think as good as he used to. Also, his temper is very bad—he gets mad when you are just playing.

A: It sounds like your brother has become dependent on both alcohol and drugs. You obviously want to help him. You should talk to either one or both of your parents privately about what you have seen. You would not be ratting on him. You are actually trying to save his life. You should also talk to a school counselor

so that the counselor can help you with your feelings, your
worries, and your nervousness about this problem. You can be
sure that the counselor will treat your information confidentially
and that he will at least help you live with the problem of
knowing about your brother.

Q: I have been attending Al-anon for the past six months to help
me put up with the alcoholic problem in my family. The
particulars are that my older sister is an alcoholic and my father
is an enabler.

At the present time we are all living under the same roof.
Actually, our life is more like a three-ring circus. I am thirty, my
sister is twenty-nine, and our father is fifty-five. Although he has
terminal cancer and cannot function on his own, he feels
emotionally obligated to support my alcoholic sister in our house.

The ideas for living which I have learned in Al-anon have been
enlightening, and they have begun to help me. But I would like to
enter into treatment with a psychiatrist in order to come to a
more definitive point of action.

My problem is that when I recently consulted a psychiatrist
and asked him if he specialized in alcohol-related problems, he
said that psychiatrists do not specialize in that kind of problem
because ''alcoholism is a symptom of an underlying problem—
not the cause.'' He theorized that my father is using my sister's
problem to deny his own fear of dying, and that I need to work
on my sibling rivalry. He offered to treat me alone, but not the
alcoholic family problem.

I felt uncomfortable with his interpretation. Am I correct, and
if so, can you direct me to a psychiatrist you would recommend?

A: The theory that your father is prolonging your sister's
alcoholism in order to not deal with his own dying, and that you
resent the attention he gives her is probably correct. Regardless of
the psychodynamics, what you need right now is a therapist who
has the skill and the time to take on the treatment of your family

and thereby get your sister into treatment.

To treat you alone would be converting your three-ring circus into a four-ring circus: You would be learning to leap through the psychoanalytic hoop with your therapist, while the other two rings (your sister and your father) would continue their own drinking and denying act until one or both are dead from their diseases. And after one or the other dies, you would need treatment for your guilt, because your superego would tell you that "you let him/her die." Also, if your sister survives your father, guess who would then be supporting her while she is drowning her own mourning in alcohol? You, of course.

The good news is that Al-anon has taught you to see right through the psychiatrist's lack of understanding. The appropriate concept of alcoholism/drug addiction is to see it as a primary disease for the person who is dependent on alcohol (your sister), and as a family disease for those persons who suffer and malfunction with the alcoholic. That makes you and your father co-dependents in the three-ring circus.

As for the notion of alcoholism as a symptom of an underlying disorder, Dr. George E. Vaillant, a professor of psychiatry at Harvard Medical School has this to say, "I would not deny the importance of psychopathology in the genesis of alcoholism but would instead emphasize the importance of alcohol abuse in the genesis of psychopathology. Too often, psychiatrists forget that alcohol in large quantities is the antithesis of a tranquilizer. The average alcoholic does not drink as an adult because his childhood was unhappy and he was unusually anxious. Rather, he is unhappy and anxious in adulthood as a result of his past alcohol abuse."

Alcoholic families never die—they just pine away—by passing on the tradition of noble suffering. Get into action now—and break the chain of misery.

Q: My drinking has become an uncontrollable problem in my personal life, although I'm still able to hide it pretty much at work. What stops me from getting treatment is that I am from New England, which means I would not be comfortable running around town announcing to everybody, "I am an alcoholic." It runs against my grain to air such personal problems.

On the other hand, I usually do things well if I learn them in a "structured" environment or program. That's why I suspect that a treatment program would accomplish the results necessary in my case. Do I have to "go public" like some celebrities do? All I really want is help so that I can help myself.

A: You sound like an ideal treatment case. You can start to help yourself by paying a visit to an alcohol rehabilitation facility. There you will see that confidentiality and anonymity are part of every good treatment program. Your medical records and your personal identity will be protected.

I have treated some very famous personalities whose recovery has never become public knowledge. Others, by their own choice, are open and very public about their own recovery, partly because it seems to help them, and partly because it helps others. But that number is very small. As a general rule, recovering alcoholics are successfully abstaining, their lives are changed, and only their families and close friends know about their recovery from alcoholism. In other words, what they got from treatment is exactly what you're looking for, which is "help to help myself."

Q: My husband and I need a clarification of viewpoints. We agree that our son-in-law is an alcoholic, but I say that alcoholism is a disease and our son-in-law shouldn't be blamed for having it. My husband says it would be better not to call it a disease because it gives the boy license to keep on drinking "because he can't help it." Who is right?

A: There is some validity in each of your viewpoints. Alcoholism is a disease (a terminal disease at that—it kills people, doesn't it?), and a person shouldn't be blamed for somehow having gotten it, any more than we blame a diabetic for having somehow gotten diabetes.

But, like the case of the diabetic, it is both humane and therapeutic to expect the alcoholic to do what is necessary to arrest his illness. We expect the diabetic to change his lifestyle by modifying his diet, sugar intake, sleep pattern, work habits, exercise routine, etc. In the same way (through rehabilitation), we hope the alcoholic will become abstinent and change his lifestyle. Neither the diabetic nor the alcoholic is responsible for having gotten the disease, but each is equally accountable for doing something positive about it.

Q: My family and friends all agree that my father is an alcoholic. He is a nice man, a quiet man who suffers his alcoholism silently. We've dropped hints or alluded to this problem in our conversations, but we've never quite known how to effectively approach him.

It's funny how we have all rallied around my uncle when he had a heart attack. We even got actively involved in his recovery. But for some reason it's hard to do something for my father, maybe because alcoholism is more chronic and less dramatic. How can we change this?

A: The basic problem with your family and your friends is your attitude about alcoholism. You are afraid to approach your father because all of you are ashamed, and because you don't see alcoholism as a disease.

Alcoholism is as fatal as heart attacks. Also, regardless of what your family and friends think, your father is drinking the way he does, not because he wants to, but because he doesn't know what else to do or how to change it. Nice alcoholics never quit, they just slowly die—unless their loved ones do something about it.

You need advice from a treatment center, a doctor or a member of the clergy to help you plan an intervention. With proper treatment and a change in family attitude, recovering alcoholic patients have a much better prognosis than recovering heart attack patients.

Q: I take exception to a statement you have made about depression and drinking. You said that a drinking patient who is depressed should stop drinking until he and the psychiatrist have cleared up the problem that caused the depression. More specifically, you suggest that the patient can start drinking again after he is cured.

A: I was referring to the depressed patient who had a long history of social drinking which became excessive with the onset of his depressive reaction. If such a patient can stop drinking completely and through psychotherapy clear up and accept the circumstances surrounding his depressive reaction, then that patient may well be able to return to his previous level of social drinking, provided he does not continue to require any psychoactive medication.

If the drinking becomes pathological again even though the problem seems to have been cleared up, then that patient may well be a previously undiagnosed alcoholic. Like other alcoholics, he then has to get whatever treatment is necessary so that he can live comfortably without wanting to drink again.

Q: Is it possible for a person to suffer mental depression from alcohol consumption even if that person is not a true alcoholic?

A: Yes. Anybody who has a high alcohol intake will manifest signs and symptoms of depression, regardless of why he drinks, or whether we call that person an alcoholic or a troubled drinker. The reason is that, pharmacologically speaking, alcohol is a depressant medication. In heavy doses, it will cause "mental depression" in anybody, even if a person has no obvious reasons for a reactive depression, or biological causes for an innate depression. Thus, after several weeks of heavy drinking, a previously normal person will show signs of depressive reaction such as mood swings, irritability, poor appetite, sleep disturbance, impotence, or loss of interest in sex.

A dangerous aspect of this problem is that if an alcoholic or heavy drinker presents the above symptoms to a doctor—and at the same time denies his heavy drinking—he is frequently misdiagnosed as having a depressive reaction. Not surprisingly, such a patient will then be put on antidepressant medications, which unfortunately creates a whole new set of problems because of the negative effect which alcohol has on antidepressant medications. Predictably, that kind of patient will not respond favorably to the treatment until the primary cause, namely his alcoholism, has been successfully treated.

Q: I have read that some alcoholics also have an overeating problem. I have been living the Alcoholics Anonymous program for ten years. As a result, I have changed my behavior in almost every way. But I'm unsuccessful in learning how to eat food normally. Is there any help or information for people like me?

A: About 20 percent of recovering alcoholics also have a compulsive overeating disorder. Some alcoholics were overweight all along, but the problem seemed minor in comparison to the alarmingly destructive effects of their alcoholism. Other alcoholics were too thin or normal in weight until they stopped drinking.

In any case, the compulsive overeater/alcoholic, after achieving abstinence, is apt to gain a large amount of weight and keep it, even though other areas of his life have improved dramatically.

You should contact a local group of Overeaters Anonymous (OA). There are more than 6,000 such groups in the United

States. They are listed in your telephone directory. They use the same 12 Steps and the Big Book of AA. Many people attending OA meetings are recovering alcoholics who are able to successfully work both programs (AA and OA) and maintain a desired body weight for the rest of their lives in the same way that they maintain sobriety and abstinence of mind-altering drugs.

Write to the OA General Office for free literature. Here is the address: Overeaters Anonymous, World Service Office, 2190 190th Street, Torrance, California 90504.

Q: Every time I drink too much alcohol, I go on a food binge. Does alcohol turn to sugar in the bloodstream? Could I be allergic to sugary foods? Does alcohol react the same as sugar?

A: Small amounts of alcohol raise production of blood sugar slightly. But even small amounts of alcohol taken with small amounts of food raise insulin production significantly. However, according to gastroenterologist Max Schneider, M.D., most people can do this without gaining weight.

Your basic problem is your occasional inability to control your drinking which then leads to food binges. In other words, if you didn't drink, you would have no weight problem. Any fat person, given that clear choice, would immediately stop drinking and live slim, trim, and happy forever after.

Now, that's what I call an offer you can't refuse. And if you can't do that comfortably for at least six months, you need to do something about your drinking problem.

Q: I am a forty-year-old registered nurse, a recovering compulsive overeater, and alcoholic. I believe compulsive overeating is a disease similar to alcoholism. When I joined Overeaters Anonymous, I realized that I was also alcoholic because I drank a lot of wine. Working both the OA and AA program, I have maintained a fifty-pound weight loss for five years.

I see a number of fat people in AA meetings. Please publish

this letter so that OA becomes better known as a real source of help for fat people, including alcoholics.

A: I'm glad to publish your letter. I agree that compulsive overeating is a disease like alcoholism. I've seen many fine recoveries through OA. I'm glad to see that OA meetings are becoming more and more available all over the country.

Q: Two months ago I went through drying out for a drinking problem. Early in treatment, the neurologist ordered psychological testing that showed I had brain damage. Now I'm not drinking and I feel good. Everybody who knows me says I'm normal. My family doctor thinks so, too. Last week he ordered psychological testing by another psychologist. It shows "no brain damage."

Who is right? If I'm honest when I fill out my driver's license questionnaire, my license will be in jeopardy. I'm a taxi driver.

A: Probably both psychologists were right. Clinical experience shows that most alcoholics who need detoxification will show no evidence of brain damage if the psychological testing is done within 30 days of their last drink. The reason is that alcohol is toxic (poisonous) to brain cells. That is, if we tested the population of the United States on New Year's morning, we would find a high percentage of brain damage. But in people who get drunk occasionally, the measurable brain damage is gone in two to three days. On the other hand, for chronic alcoholics, because of the cumulative effects of drinking, it may take up to six months for the brain damage to clear up.

You probably had brain damage two months ago, but you don't have any now. You should, therefore, use the more recent psychological test data and your family physician to help you solve any driver's license problems you may encounter.

The more important part of your problem is for you to get into Alcoholics Anonymous and some outpatient alcoholic program to help you maintain your abstinence and sobriety because if you drink again, you will get brain damage again. And every time you do that, the brain damage will be more serious and take longer to clear up.

Q: In a recent column you described a taxi driver who had alcoholic brain damage on psychological testing. But after treatment and abstaining from alcohol, he was retested and said to have "no brain damage."

I am an instructor in a drunken-driving program. We teach our clients that damaged brain cells can't be replaced. Is this correct?

A: Certain areas of the brain are responsible for how we act, think, and feel. Neuropsychological testing of these cognitive, affective, and motor areas shows the extent and source of the impairment. Actually, it measures the behavioral manifestations of brain disruptions rather than actual brain-cell destruction.

The difference here lies between destruction and damage. Impairment because of brain cell destruction, e.g., Korsakoff's psychosis or Wernicke's encephalopathy, is permanent because destroyed brain cells don't regenerate. But impairment because of swelling of the brain or damage to nerve pathways (which is common in alcoholism) improves when drinking is stopped. As the swelling subsides, or as the nerve connections regenerate, there is improved function and behavior.

We are born with about ten billion brain cells, some of which we normally lose as we get older. Alcohol abuse substantially increases the normal rate of brain cell loss, but it may take three to six months for brain function to return after drinking stops. I have seen improvement of brain function even after one year of not drinking. Undamaged areas of the brain seem to take on some of the functions of other areas of the brain that were destroyed, much like an employee taking on the added tasks of a co-worker who has left. But this never happens in the alcoholic who still drinks. He can only get worse.

Q: My doctor said my husband is not an alcoholic because he gave only two "Yes" answers on the twenty-question test. I know that my husband could easily give ten "Yes" answers. What can I do?

A: Two people living together usually know each other's lifestyle so well that one could easily take the test for the other. In my practice I first get a history, then let the patient take the test alone. After I scan the test, I call the spouse into my office so that all three of us can go over the questions together.

I then read each question aloud along with the patient's answer, then ask the spouse to elaborate on what she thinks the answer should be, and why. The ensuing three-way discussion is usually very revealing (always brings out the denial, rationalization, distortion, and confused thinking, all of which are part of the drinking problem). This added knowledge helps me to help the patient into treatment. Take this information to your doctor and have another try.

Q: My husband and I went to a psychologist-marriage counselor. We had one individual session, one joint session, and psychological testing. He never asked me about my drinking. He did, however, call my husband and ask some questions about our drinking habits. The psychologist's conclusion was that I was an alcoholic but not otherwise mentally ill.

I cannot accept this diagnosis, but I don't know how to disprove it. I feel like I've been convicted without a trial.

A: The psychologist may have based his decision partly on psychological test data like the MacAndrews Scale. Also, he may have asked you some things about your drinking style without

you being aware that you were actually talking about drinking. It
is more likely, however, that he made his diagnosis clinically by
inference from your drinking history as given by your husband.
Often, the most important information about an alcoholic is
obtained from other people; but this information then has to be
discussed with the patient.

See the psychologist again together with your husband so that
you can understand what the problem is. Be sure you approach it
as a patient looking for a diagnosis, not as an "accused" who is
demanding to face his accusers.

Q: My husband is a practicing physician. I think he is an
alcoholic, but he insists that so far he is only a problem drinker. I
want him at least to attend several Alcoholics Anonymous
meetings so he can find out a little more about it, but he says he
is afraid he would be recognized. Also, he thinks that he is too
educated and the things ordinary people in AA talk about would
be too simple to benefit him. Is there any place I can send him in
view of these arguments?

A: Many "educated" alcoholics, such as physicians, lawyers,
professors, etc., voice objections just like your husband when
they first hear about Alcoholics Anonymous. In most large cities
you will now find Alcoholics Anonymous groups that hold closed
meetings in which all group members are physicians. There are
similar groups in the same cities in which all group members are
lawyers or pilots. Your husband should make an agreement with
you that he will attend at least 20 such meetings before he makes
up his mind about whether he has a significant drinking problem.

I have never seen anybody who was too dumb to recover from
alcoholism. But I have seen a number of very intelligent, highly
educated alcoholics who continued to look for "causes" of their
drinking, pursuing existential searches and intellectualizing their
way through new kinds of treatments while they drank themselves
to death. Your husband should go to AA and through rehabilita-

tion because, if he is alcoholic, he will eventually lose his medical license and his life.

Q: I once read a famous quote by Abraham Lincoln which supported the idea that alcoholism is a disease. Can you publish that quote?

A: Lincoln never flatly stated that he saw alcoholism as a disease, but he apparently knew that non-alcoholics have no grounds for being smug or proud of the fact that they do not have alcoholism. He also was of the opinion that in terms of character and other personal virtues, alcoholics are as good as or better than other people.

Here is the quote from Lincoln. "In my judgment such of us who have never fallen victim to alcoholism have been spared more by the absence of appetite than from any mental or moral superiority over those who have. Indeed, I believe if we take habitual drunkards as a class, their heads and hearts will bear an advantageous comparison with those of any other class."

"I've tried everything," Judy (Belushi) said in her high-pitched voice, shaking her head. "I've tried doing drugs with him. I've tried not doing drugs with him. I've tried going to a shrink and not going to a shrink. We tried going to a shrink together, and we've tried going to a shrink separately."

Wired
Bob Woodward on John Belushi

3

Chemical Dependency –
It's All in the Family

It's impossible to live around an alcoholic or drug addict for very long without becoming sick yourself. That's why chemical dependency is called a family disease. In the jargon of therapists, the parents, spouses, and children of chemically dependent people are known as co-alcoholics or co-dependents. The idea is that family members suffer almost all of the same symptoms that the drinker or user does even though such family members drink socially, or in some instances, don't drink or use drugs at all.

Much like chemical dependency itself, the family's way of getting sick is predictable and progressive. As the mind-altering and physiological effects of alcohol and drug abuse slowly—or swiftly—take their obvious toll on the drinker or user, they also poison the family atmosphere. The family shame and the coping maneuvers which the co-dependents deploy to "live with the problem" cause the family to become isolated from the community. As the disease gets worse, individual family members suffer emotional strain, develop health problems, and eventually economic hardships.

More specifically, we have learned from patients who are now clean and sober that the abuse of mind-altering drugs is a major cause of all sexual dysfunction (including impotence and frigidity), and that it plays a major role in child abuse, molestation, and other such pathology. Another manifestation of the family aspects of this disease is the rising incidence of addiction among women. Also, there is now 20 percent incidence of alcoholism in nursing home populations.

Most co-dependents come from family backgrounds in which chemical dependency or a similar maladjustment was the family lifestyle. It is this psychological conditioning which predisposes co-dependents to finding the kind of partners they end up with, namely spouses with compulsive problems (booze, drugs, gambling, work, etc.). Predictably, they (co-dependents) spend most of their adult lives unwittingly helping one alcoholic or drug-using partner after another get sicker. They do this mostly by covering up and by protecting their chemically dependent partners from the consequences of their illness. The co-dependents do this "enabling" almost by second nature. Therefore, they're astounded when a therapist points out what is obvious, for example, that a woman has been married to three alcoholic men in a row.

In my own practice I have treated many a family in which the husband is covering up for his drug-addicted wife, while their oldest daughter is taking care of a falling-down grandfather (alcoholic) who lives next door. It's like watching a chemical soap opera in which the primary patients (wife and grandfather) sink deeper into their addiction while one co-dependent (the husband) gradually becomes psychosomatically ill and the other co-dependent (teenage daughter) is learning the skills she will need to someday cover up for her future alcoholic husband.

Until a decade ago the major focus in treating chemical dependency was on the primary sufferers, namely, the addicts themselves. But modern treatment programs show very clearly that through education, rehabilitation, and attendance in Al-anon or Adult Children of Alcoholics meetings, co-dependents can recover from their own pathology. And it's a good thing, too, because clinical experience shows that without such help, the children of alcoholic families usually *become* alcoholics, *marry* alcoholics, or *rescue* alcoholics. (They often do the latter by becoming doctors, preachers, social workers, therapists, etc. And while I'm not saying that most people in the helping professions actually are co-dependents, there is no doubt whatever that most of them deal with addicts the way untreated co-dependents would.)

In other words, untreated co-dependents almost always carry out the alcoholic or drug-using family patterns because they never saw their roles clearly in their own primary families.

The Co-dependent Twenty Years Later

Her name is Jane, and her husband Dick is an alcoholic. It is our first session. I must have pushed too hard, too soon, because she momentarily rears up with indignation. "Doctor! If I had known he was gonna be an alcoholic, I never would have married him," but then she crumbles back to self-pity. "I don't know what I've done to deserve all this."

Jane herself doesn't drink, but she is what we call a co-alcoholic or a co-dependent because she lives with and cares about an alcoholic. She is also a middle-aged, sweet, and sad woman. Although she describes their 20-year marriage as an ideal childhood sweetheart marriage, right now she feels angry and wronged because Dick's drinking has almost destroyed that marriage.

In the course of treatment, she will come to understand that she did nothing to "deserve all this," that the die was cast generations ago. She will also come to understand that Dick's drinking problem was obvious even during their courtship, and that his and her problem grew day by day, hand in hand—together.

Alcoholism has genetic, biochemical, and learning aspects. To see how the alcoholic and the co-alcoholic grow together and become sick together, let's go back 20 years and look in on Dick and Jane during their courtship. It's 1960 in Smalltown, U.S.A. It's their first date. They're going on a picnic.

"Hi, Dick and Jane," their friends welcome them. As they settle down by the marshmallow fire, one of the guys sidles up to Dick. "Let's go behind the bushes," he says. "Harry's big brother brought some booze." (At every picnic since Neanderthal times there is always somebody's big brother—usually a psychopath—who brings some booze "for the kids.") It's the alcohol part of pubertal initiation rites.

At picnics all over America the initiation ritual goes something like this: In ominous tones a boy whispers to his girl, "I gotta go and see a man about a dog." He's learned such macho talk from cowboy movies. It means that he's gonna go behind the bushes to drink some booze.

The same culture teaches girls what that kind of talk from a boy means, and how girls are supposed to react. Like a silent movie queen, she has to arch her eyebrows in mock alarm, cover her mouth with the back of her hand and say, "Oh, you guys!"

The boy then stalks off into the bushes to have his first beer. The beer is neither hot nor cold, but it tastes bitter and it burns and stings his throat a little. "What's supposed to be so great about it?" he wonders. But he wouldn't dare say so out loud. Instead, he hooks a thumb in his belt, stands up straight and grins. "Oh, boy, this stuff is real good." He then takes another sip and struts back to the fire where he breathes on his girl. "Wow! I just drank a whole bunch of booze. Boy, am I drunk." In response she does her "Oh-you-guys" routine again, except now she is also supposed to look a little worried. But nothing really bad happens for the rest of the evening because the boy actually drank very little booze.

With Dick and Jane, however, the story is different. When Dick goes back to the bushes and tastes his first beer, he, too, says, "Boy, this stuff is great," but he really means it. Somehow he ends up talking with Harry's big brother. Before long, Dick has drunk a six-pack all by himself.

When he returns to the fire and breathes on Jane and says, "Wow, I just drank a whole bunch of booze! Boy—am I drunk!" he isn't kidding. Jane can see how his personality has changed. Instinctively she seems to know that she'll have to watch him and take care of him.

And a little while later, almost as if she had learned all this in a previous life, she carefully walks him back to his car and puts him in the righthand front seat. With loving thoughts she drapes his jacket over his chest and tucks it neatly behind his shoulders. She closes the car door carefully and pushes the button down to lock the door, then notices that the window is partly open. "Oh, my God! He could have caught cold if I hadn't noticed that," she says to herself. She carefully rolls the window shut and locks him in safely once again.

She then gets behind the wheel of the car to drive him home, even though she has had only three driving lessons and has a student permit. As she starts the car, one of the guys comes over and says, "I guess Dick got pretty bad, eh?" but Jane looks straight past him—as if he'd said nothing. "By the way, Jane, are you and Dick coming to Andy's house Saturday night? We're gonna have a party. His folks will be out of town."

"Oh, I don't think we can," Jane says sweetly. "Dick and I already have other plans." (Actually, Dick and she have no plans at all, but she's already keeping him away from "bad company.")

Twenty minutes later she helps Dick up the front porch of his house and rings the bell. Dick's mother is all smiles as she opens the door, but her face falls as she gets the picture. She knows the picture well from long experience. (Dick's father is a chronic alcoholic, like her own father was.)

But Jane is no slouch herself in the art of co-alcoholism. For years now she has watched her own mother take care of "Daddy's problem." Without waiting for Dick's mother to have

to come up with a face-saving lie, Jane quickly explains:
"Ma'am, I brought Dick home because he got a little light-
headed at the picnic. It must have been the egg salad that the
Wagner girls brought. We had a real good time, though."

Dick's mother smiles and tunes right in on Jane's co-alcoholic
frequency. It's like one diplomat talking to another. "Oh, yes,"
she says, "that sometimes happens to Dick. Maybe his allergy is
back, too. You're such a sweet girl to bring him home like this,
Jane. Some day you'll make somebody a good wife." Dick is still
more or less out on his wobbly feet as both co-alcoholics—
present and future—help him to his bedroom.

In the coming years Dick and Jane will replay this scene with
infinite variations. From time to time when they have a lovers'
quarrel and decide to date other people, Jane will meet some light
drinkers but she will find them "boring, stubborn, or too bossy."
And Dick will find that his dates are "ungiving, conceited, and
too independent" because when he gets drunk, they let him find
his own way home. But always Dick and Jane are drawn back to
each other—or to people with similar personalities—until treatment helps them both understand their alcoholic lifestyle.

It's all in the family.

A Dialogue with Drinkers Is a Broken Record

Spouses, lovers, and friends—even doctors, lawyers, and bosses—
don't understand that the alcoholic has a disease, that his
drinking is beyond will power, that he probably has blackouts
(amnesia when drinking), and that he knows he shouldn't drink
but doesn't know how to stop.

As a result, these well-meaning helpers spend decades asking
the alcoholic the same dumb questions. If you're tired of playing
the same old drunken record, here are some questions you should
never ask an alcoholic. The dialogue which follows is between a

well-meaning caretaker (WCT) and an alcoholic known as a poor problem drinker (PPD). The alcoholic's private thoughts are in brackets.

WCT, angry, warning: "You're going to feel like hell tomorrow morning."

PPD, angry, defiant: "Don't talk to me until I've had another drink." [I don't care about tomorrow, but I'm gonna feel good tonight. Besides, I'm going to feel like hell tomorrow anyway, unless I drink again.]

WCT, trying to reason: "You won't be able to wake up in time for work!"

PPD, reassuringly: "I'll be okay." [I won't have to wake up on my own. You'll make sure I get up. You always do.]

WCT, the morning after, reproachful: "Where were you last night?"

PPD, puzzled and play-acting: "Wait a minute, let me collect my thoughts." [I can't remember. I was either with my buddies, with my girlfriend, or I was drinking alone. In any case, I was in bad company. So what's the difference?]

WCT, icily: "How much did you drink last night?"

PPD, brusquely: "Not enough!" or "Just the usual." [Obviously, I didn't drink enough because you're still getting on my nerves.]

The PPD's answer to "How much did you drink?" is always vague. If the answer is specific, it's usually not true. The most popular one is "two beers." Father Martin's advice to brewers is to switch from manufacturing six-packs to making two-packs instead, because that's what alcoholics seem to drink.

WCT, with a hint of glee: "Do you know what you did last night at the party?"

PPD, startled: "No." [I haven't the vaguest idea. But I have a feeling it wasn't good. So, I'd better make a swift denial and hope for the best.]

WCT, ashamed for him: "Has anybody ever told you . . . ?"

PPD, cutting in: "No! Well, maybe, kind of." [You bet they have, time and again; and I'm getting sick of hearing it.]

WCT, reproachfully: "Aren't you ashamed of yourself?"

PPD, feeling awful: "Yes, I am." [But nothing I try seems to work. I'd do anything to change, mostly because of the shame and guilt.]

WCT, self-pityingly: "Do you know how this makes me feel?"

PPD, looking hang-dog: "Yes. I'm sorry." [No, but I can guess; you've told me often enough. The trouble is, you always tell me when I'm drunk, and that's too confusing; or when you're mad, and then we fight.]

WCT, threatening: "If you do that again I'll leave you."

PPD, feigning concern: "Please, just give me one more chance." [No, you won't. You've threatened many times. You even left once, but you came back. We need each other the way we are.]

WCT, hoping against years of evidence: "Will you promise not to do that again?"

PPD, eagerly: "I'll be glad to promise that again." [Don't you remember I promised that last month and many times before?]

Sometimes the WCT (well-meaning caretaker) is the doctor. Then the conversation goes like this:

Physician WCT: "Don't you know you're killing yourself?"

PPD, feigning surprise: "It's gotten that bad, Doc?" Or with a cynical shrug, "So what else is new?" [He tells me the same thing every time he sees me. I'm going to get a new doctor so I can get more tests and more pills.]

The dumbest question any well-meaning caretaker can ask is, "Why do you drink the way you do?" If the alcoholic knew that, he wouldn't drink that way. He drinks the way he does because he's an alcoholic. He cannot drink otherwise. If he could, he would.

All too often, the answer is a flippant rationalization, barely disguising his growing irritation: "With a wife like mine, you'd drink too."

There is only one question that makes sense. It should be asked only once, clearly and dispassionately, when the alcoholic is not drunk. "What are you going to do about your drinking?"

Fortunately, there is only one correct answer. "I'm going to get some help for my drinking problem today."

If you are a WCT and you get any other answer, you have to ask yourself the question: "What am *I* going to do about *my* drinking problem?" (You see, you, too, have a drinking problem. You've been talking to your drinking problem for years now, as the above questions and answers should tell you.)

The answer that you have to give is the same one you were expecting from your PPD: "I'm going to get help for my drinking problem today." And that's when you start going to Al-anon for self-help and to an alcoholism treatment unit for counseling.

The Real Solution to the "Morning After"

If you are an average social drinker, "the morning after" usually means a hangover, maybe the only one you had this year. Maybe you had nausea, lack of appetite, and a throbbing headache. To make your misery somehow seem worthwhile, you probably laughed with your wife about the silly things you did last night.

But if you're an alcoholic—the morning after is no laughing matter. It has to do with pains of the soul: guilt, remorse, and hopelessness. Deep down you also know that you are going to have to drink again . . . and that it's going to be bad again.

What you dread most on the morning after is having to sneak into the kitchen, unobtrusively getting yourself a cup of coffee, and silently waiting for the bombs to fall. As you sit by the kitchen window, your wife is silently fixing breakfast for the kids. The impassive look on her face makes you wince. You try to catch her eye, to break the ice—but there is not a hint of recognition, not even a flicker of that out-of-the-corner-of-her-eye contempt you've come to know so well.

Since your alcoholism has reached the blackout stage, you quickly rule out the most ominous possibilities: there are no bruises on her face; the kids look okay; the furniture seems intact; the car is in the driveway. You quietly fetch the morning paper and casually inspect the car. The bumpers and fenders look okay. You settle down again at the kitchen table. The kids are gone, your wife is silent. You finally can no longer contain yourself. "All right, Betsy, cut out the holier-than-thou attitude."

Your tone of voice says that she's overdoing it again, she is being melodramatic. But then she starts to recite a litany of incidents: "You promised you'd come straight home from work last night . . . the life insurance salesman was here to re-do our policy." You sigh heavily as she continues: "Bobby pitched in the Little League playoffs at 7 o'clock." The proud father in you would like to know how Bobby did and who won the game—but you feel too guilty to ask, and there is no pride left.

"On the way home," she continues in her masochistic monotone, "I had a flat tire—with a station wagon full of kids." Oh . . . that really hurts. And as she moves on to the next gripe on her list, she puts her soft little dish-water hands on her seven-months-pregnant tummy. It's enough to make your liver quiver.

You're in agony. You look out the window. Everything she says is true. Worse yet, even her interpretation of the truth is correct. Worst of all, so far she's only told you what you *didn't* do last night; wait till she gets around to the super-terrible things you actually *did* do! It's enough to drive a man to drink.

There are many solutions for the morning after: denial, arguments, apologies, promises, going on the wagon, blaming others, moving to the West Coast, making New Year's resolutions, switching from Scotch to beer—the list goes on ad infinitum, ad nauseam.

A famous movie star said in her biography that on the morning after when you find out what you did the night before, the only choices are to drink again or kill yourself.

Well, we all know that drinking again doesn't work; and suicide somehow seems too final. The only solution that really works is to get treatment and go to AA. The many stored-up "mornings after" of guilt and self-recrimination, of physical and mental cruelty, of anger and disappointment—they all have to be worked through, i.e., you have to learn to accept yourself and forgive yourself—and so do your spouse and other family members—before you can start to live again.

Saturday Night Dead

> Jake Urban, 39, was fatally shot by his son Rob, 16, during a family altercation Saturday night. The shooting was accidental, the boy's mother said. Rob is in custody of juvenile authorities pending psychiatric testing.
>
> Weekly Gazette, Smalltown, U.S.A.

This news item appeared on page 7 somewhere in America. It reads innocently enough. But when you work with alcoholic families, you learn to smell between the lines. Here's how the case unfolds when the court psychiatrist interviews Rob:

"Doctor," Rob says, "Jake was actually my stepfather. My real dad, I remember only as a big chest . . . and powerful arms. He would crush me or cuddle me—depending on how drunk he was. The rest of my childhood is a blur, just a haze . . . of scuffling, and fighting, and night noises. Then one night my dad went out to get a pack of cigarettes. We never heard from him again."

There followed a fatherless period during which Rob's mother managed the best she could. When Rob was 6, Jake appeared on the scene. "I liked him right away, Doc. His powerful arms and his hearty laugh made his chest pound like a drum when my head was cuddled against it. A week later he married my mom.

"Almost overnight, things changed abruptly. Jake made me call him Dad, and his drinking got real obvious. He started beating Mom when he was drunk. All I could do at that time was hide in the back yard or run to the neighborhood playground and watch a ball game." The midnight beatings were harder to ignore. All Rob could do was press his face into the mattress and tightly clamp a pillow over his ears, but he could still hear the thuds and the screams through the thin walls.

At such times he'd sob and vow to himself, "Someday when I grow up—I'll stop him from beating her." By morning, with Jake still asleep, his mother would unload her emotions on Rob. Some of the things she told him in the morning were worse than the things he heard at night. He hated her for doing it.

Since he was an only child, he wrapped his pain in daydreams and sadness. But it got more and more difficult to hold it all in. Of late, his head wrapped under the muffling pillow, he'd feel torn with fear and joy: joy in the budding manhood of his puberty, the rippling muscles of his coming manhood; and because he knew that since he was no longer a child—he'd have to do something about Jake and the beatings. He felt almost like two people: no longer a child—and not yet a man.

The night of the shooting, Rob (the child) was sound asleep when Jake came home drunk. Minutes later Rob (the man) awoke to the sounds of another Saturday-night beating. Filled with rage he jumped out of bed, grabbed the shotgun from the hallway rack, stormed the kitchen door and aimed the gun at Jake's chest. Rob's mother, stunned in disbelief, stifled a scream; and Jake, a silly drunkard's grin on his face, eyed the muzzle of the gun, and raised a casual hand to—"Oh, shucks, boy"— minimize the whole thing.

But for reasons too deep for understanding, Rob (the person) pulled the trigger and Jake crumbled, a gurgling heap on the kitchen floor.

Rob the child—and Rob the man—softly answered more of the doctor's questions. "You know something, doctor," Rob said in the end, "for the past year, every time they fought—and I had to hear it again through those thin walls—I always had two recurring thoughts. One thought was that someday when I'm big enough to stop him, I hope I won't hurt him. The other thought was, I pray to God I won't grow up to be like him."

Like (Drinking) Father, Like (Snorting) Son?

I looked at the family sitting in my office: Randy, a freshman at Ivy Hall U., had rich parents and handsome athletic looks, but he was a cocaine addict; his mom, comfortably dressed and sweet, was scared; and his dad, a self-made land developer, looked frankly disgusted. "I never thought I'd be sitting in a shrink's office with my son—the pusher." He shot Randy a hard glance.

Mom, dabbing her tears, said, "He is not really a pusher—as such."

"Stop defending him. He was selling cocaine on campus. That's illegal. That's what I call a pusher. I still can't believe it!" Dad growled, venting more anger and disappointment.

"Dad, I wasn't in the drug business, you know. I only sold to fraternity brothers; and I sold just enough to cover my own use," Randy said meekly.

Mom looked up hopefully. "There," she seemed to say, "you see, he's not a real pusher."

***

The story of Randy's addiction is routine enough. He was always a good boy, never did anything wrong, drank a little beer in high school. But when he tried cocaine at Ivy Hall, it was love at first snort, almost like he had the genes for it. It seemed to make him into everything he secretly feared he wasn't: smart, tough, energetic, funny—all the things he admired so much in his dad.

For about six months it was great, but then he started to worry. Sometimes he couldn't stop using all night, then had a terrible time in class the next day. Soon he needed more coke, more often. That's when he started dealing. At first he sold only in the frat house. Then word got out, and . . . then he got caught. Because of Dad's name and because Randy agreed to get help, the school dropped the charges.

This case is complicated by what Randy told me in private session yesterday. Here's a quick sketch of his dad: puts away a pint at night; has one drunk-driving arrest; some weekends he drinks through the night; has blackouts; pushes Mom around sometimes, then feels remorseful the next morning; has occasional hangovers, but makes it to the office no matter how bad he feels. Business is better than ever—but the family is miserable.

After I explained the similarity between drug and alcohol addiction, I asked Randy if he thought his dad had a problem. "He's an alcoholic," Randy said. "I've known it for years. Mom knows, too, but she's afraid to admit it."

***

I looked again at the family sitting before me. "While we're treating Randy," I said to the parents, "I want both of you to take part in some groups and educational sessions."

"That's out of the question," Dad cut in. "I've got work to do. Besides, I don't have any problems. If I'd ever had even a *similar* problem, I maybe could see some value in my participation."

"Dad, in some ways you and I are very much alike. You see, when you were my age, you were a pusher just like me."

"What in (bleep) are you talking about? In my day we didn't use drugs—we drank beer!"

"Yes, but beer was illegal in your frat house, Dad. Many times we've heard you tell about the small fridge you kept hidden in your room stocked with beer which you sold to frat brothers for enough extra to buy your own liquor. In other words, you bought, stored, and sold an illegal drug in your frat house 30 years ago. And you're still using the drug. And when you drink, you . . ."

"That's enough!" Dad yelled. But for the first time he looked at Randy with a hint of admiration. Then, almost gently, he said, "Look, Randy, since your mother is crying, maybe we'll try a few sessions, anyway."

And as we shook hands he said in an aside to his wife, "That's the first time I've seen that kid stand up to me like a man." And Randy said, "Mom, it's gonna be all right. I guess I'm just a sip off the old block." And with a wink at me he added, "Things go faster with coke."

The Alcoholic's Wife: Before and After

Sometimes the wife of a recovering alcoholic will pray that her husband drinks again simply because when he was drinking, at least he was easier to live with. The reason for her continued unhappiness is that he went through treatment—and she did not.

Let's look in on John and Mary during his drinking days. It's Saturday morning. The minute John wakes up, he knows he must have tied one on last night—he has that "floor-of-the-bird-cage" feeling in his mouth and only a hazy recollection of what he did last night.

He carefully opens the bedroom door, sniffs coffee and hears Mary clattering at the breakfast stove.

He quietly gets himself a cup of coffee. Mary just gives him a silent look. John goes into the family room where he tries to look invisible. He hides deep down into an easy chair and turns on the football game. He keeps the volume low because he doesn't want to provoke her in any way. He's trying to concentrate on the game and at the same time is hoping she won't mention anything about last night.

But Mary is fuming and angry. "Some people I know sure sleep late these days," she hints darkly from the kitchen. "Since it is getting to be fall weather, our storm windows should probably be put up this morning. Also," she adds in a firm voice, "my father down the street—who is getting on in years—could use some help with their storm windows."

Trying to act like a good little boy, John immediately flips off the T.V. Even though he's furious on the inside (because he feels that she is emasculating him again), he's smiling on the outside. I'd better please her, he's thinking. Who knows what I really said or did last night, or what she actually has on me? She's apt to do anything.

He is also angry because he is slowly coming to realize that he never has been able to stand up to her, or to his own stepmother, or to women in general, for that matter—except when he's drunk.

When he finally enters alcoholic rehabilitation, Mary refuses to become involved as a co-dependent or as a co-patient or co-alcoholic. By now she is chronically angry and heartbroken. During the intake interview she's apt to say something like, "He is the drunk and he's had the fun. I don't have a problem myself."

In rehabilitation John has to get couples' therapy without her. He tries to learn about the alcoholic family dynamics by working with other wives and their husbands. As he learns to live without alcohol or other sedative drugs, he also comes to learn about what makes him tick and drink. Through group interaction he also comes to learn a lot about what makes his wife tick, and how she controls him. In the role-playing sessions he learns how to be assertive so that he won't have to become drunk and aggressive when his "hurt feelings" flow over.

Now let's look in on John and Mary several weeks after he completed rehabilitation. On Friday nights he enjoys warm fellowship, gets good feelings, learns about himself and grows emotionally by attending an AA meeting or by going to a follow-up outpatient session at the treatment center. When he comes home from such sessions he talks to his family, catches a brief T.V. show and gets a good night's sleep. The next morning he wakes up with a feeling that life is worth living. He walks downstairs. "Ahh, fresh coffee! Good morning, honey." He gets himself a cup of coffee and affectionately pats Mary's shoulder. He switches on the T.V. and when he hears Mary saying, "Some people sure sleep late around here . . . ." he says politely, "Just a minute—they're about to score a touchdown here." He intently watches the play to its completion, then turns to her and listens to her remarks.

He smiles. "Yes, fall weather is coming on. As soon as the game is over, I'm going to check out the storm window situation and decide what to do.

"As for your 'aging father,' he is now all of 56 years old and still beats me in singles tennis. After I've hung our storm windows, I'll call him and remind him that he might want to think about their storm windows, too, being as it's getting to be fall.

"And now, to see me through this game, honey, I'd like another cup of coffee, cream only, please."

And that's when Mary stands there with her hands in the dishpan. Her heart is still full of anger for all the mean things he did during his drinking days. It somehow doesn't seem fair. She has nothing to say to him, and since he quit drinking, she has nothing on him with which she can control him.

And that's when she wishes he were drinking again.

Sexual Performance and Drinking

Folklore and the media say that drinking booze makes you sexy.
The clinical truth is that the chronic drinker's most personal
worry is impotence. As a matter of fact, one out of three is
impotent. But now we have learned that even moderate drinking
impairs sexual performance.

The folklore about booze and sex stems from the everyday
observation that a couple of drinks will increase your sex drive.
That's true because 80 percent of impotence and frigidity is due
to psychological or attitudinal problems. That's why after a drink
or two the reluctant are willing, the rigid relaxed, the pious are
joyous, and the righteous feel blameless. Booze also removes
emotional-cultural-religious blocks that cause sexual inhibitions.

Thus, many a young stud gets his initial "macho" from the
bottle; and many a shy lady surrenders first to the booze—and
then to the man. To that extent the media myth is true.

However, anyone who over the long haul can't enjoy sex
without booze, pot, etc., is a chemical lover. He has a problem
and needs an attitude change, not Happy Hour.

If there is no emotional maturation and attitude change, then
booze remains the aphrodisiac, the turn-on, the necessary ingredi-
ent for enjoying sex. Unfortunately, as drinking becomes a habit,
the cure becomes the problem because of alcohol's effects on the
body.

By direct effect on hypothalamic-pituitary-gonadal function,
alcohol reduces the amount of testosterone (male sex hormone) in
the male. Even 24 hours after heavy drinking, there is a
measurable drop. In young men this is not noticeable. (Ironically,
it may even help the premature ejaculator delay his climax and
thereby make him seemingly into a more desirable lover.) But
after age 30, the negative effects of heavy drinking on sexual
performance become undeniable.

Thus, with chronic drinking come a whole host of problems: premature ejaculation, poor quality of erection and retarded ejaculation, along with poor judgment, poor body hygiene, clumsiness, and disregard for the pleasures of the sexual partner.

As if this weren't enough, heavy drinking has feminizing effects in men. A healthy male who does not have a drinking problem normally has a certain amount of estrogen (female sex hormone) in his body. The estrogen is produced by the adrenal glands, and the level is kept in check by low production and high rates of destruction (which normally take place through the patient's healthy liver). In that way, in healthy males, the scales are continually tipped in a masculine direction, that is, the sex drive, muscle mass, body hair distribution, etc., are masculine.

But in the heavily drinking male, the opposite happens: estrogen is produced at an increased rate, and because of liver damage, the destruction of estrogen is decreased. In that way the heavily drinking male ends up with more female hormones and less male hormones in his body.

On physical examination there is a decrease in male body hair (chest, auxiliary, and pubic), increase in breast size (gynecomastia), and the testicles have atrophied, that is, they have shrunk in size from plums to marbles.

Add to this the loss of muscle mass (especially in the shoulder, thigh and buttock areas), and you have a female body outline. The "macho" man who used to strut on Muscle Beach scratching his hairy chest, ogling the girls, and sipping his brew with gusto is now shuffling through the sand on spindly legs with a wino walk, bulging belly, sagging breasts, and glassy eyes.

Over the years he shows less and less interest in sexual intercourse, because he finds it increasingly more difficult to engage in sex. Finally, he is totally impotent.

What should be done? Testosterone shots or pills are only good for about six hours. Therefore, they don't work unless you have a live-in urologist. As a matter of fact, they are dangerous because they cause the testicles to lose whatever hormone-producing capacity they might still have.

The good news is that if your liver is not completely gone, and since much of the problem is psychological anyway, it will get better if you stop drinking and, together with your partner, get counseling.

Although this is a gradual process, in some cases it seems to happen suddenly. Carlotta Monte describes her life with W. C. Fields in her book *W. C. Fields and Me*. She says " . . . quite early in our relationship, as the flame that once ran through his loins was gradually reduced to some faintly glowing embers, I began to think that in the run for his affections, the martini pitcher came first, the ice box second, and yours truly an out-distanced third. Naturally his virility drowned as his libido became soaked in alcohol. And it didn't go down the customary three times, it just sank."

Women Who Drink Too Much

Alcoholic women are different from alcoholic men in several respects: society stigmatizes them more heavily; they develop more serious organ damage in less time; and doctors are extremely reluctant to diagnose them.

Here are some clinical features of the woman alcoholic.

She frequently comes from an alcoholic home and was probably an abused child. She tends to relate her drinking to depression or to a recent loss such as divorce, death in the family, etc. She may drink in order to feel more sexually uninhibited. Her marriage is probably unstable, and even though she is upper middle class, she may, as a result of sexual involvement while drunk, have venereal disease or a pregnancy of uncertain paternity.

She usually drinks more heavily when she has pre-menstrual tension. Unlike alcoholic men who may have alcoholic blackouts for years without being particularly bothered by them, the alcoholic woman usually begins morning drinking in connection with blackouts, simply because of a sense of shame and guilt.

In the examining room the physician will see an anxious, depressed, chronically fatigued woman with weight loss, anemia (which he tends to ascribe to excessive menses), slight liver enlargement, and high blood pressure. She may have bruises. When he asks her about them, she might admit that she has no idea how she got them, but she's more likely to fabricate an explanation on the spot because the injury occurred during a blackout or during a scuffle with her husband or someone else. There may also be an unexplained rib fracture found on the chest film which was ordered because she had a mild cough.

The doctor may recall that during a recent hospitalization she had increased drug tolerance (she required unusually high doses of medication for minor pain; and in surgery she needed a larger amount of anesthetic than her body weight would indicate). These findings suggests drug addiction or alcoholism, but since her hospital stay was brief, and because she is a nice, upper-middle-class lady, her doctor was reluctant to bring this up to her or her husband.

An added problem for the woman alcoholic is that the clinically unskilled or busy physician will probably react to her symptoms by prescribing tranquilizers or anti-depressant pills, which will only compound her problems. That is why up to 70 percent of women alcoholics are dependent on tranquilizers or sleeping pills.

Because of the stigma and the unexplained tendency of the woman alcoholic to become sicker faster, it is important that her family, her friends, and her doctor pool their findings about her. Getting the complete picture plus family support will help the doctor get her into treatment faster.

It is also important for the physician to know that for purposes of confrontation and for motivating the alcoholic

housewife into treatment, the doctor should consider the husband
and the family as her employer. The doctor may have to persuade
them to use love (as her family), as well as coercion (as her
employer) to get her into treatment.

Unattached, Employed, Alcoholic Woman

A growing phenomenon in my practice is the middle-aged,
unattached alcoholic working woman. She drinks as much as she
can get away with on a daily basis, and she drinks quite heavily
on weekends. She needs more and more face makeup not to look
hung-over, and she walks in a cloud of perfume to deceive
diagnostic noses.

For a while, she seems to be fooling the world successfully, but
more and more she begins to send out additional smoke signals
which quite clearly telegraph her growing disability to anybody
who is observant at all.

For example, she sustains injuries such as a broken wrist
(especially on weekends when she gets very drunk because she
knows she won't have to go to work for two days). She volunteers
to work on the night shift because her drinking problem is less
apt to be noticed then. She comes to work in a taxi because she
has lost her driver's license. She is less and less involved in social
functions at the office and avoids even the informal gatherings
with the "girls." Usually, each of these red flags is noticed by,
and known to, one or more people at the office.

When co-workers see her carrying her large handbag into the
ladies' room, they snicker "There goes Arline again for the
fourth time this morning." As far as job performance is concerned, her effectiveness goes from excellent to marginal. Even
though the level of performance in such an employee is still
acceptable or even marginal, it means something is definitely
wrong with that worker, and something needs to be done.

Eventually, Arline ends up living alone with her cats, her canary, and her television; or with family members who have begun to live their lives around her, and are waiting for her boss to do something. In actuality she ends up living alone, chronically sedated by her bartender and her doctor, and continuing to wait for "somebody to do something."

Long before she reaches this point she should be called in by her employer for a firm talk or confrontation which should be related to her job performance. Frequently, I have found that managers are unconsciously hiding behind Civil Service regulations or other regulatory employee protections by pointing out that her "performance was still acceptable."

It is the supervisor's job to look into it. To wait until Arline's performance goes below marginal—simply because she is a woman—is probably sexism of the worst kind. Arline has two problems: she has chronic alcoholism, and she has a lousy supervisor. And the combination can kill her.

There's no doubt that alcoholism among women is on the increase. It may be the first area in which women will achieve equality. To make all things equal, we must meet the special needs of women as effectively as those of men. In this particular case, it's time to start dealing with employed alcoholic women as female employees rather than employed females.

Some Signals of a Drinking Housewife

Since most women alcoholics work in the home, they are usually diagnosed much later than the male alcoholic. For instance, there is no employer to notice a decline in job performance and raise some questions about it. Here are some pointers on how family members can tell when a woman's drinking is getting out of hand:

Carol, 35, began drinking shortly after she got married because it took away her hand-wringing, tongue-tying nervousness at social functions. The sedative effects of alcohol enabled her to be the humorous, vivacious Carol in public that John, her husband, knew her to be in private. It also made her sexually spontaneous and, at times, even titillatingly aggressive—and John really liked that.

As her drinking increased, she became less and less interested in sex and more interested in liquor. Also, she started a habit of late-night reading so that she could drink herself to sleep unobserved after John had gone to bed alone.

Her good morning moods, which early in their marriage had made her a delight to wake up, now changed. Most mornings, she was either still in a stuporous sleep because she had been drinking until 2:00 a.m., or she was grouchy or agitated because she had passed out at midnight and her body, after several hours of abstinence, was now craving alcohol. On such mornings, she could usually not remember last night's events, and she seemed in a great hurry to get John and the kids off to work and school so that she could start her day with brandy in her coffee and follow it up with wine for lunch.

She began avoiding luncheons, and she had groceries delivered to the house so as not to have to face the store clerk. At times she had liquor delivered from several different stores in order not to call attention to her problem. Unbeknownst to John, she also started to refuse invitations to evening functions because there had been several scenes due to her drinking.

Gradually her girlish disposition was replaced by crying, mood-swings, and paranoid outbursts. She went to several doctors but was given vague diagnoses, and no effective treatment. She avoided dental visits altogether because she was afraid the dentist might detect her problem. Also, she couldn't handle the anxiety of going there without booze or pills in her system.

The last thing to deteriorate was her ability to do her housework. Without being aware of it, the family helped her in her denial by gradually absorbing the load: the oldest daughter took charge of the cooking; the next oldest was doing the cleaning; the boy took care of the pets, and John did all the rest. Carol was still living in the house, but she was out of the picture as a family member. Everybody knew she was sick, but nobody knew what to do. Even John's mother was on to her, but John wrote that off as mother-in-law hostility while he was hoping against hope that "something" would happen.

In self-defense they all lived their lives around her until the neighbors broke into the house one afternoon because smoke was pouring from the kitchen window and no one answered the phone. They found Carol drunk and passed out in the living room.

Fortunately, John's company had an employee assistance program through which Carol entered an alcoholism recovery hospital where the whole family was able to get treatment for the disease from which all of them were suffering, even though Carol was the only one who was doing the actual drinking.

Drinks, Drugs, and the Incompetent Mother

From time to time I get a letter about a woman losing custody of her children through court action because her alcohol or drug dependence has made her into an incompetent mother.

The type of alcoholism that leads to such heartbreak usually begins as social drinking, then becomes a habit, and eventually a disease. In some cases, the mother was an immature child-woman from a poor family. She started drinking and using to treat her emotional immaturity and the squalor of her lifestyle. On the other socioeconomic extreme is the intelligent, neurotic country-club mother who drinks to tolerate her phony lifestyle and to avoid thinking about her thwarted personal ambitions.

Most cases fall somewhere in between. Where the woman comes from makes little difference—the end result is the same:

excessive booze or other drugs impair her job effectiveness as a homemaker and a mother.

Many an incompetent mother never comes to the point of having her children taken away, usually because others cover up for her by taking over most of her responsibilities. Ironically, the helpers who do the covering up usually do it for selfish reasons, rather than "for the sake of the children," which is the usual explanation they give.

Often the enabling person is the husband. More than likely he is a workaholic, obsessive-compulsive, overachieving neurotic who may even be admired by the community. As his wife gets sicker, he slowly becomes both father and half-time mother.

The dynamics of this kind of alcoholism are illustrated by the case of Sarah. Starting as an occasional drinker, she became a habitual drinker who embarrassed her husband at social functions. He was extremely career-oriented. In order to rise high in his corporation and to fulfill his own ambitions in spite of her alcoholism, he wangled a company transfer to another part of the country near his mother's home.

For several years he literally hid his wife at home while he excelled at the office. He did half of her chores and pinched pennies to hire a part-time maid while his mother ran the show. This added insult to humiliation for Sarah. She increased her drinking in order to cope with her idle hands and sinking self-worth. When she finally died in a single-car crash, he and his mother honestly and openly took over the management of the children.

In other cases it is the woman's mother who gradually takes on the cooking, cleaning, and child-rearing because she and her own husband are ashamed to admit they have an alcoholic daughter.

Sometimes the helper is a lonely busybody neighbor woman who denies her own advancing middle age by taking on the child-rearing of the incompetent young mother next door. At other times the helper is a 15-year-old daughter who is a pseudo-adult.

She takes over the raising of her younger sisters because her own mother is alcoholic and non-functioning, and her father doesn't have the emotional wherewithal to do what should be done.

In any case, the children who are raised by an incompetent mother often become marginally functioning adults who are alcohol or drug dependent because they are emotionally inadequate for the demands of modern-day living.

How do you remedy this situation? Prevention is the best solution. I have treated many a middle-stage alcoholic woman who came into rehabilitation because one of the helpers could no longer go on with the cover-up. While that mother is in treatment for a month, the children are cared for by the same helpers who had actually been doing it all along as part of their cover-up. Even after she comes home from the hospital, the same people are still doing part of the child-rearing, but now they're also supporting her emotionally and helping her to restructure her life as she gradually assumes more and more of the mothering and wife roles.

The prognosis for the incompetent mother is excellent if the mother and all her "helpers" are involved in the after-care program of the facility in which the mother herself was treated. However, unless every actor in this drama begins to understand the illness and his own contribution to it, the propensity for the alcohol- or drug-dependent mother to slip back to using chemicals is great.

Ironically, the prevention of this kind of incompetent-mother syndrome often depends on mother's little "helpers," usually on people like you and me who don't have alcoholism, but who unwittingly enable the slowly deteriorating mother to sink deeper into her drinking and pills.

A good analogy is the alcoholic airline pilot who is finally disqualified from flying (just like a mother losing her children) because he has irreversible brain damage. In retrospect, it becomes clear in almost all cases that for a long time the pilot was allowed to fly in spite of the fact that his drunk–driving problems, alcohol-related family problems, absenteeism, and health problems had become known to various people in the airline. The only way such a pilot can deteriorate from early stage alcoholism all the way to brain damage is when co-workers and people in places of responsibility continue to look the other way.

By way of returning to the topic, it should be pointed out that for every alcoholically incompetent mother, there are probably a hundred alcoholically incompetent fathers, but they seldom come to legal attention because society doesn't see fathers as being essential to the task of child-rearing.

Husband's Burden: His Drinking Wife

The best example I know of man's inhumanity to woman is in the plight of the alcoholic wife. Why does this happen? Because when it comes to alcoholism, most men suffer from a curious but fatal mixture of chivalry, fear of women, and economic expediency.

What keeps the alcoholic wife going? Or rather, who keeps her going? Why, it's Bob, her compulsive, letter-perfect, overachieving husband, that's who. He does this by gradually changing their daily routine so that all her work gets done. At the same time he covers up a thousand details, which if discovered would make it necessary for her to get into treatment. He keeps tabs on her mental functioning by telephoning her at least four times a day from his office. When he does so, he always uses a pay telephone in the hallway. (He avoids using his desk phone because if someone accidentally got in on their conversation by picking up an extension, they might overhear that Mary sounds angry, slurred, obscene, or even suicidal.)

At lunchtime he leaves the office early because he needs extra time to change his clothes in the corner gas station. Ten minutes later he is in the supermarket dressed in Hawaiian sports shirt and tennis sneakers, casually pushing the grocery cart down the aisles, giving the impression that he is on vacation. Actually, he looks harried. Shopping for all the groceries takes the whole lunch hour, with no chance to eat, and with barely enough time left over to stop in the gas station and change back into his business suit.

Two hours later he is back at his desk—hungry, smiling on the outside, and furious on the inside. After two more pay telephone calls and a preoccupied afternoon at his desk, it's finally time to go home.

As he drives up to his house, he hopes for the best and fears the worst. Rushing up the front steps, he gives a casual, phony wave to the neighbor: "Hi, Jack! Mary isn't feeling too well." In the living room he finds that Mary is out—on the couch. Thank God, he sighs, at least she is asleep. It gives him a chance to pick up after the kids and start supper. With grim efficiency, he cleans the house, feeds the children, bathes them, and puts them to bed. He's just about ready to drop into bed with the "tired housewife syndrome" when Mary, having had six hours of stuporous sleep, wakes up.

She can see that the house is clean, she can smell that food had been cooked, and she can see that the kitchen is clean. She is furious. That son-of-a-gun has done it all by himself again! Now, in order to unload her guilt, anger, and self-hatred, she has to pick a fight.

But Bob, a congenital conflict-avoider and an obsequious company man, doesn't want to argue. He tries to avoid her by covering his ears with his hands and dodging her from room to room, but she doggedly keeps after him, hurling insults, crying and drinking heavily from a fresh bottle. By 3:00 in the morning, he is so angry he could murder her. In desperation he decides to "join her." He knocks back a large tumbler of cognac which burns his throat. Actually, Bob seldom drinks, but now he sardonically thinks, "Boy, this is enough to drive anybody to drink."

Just about then, Mary passes out, drunk again, and he falls into stuporous sleep helped by the angry slug of cognac. But first he sets the alarm, hoping that his tardiness and long lunches have not been noticed at the office. At 7:00 the next morning—barely four hours later, he is on the job, unaware that when the boss leans over him at his desk, he can smell alcohol on Bob's breath. All the while, Bob is working hard and secretly hoping that nobody finds out about Mary's drinking problem. If he can only hang on until October, his promotion will be official.

Actually, Bob didn't get promoted that year. When the promotion board studied his file, the discussion revealed that although Bob had been "a comer" for several years, there was something going on with him lately. No one could put a finger on it. He had undergone some kind of personality change in the past six months: taking long lunches, quitting early in the afternoon, making numerous calls from a public phone, showing signs of nervousness, irritability, absent-mindedness, having difficulty getting along with others, and smelling of alcohol on more than one occasion.

The consensus of the board was to mark Bob's file as "still a promising candidate," and to consider him again next year. Also, since Bob's performance had obviously declined, his boss would look discreetly into the possibility that Bob might have personal problems.

Actually, Bob was never confronted by the boss because soon after the board meetings, Mary's drinking stopped. Ironically, Bob's problems remained a secret.

What happened, you see, was that one morning Mary found a spare set of car keys in the kitchen drawer. She was killed in a single car crash on her way to the liquor store because she was in alcoholic withdrawal and driving erratically. On her death certificate the cause of death was listed simply as accidental, with "internal injuries, multiple, extreme."

Grandma Has a Drinking Problem

Alcoholism is the second most common reason for admitting elderly patients into psychiatric hospitals; and the rate of drinking problems among elderly patients who have other medical problems is about 25 percent. The good news is that older alcoholics have a good prognosis for recovery if the problem is addressed correctly.

The biggest hurdle that we have to overcome is the problem of diagnosis. The usual guidelines for diagnosing alcoholism—family problems, legal problems, job problems—don't apply to older people. Family problems, for example, are not a good indicator because 47 percent of women over age 65 live alone, with non-relatives, or in nursing homes. Legal problems are not a good marker because unlike younger drinkers, older people don't drive their cars very much, and they don't get into bar fights. And even though intoxication is the number one reason why senior citizens are arrested when they are found confused and wandering the streets away from their residence, police don't book them for being "drunk in a public place"; they take them back to their residence because it's simpler for everybody concerned to do it that way. Finally, since most of the elderly are retired, they don't have job problems.

That leaves health problems as the most likely reason for making the diagnosis. Unfortunately, such common symptoms of alcoholism as injuries (from home accidents), malnutrition, anemia, and mental deterioration are easily ascribed to aging, especially if the patient lies about his or her drinking.

Thus, most elderly alcoholics remain undiagnosed and quietly die of alcoholism. The few lucky ones who end up in treatment

were diagnosed when a concerned family member or friend
realized that there might be a drinking problem and then did
something about it. Here are some things to look for:

1. Grandma (or Grandpa, of course) acts confused, forgetful,
   or slurred on the phone or in person.
2. She has a history of falling, getting injured, or wandering
   away from home.
3. She behaves inappropriately with friends or strangers.
4. She has poor eating habits, malnutrition, or failing health.
5. Sometimes she acts as if her medicines are too strong.
6. She looks, smells, or acts drunk at times.

Any of the above five are *not* due to senility unless they
continue to occur after Grandma has been off booze and drugs
for several weeks. In a case like this, you have to outline in detail
the above history in an eyeball-to-eyeball talk with one or all of
the following people: Grandma's doctor, the nursing home
manager, or the friend or relative she lives with. The goal should
be to get Grandma to stop drinking. (You may get initial
resistance from the doctor or the nursing home manager; they
may feel that Grandma is easier to manage if she is drowsy or
tipsy.)

In case you are planning to confront Grandma by yourself,
beware of the foxiness of a denying alcoholic, even if she is
thought to be "elderly" or "senile." I know of one such case
where a concerned daughter took her alcoholic "senile" widowed
mother to Alcoholics Anonymous meetings. After several meetings the daughter said, "I like these meetings, Mom. What do
you think about them?"

"Why, my dear daughter . . . I am truly touched. I can hardly
believe that in all these years—you and your father never once
told me that you had a problem with booze."

Dear Doc...

Question: My mother, age 62, has been an alcoholic for at least 20 years. She also overuses prescribed drugs. My father, age 65, has, over the years, continued to bail her out of her troubles. He, too, drinks every night and has never been able to quit. However, his drinking does not affect his personality as much as mother's drinking affects her behavior.

Several years ago, after attending alcohol counseling and Al-anon, I confronted my father with the facts of mother's illness and our options for getting her into treatment at that time. He reacted with denial by saying that she was "getting better again." Of course, it didn't last.

Is he also an alcoholic or is he just a severe co-alcoholic? Is there any hope for these two people at this late stage?

Answer: The answer to all three questions is "yes." As Jean Vandervoort Hubbard likes to say, "There is only one breath test when it comes to alcoholism: You lean over close to the patient, and if he or she is still breathing, there is still hope."

The same applies to your parents. There is very little doubt that your father is co-alcoholic (which means that he has been enabling her to keep on drinking). Your description of him (drinking every night, never having been able to quit, and showing personality changes when he drinks) marks him as a functioning alcoholic. No wonder your confrontation several years ago failed.

Do not be discouraged. I know many patients who are sober today, but they have to have four or five interventions before they finally accept treatment. You will obviously need people other than your father to help you with your mother's intervention this time. Good choices would be other family members, friends, neighbors, a family doctor, and a clergyman. Probably, your best ally at this point would be the family doctor because it's almost certain that your mother has signs of physical damage.

If her doctor can get her into the hospital to study her physical problems, an intervention can be done much more effectively. This usually results in the spouse (your father) accepting his own problem. Part of your father's motivation for drinking might be that he's afraid to stand up to your mother's drinking.

Most important of all, though this is a chronic, relapsing disease, nobody is ever too old to recover.

Q: I divorced an alcoholic husband two years ago because I couldn't stand living with him any longer. I am now engaged to a very nice man. We were in love right away. My mother seems convinced that my fiance is also an alcoholic. She says wives of alcoholics tend to marry more than one alcoholic. (By the way, my father was also an alcoholic.)

I agree that my fiance drinks a little too much, but when I told him about it recently, he said that he would cut down as soon as we are married because married life would help him settle down. What else can I do?

A: Alcoholism is a family disease. If your fiance is alcoholic, then it surely will affect his family, and that means you after you are married. In view of this, all three of you—yes, your mother included—should go to an alcohol treatment facility and ask for an interview and evaluation with an impartial, professional counselor. With all three of you interviewed, either jointly or individually, it is possible to make the proper diagnosis.

You would certainly consider having a professional evaluation if your fiance had some other problem that has hereditary, family tendencies and consequences such as abnormal babies, epilepsy, or any other such illness. If your fiance refuses to go to such evaluation, then this should be a warning. If he were to ask you to go for such an evaluation because he thought you might be alcoholic, wouldn't you be glad to go? Also, in view of your father and fiance, you should be going to Al-anon.

Q: Recently I learned that my natural father (I'm adopted) was an alcoholic. Is alcoholism hereditary? What should I do about drinking?

A: Yes, it runs in families, but the mechanism isn't clear. Since you didn't give me any details about your drinking problem, I'll have to give you two answers.

If you haven't started drinking—don't! Your father's problem puts you in a high-risk category. Why invite trouble?

If you are already a drinker and you don't want to stop, get some education on the subject and ask your spouse or people close to you to help you detect early signs of the disease if you develop them. Among them are an increase in amount or frequency of drinking, change in personality, arguing about it, getting drunk, or having blackouts or hangovers.

Unfortunately, lying about drinking is also one of the cardinal signs. That's why you need the help of others.

Q: My brother and I are both adopted. Although we don't know who our parents were, we know pretty definitely that our father was an alcoholic. What puzzles me is the difference in my brother's drinking and mine. I drink very little because after one or two drinks I don't like how I feel, and the next morning I almost always have a hangover. My brother, on the other hand, is able to drink a lot. Even when I know he is drunk, he seldom acts drunk, and he never has a hangover the next morning. When I point out to him how much he drinks, he says the fact that he never gets sick from it proves that he won't become an alcoholic.

A: Recent studies indicate that people who are "born" to be alcoholic often react to alcohol differently than normal people.

One such study involving more than 1,000 drinkers showed that only 50 percent of the heavy drinkers ever had hangovers.

My theory is that people who early in their drinking careers have hangovers (headache, nausea, vomiting, dizziness, etc.) don't become alcoholic because they never learn to drink enough alcohol. Another way to look at it is that a high percentage of people who remain non-alcoholic actually have a biological, built-in aversive response to alcohol. After just a few drinks they feel tired, bloated, unsteady, flushed, nauseous, or drunk.

Alcoholics, on the other hand, can be thought of as people who were biologically and/or psychologically predisposed to becoming alcoholics because when they experience the initial "good feelings" from one or two drinks (euphoria, talkativeness, energy, etc.), they are able to keep on drinking for the rest of the evening to keep those good feelings going.

Q: Three years and two weeks ago, my alcoholic husband of 36 years walked out of my life while he was in an alcoholic fog. At first I thought of killing myself, but then I decided to try one more thing—Al-anon.

Well, Al-anon saved my life.

One year later, I found my ex-husband living with a 70-year-old woman (he was 57 at the time). She was a widow who had sold her business and wanted "a warm body" to be her traveling companion. She gave him a new car, clothes and money, then took him abroad. After I found him, he filed for divorce.

I still love him. I no longer meddle in his life, but I haven't let him go in my mind. I can't. Therein lies my problem.

Do recovering alcoholics ever go back to their former wives?

A: Some do and some don't. It depends, among other things, on the quality of sobriety and lifestyle that both the alcoholic and his former wife have. For example, a successfully recovering alcoholic man will refuse to return to his former wife if she has not recovered from her own maladjusted lifestyle. When I interview him, he will tell me that he still finds her too dependent, too self-pitying, too controlling, etc.

I also know many a non-alcoholic wife who has recovered from her own maladjustment by using Al-anon and/or counseling and is now living happily but without her non-drinking alcoholic husband. Why? When I interview her she usually tells me that even though he has stopped drinking, he has not significantly changed his maladjusted lifestyle. The story is the same. He is still over-bearing, dependent, self-pitying, too controlling, etc.

As for your situation, you may no longer be meddling in his life, but you admit that you have not been able to let him go in your mind. You also sound envious and angry at the other woman. Even though you've never met her, you speak of her in a disparaging manner. You're still "grasping at straws." Get some counseling so you can bury your dead marriage, complete your mourning, and get on with your own life.

Q: You must write about prescription drug abuse, because this is a greater threat to public health than street drugs.

In 1977 our newly married daughter began psychiatric treatment at a famous clinic because she had marriage problems and migraine headaches. At that time she had no known emotional problems. In the next few months she got electric shock treatments, repeated psychiatric hospitalizations, and was prescribed many different kinds of mood-altering drugs. At one time she was taking 23 pills a day.

Two years later, she went through four weeks of chemical dependency treatment and was fine for one year. She was happy, positive, productive, and had again become the kind of daughter we had always known her to be.

Then she visited one of her former psychiatrists and was put back on drugs. Now she can't work, she visits a lot of psychiatrists and is in and out of hospitals again.

My husband and I want her to go through chemical dependency treatment again, but we have no legal right to insist on it. Only her husband can do that, through a court order. The problem is that he's a pharmacist.

The other problem is that her "doctors" are totally opposed to detoxification or any other procedure which is not centered around prescribing mind-altering drugs. It makes a farce of the Hippocratic oath.

A: The history of your daughter typifies a common dilemma: was the patient mentally ill to begin with, or are the current mental symptoms a manifestation of the effects of drugs (including alcohol) which the patient is using now? Possible answers are: (1) the patient is mentally ill, (2) the drugs are making the patient ill, or (3) both are true.

The significant elements and the tone of your letter indicate that in spite of the present treatment regimen: (1) your daughter is not functioning well; (2) you, your husband, and others are angry, hurt, and frustrated; and (3) by now several emotionally upset parties have drawn up battle lines. To some extent these lines are designed to save face and justify a certain course of action, or belief in a particular treatment system, whichever the case may be. The real problem is that in this battle of pills versus the couch versus the rehabilitation hospital, the important person, namely your daughter, has been lost sight of.

The fact that your daughter was able to function normally for one year following her detoxification and rehabilitation indicates strongly that she can function without mind-altering drugs, although there is a remote possibility that she was in remission from an innate mental illness such as schizophrenia.

At this time the only real hope for resolution of your daughter's problems is that you arrange for a consultation conference involving you, your husband, your son-in-law, and at least one dispassionate member of your daughter's psychiatric treatment team. The purpose of such a session would be not only to ventilate and discuss your fears, angers, and prejudices, but more importantly to agree on the most intelligent course of action for helping your daughter.

The conclusion will probably be that your daughter begin treatment again at a site which, although in a psychiatric treatment facility, is nevertheless run along the principles of a chemical dependency treatment unit. It is essential that a psychiatrist who is knowledgeable in the treatment of addictive disease be involved in the case. He could also advise you on the use of a court order to make such treatment possible.

A most important part of your daughter's follow-up treatment, regardless of whether she turns out to be addicted to drugs or mentally ill, will be ongoing family involvement and family treatment because the bruised egos of all participants need time for healing.

In any case, 23 pills a day is not the answer for an out-patient, no matter what her basic illness.

Q: I'm a recovering alcoholic and I found your columns on alcoholism very helpful. I have a friend who also has an alcoholic husband. They are both suffering a lot from his disease. How can I give her some information without offending her?

A: Alcoholics and their loved ones are equally ashamed of the disease. The best way for you to help her is to talk to her privately in a kind, matter-of-fact way. Describe to her your problem and your experience so far. This would minimize any fear or shame she has about the problem. You could then give her the information. You would be doing what alcoholics have done since AA was founded—namely, helping somebody else by sharing your own story.

Q: My dad is an alcoholic. I often feel as if you've been sitting at the dinner table in my parents' home. In my childhood even a discussion of alcohol or drinking was a sore subject. Your columns have made me realize that I have learned a self-medicating behavior pattern from my dad. I rarely drink more than four glasses of wine or beer, but I realize that most of the time I drink to relax after a hard day's work. How many times has that line been spoken? I am keeping a watchful eye for any potential problems I might develop.

A: As you can see, one alcoholic in the family can have a gradual, even though subtle effect on other family members. Also, there is usually a problem drinker in the family if discussion of alcohol turns into a "sore subject." People get "sore" about this subject because it touches a raw nerve kind of like an adult-teething problem.

The difficult problems caused by being a child of an alcoholic are being recognized now. One good source book on the subject is Claudia Black's *It Will Never Happen to Me!* (M.A.C. Publishers). Reading this may help you get perspective on your own situation.

Q: I grew up watching my father's alcoholism. My husband doesn't drink every day, but on weekends he drinks two six-packs. It bothers me a lot. He says there is no alcoholic problem. What do you think?

A: Two six-packs in one day even once or twice a week causes physical damage in the long run. The tone of your letter suggests that you're onto something much more immediate. You are asking, "How come he can't enjoy a pleasant weekend without a lot of drinking?"

Your husband might drink too much to handle boredom, free time, or intimacy. In any case, your marriage is seriously disrupted because of the way he drinks and because of your thoughts and feelings about it. Together you should get a diagnostic opinion from an alcohol treatment center. If your husband refuses, you need counseling to help you decide whether to stay in that marriage.

Q: I am a recovering alcoholic, but I go to Al-anon because my husband is unquestionably an alcoholic too. I'm staying sober for myself, but it's hard to see him deteriorating. What can I do other than go to Al-anon? Is it unusual for two alcoholics to be married to each other?

A: In my experience up to 30 percent of the alcoholics' spouses have alcoholism or drug dependence themselves to varying degrees. It is one of the reasons why I always interview the alcoholic and the spouse separately and then together so that the eventual treatment for both becomes more acceptable.

Since your husband appears to be a more difficult case, see a counselor or a physician who works in alcoholism, then ask your husband to go with you for a couple of sessions to "help" you and your therapist with your problem. Also, ask your husband to join you for a few AA meetings. This is not a subterfuge. It is actually good medical practice. Any normal husband will gladly go with his wife to her doctor or therapist to help her with her diabetes, her heart disease, her depression, etc.

If your husband adamantly refuses, then the diagnosis is probably correct. You then have to get education and treatment for yourself and your family so that you can eventually do an intervention.

Most important of all for you, in my experience a recovering alcoholic cannot have serenity and a happy life while living with a spouse who is drinking alcoholically.

Q: I was surprised by the answer you gave the woman whose husband has been drunk every day for years. How can you say she made it "possible for him to be drunk"? It is not her responsibility to control his drinking. One of the main steps of the Al-anon program says "hands off" your alcoholic. There is hope for her alcoholic, but only if he wishes.

A: You are right. She can't control his drinking. I suggested Al-anon because the woman's letter made it obvious that she needed help first, and because (here I agree with you again) Al-anon helps those people who carefully follow the steps of the program.

I said that she'd been making it "possible" for her husband to be a drunk because that's what my work with alcoholics and their families has shown. Not surprisingly, Al-anon and rehabilitation for family members is the best way for spouses and family members to realize that they have been "making it possible" by covering up, and that that's what they have to stop doing.

The notion that there is hope for the alcoholic "only if he wants it" is *your* idea, not Al-anon's idea. To my knowledge Al-anon says nothing about that one way or another. Seventy percent of my patients are pressured into treatment against their wishes by the judge, the family, or the employer, but their recovery rate is the same as it is for patients who "volunteer."

Q: My husband is clearly an alcoholic. Here are the things I have done so far:

- I have let him know the change I see in him, and what my feelings are about his drinking.
- I have explained to him his employer's treatment policy for troubled employees, and I have promised that I would cooperate in rehabilitation.
- I've had our family and a counselor talk with him, but he walked out and has not talked to his parents for a year now.
- I've gone to family counseling and Al-anon for my own benefit.

I feel good about myself again, and I've learned that I can't control him. I'm now getting a divorce, which I really don't want, but I refuse to live a sick life any more. Our children are still confused, but they are beginning to feel better. They seem to understand. I still love my husband and want him back healthy. I pray that something will click and that he will get help just for himself. Is there anything else I can do?

A: You've done all the things that you could possibly do, and you have done them correctly. You sound like a compassionate woman who has come a long way. If you take good care of yourself and your children, and if you keep your present resolve, chances are your husband will find help for himself. I hope and pray with you that he will.

Q: My husband and I seem to have an incompatibility. I think he has a drinking problem, and I have a hard time putting up with it. I've thought about leaving him but I keep staying. Sometimes his drinking makes our life interesting because it makes him energetic and entertaining; at other times his drinking really embarrasses me and makes me ashamed of him. I'm confused.

A: You and your husband have a living problem. Part of the time he uses alcohol to make *his* life exciting, and you use his drinking to make *your* life exciting. The fact that you still find some of his drinking antics "interesting" or fascinating tells me that you have not yet learned to understand alcoholism as a family disease which can affect couples and whole families.

The tone of your letter also suggests that you are using his drinking to make up for some of your own personality defects. You badly need to go to Al-anon, but you also need psychotherapy for yourself. Get off the "pity pot." The best way to resolve your own confusion and doubt is through action.

Q: Your response to the woman whose daughter was molested by her drunken stepfather was inappropriate in my opinion. By focusing on the stepfather's "drinking problem," you took the focus away from the real issue which is that the child needs treatment for the sexual abuse. In my opinion, it is more appropriate to say that the stepfather drank to molest her—rather than to say that he molested her because he was drunk.

A: Your letter was one of many which commented on the same issue. All the letters agreed that the child needs treatment. Some of them did not agree that the mother also needs counseling, regardless of whether she was preconsciously aware of the sexual abuse—as is often the case—or not.

Why did I focus on the stepfather's problem? Because he obviously has a drinking problem regardless of whether the child fabricated the story of abuse or not, as he alleged. I surmised this from the mother's letter which quoted him as saying, "I was drunk when I did it, and I can't remember it." In my experience with such cases, the molesting stops when the drinking stops, and it stays stopped when the whole family gets into treatment.

The handling of this case points to an overlapping problem issue in the treatment field: therapists who treat incest consider alcoholism a taboo subject because they don't understand alcoholism (many of them hate alcoholism); and alcoholism therapists consider incest a taboo subject for similar reasons.

Much education is needed for therapists in both fields. You write that: "The stepfather drank to molest her—rather than . . . he molested her because he was drunk." That's very clever, but it is not very helpful. As a patient of mine once said about her alcoholic, homicidal husband: "I could care less if he drank in order to shoot me, or if he shot me because he was drunk. The drinking has to stop before we can figure anything else out." Let me paraphrase her: if drinking causes you to molest or makes it possible for you to molest—then you should stop drinking.

Q: My mother has been a problem drinker for many years. After my father's death two years ago, she really got bad. She has many health problems. Last week she fell and broke one of the bones in her face. She is 55 and can't recover as quickly the morning after as she did when she was 30. How can I help her?

A: Women who drink heavily but still manage to function tend to become overtly and fatally alcoholic when they suffer a loss, a mutilating operation (mastectomy or hysterectomy), death of a husband, or a favorite child moving away or marrying. In a way, it is fortunate that your mother has developed health problems and physical damage from her drinking, because this will enable your family physician to get her into the hospital. Starting to treat her physical damage will be a face-saving device for all concerned.

Once she is in a hospital, he can easily get her evaluated for alcoholism treatment and concurrently get her the help she needs to finally deal with the pain and sadness of your father's death. She is very likely seriously depressed and on a self-destructive, suicidal course. Discuss this treatment plan with the doctor beforehand. Without treatment, her prognosis is poor.

Q: My wife, 25, recently stopped drinking because she's an alcoholic. I stopped at the same time to give her moral support. Now I wonder. Is this necessary, or even helpful? How long do I stay stopped?

A: You sound like you're having second thoughts. What you did is helpful unless you yourself are psychologically dependent on drinking, in which case you will resent her and see it as a sacrifice.

If, on the other hand, you are a light social drinker, you can go back to drinking again in a few months, or you may decide to not ever drink again.

Some recovering alcoholics continue to find it distasteful to live intimately with someone who smells of alcohol, even from time to time. A frank discussion with your wife and your therapist will clarify this problem in your particular case.

The bottom line is that if you can stay comfortably "quit" and never give drinking another thought, that undoubtedly is the best choice.

Q: I have a friend who frequently tells me about his fears that he might be an alcoholic. He has been on booze or pot since he was in the seventh grade—he will be a senior in high school this fall. For a while he was heavily into pot, now he's heavily into alcohol. We often have long talks about his "problem." I always give him the best advice I can come up with, but he always comes up with lame excuses and solutions like limiting his drinking to only once a week. I love this friend, and I am concerned about his future. Is there any effective way of getting him to seek help?

A: Your friend is like many of my chemically dependent patients who are in their early 20s and are now in hospitals. They started around age 13 with either pot or alcohol, then progressed from one to the other. At first they did it occasionally, then they started doing it on weekends only, but eventually they became chemical gourmands or "garbage cans" (in the teen-age drug vernacular), which means that they were using any drug they could get.

However, what's more important for you to realize is that your friend is not only using pot and booze—he's also using you. You may see yourself as a friend, but as long as he can get you to function as an amateur counselor, and as a psychological crutch, he will slowly but surely get sicker.

The only effective way to get him some help is to (1) insist that he get an evaluation from a qualified therapist or drug treatment center; and (2) stop letting him use you to avoid what you know he needs. If he refuses to get an evaluation, you owe it to him to let him go with love.

Q: In my opinion, my wife is an alcoholic. She lost her part-time job selling real estate, and then she lost her driver's license, both due to drinking. Our 15-year-old son is privately complaining to me about her drinking, and our daughter has moved out and entered an ill-advised marriage simply to get away from my wife's drinking. I am developing some guilt feelings about what her drinking is doing to our family. I have a feeling that maybe I am "allowing it" to happen.

I think I still love my wife, but I'm beginning to wonder. Every time I bring up the subject of her drinking, she throws a fit, refuses to talk about it, and then is drunk again the next day. Is she an alcoholic, and how can we help her?

A: It sounds like your wife's drinking is causing problems in her family life (the reactions from you, your son, and your daughter), her legal life (loss of driver's license), and in her work (loss of part-time job). Any of these consequences of drinking alone means that she should cut down (if she can), or quit. Since she has done neither, there are only two possibilities: she is doing all of this for the heck of it—or she can't quit or cut down because she has become dependent on alcohol.

You need to present your problem to a professional counselor at an alcohol treatment facility in your community and ask him or her to help prepare an intervention on your wife to get her into treatment. While going through the preparation for an intervention, you and your family will also learn what to do about your own reactions to her drinking. Your current efforts to get her to see the light will continue to fail because your own emotions, your guilt, and your reluctance to be firm will continue to get in the way as long as you are trying to do the confrontation single-handedly.

Q: I have a dear friend who is an alcoholic and knows it. She stays dry for a time, but then relapses when certain pressures in her life arise. She now goes into blackouts even after she's had only one or two drinks at times. Fortunately, she only drinks at home, alone, and therefore has not become a nuisance to others.

The only thing that frightens her are some large bruises which appear all over her body. She gets them from falling down while she's drunk. What can I do to get her some help?

A: Different alcoholics respond to different approaches. Your friend may be most susceptible to a doctor's explanation about how alcohol is destroying her body and brain. She is a periodic (binge) alcoholic whose drinking is causing serious damage to her liver and bone marrow. The bruising indicates that her blood-clotting mechanism is disturbed. During a fall she could bleed to death from an otherwise harmless laceration, or from internal injuries, including injuries to her brain.

Do whatever you can to get her to a doctor who understands alcoholism. If necessary, drive her to an emergency room the next time she falls—but tell the examining doctor privately what is going on. This lady is really sick, and you would be saving her life.

Q: I am a 22-year-old secretary. I wonder if I have a drinking problem. I usually drink alone in my apartment to relax around the same time every day. Lately, I drink out of loneliness in a cocktail lounge at "happy hour." It's sophisticated and makes me forget about the workday. But I never drink before 5 p.m.

A: You are developing a problem manifested by psychological dependency. You're also using alcohol as a tranquilizer to "relax" and to help you fix job problems.

Stop drinking for a month. Take daily notes on how you feel and what thoughts, wishes, angers, and daydreams you have after 5 o'clock. If possible, discuss your notes with a trusted friend. You would benefit from psychotherapy to clarify the reasons for your job frustrations and loneliness. You would also learn more about your alcohol dependency if you attended some AA meetings.

Q: I am 19 years old. I fell in love with a girl who has an alcohol problem. I convinced her to get treatment. She said she would go because she loved me. When I saw her in the hospital a week later, she was withdrawn and talked very little. Two weeks later she called me and told me not to visit her any more because she no longer loved me.

I still love her. Can you explain her behavior? Does treatment always break up relationships?

A: Treatment doesn't always break up relationships, but it always brings about changes in any relationship, especially if one person was alcoholic even before the couple met. The result of treatment in that kind of situation can be anything from disastrous to marvelous. But since the outcome without treatment is always disastrous, you have really nothing to lose.

Your friend is depressed because her brain is clearing up from the effects of drugs and alcohol, and because she is now able to more and more clearly see reality.

Write her a letter. Tell her you still love her and offer to be in outpatient treatment with her. Also, tell her you are going to Al-anon. Then the ball is in her court.

It is important for you to understand that even if she never speaks to you again, you need this treatment for yourself. The tone of your letter tells me quite clearly that you are a born helper. That means you will very likely continue to find yourself attracted to people just like her unless you come to understand this disease and your own feelings and reasons for being attracted to it.

Q: My wife is from a noble European family. We have always had only the best vintage wines. She used to sip with some of the world's connoisseurs. Over the past two years on three different occasions I have noticed that she hurriedly knocks back a whole water glass full of wine in the kitchen when she thinks she is unobserved, and then she rejoins the dinner party and sips graciously with the rest of us. Could she be developing a problem?

A: She already has developed a problem. She has gone from gracious sipper to secret gulper—and that's not social drinking.

Confront her about what you've seen her do. If she denies it, there are only two possibilities: (1) She needs alcoholism treatment because she has a problem with alcohol, or (2) you need psychiatric treatment because you see things that aren't happening.

Q: When I read your column on the alcoholic wife, I saw red! Nine months ago I would have had a drink in hand to ease my anger; now, as a recovered alcoholic, I will take pen in hand.

Did it ever occur to you that the "tedium of housework" and the "pressures of raising children" are enough to drive women to drink? That was certainly true in my case. Now I can say firmly and without guilt, "The housework is not my responsibility."

In Carol's family (that's what you called the alcoholic lady in your column), her oldest daughter *should* have been doing the cooking; the next oldest *should* have been doing the cleaning; the boy *should* have been taking care of the pets (I'll bet they were his!), and her husband *should* have been doing the rest.

I'm 34 years old and just beginning to see what effect the male-dominated medical profession has on women, causing them everything from alcoholism to drug abuse to suicide. And don't you dare print my name in your column!

A: Without revealing your identity, I shared your letter with some of my patients, both male and female. They felt that tedious housework and child-rearing are explanations for drinking—not causes of drinking. Rehabilitation doesn't change these external conditions; it only changes your reaction to them. Several male patients felt that their own drinking had been "caused" by executive stress, the meaninglessness of shuffling papers, the tedium of the production line, and the frustration of being "responsible" for how their children turned out even though they (the men) had not been around to raise them. (These men had extra jobs to raise the family income.)

One male patient—he was also hostile—asked, "If the housework is *not* her responsibility, whose is it? If her children and husband share the cooking, cleaning, pets, etc., what does she, as a 34-year-old housewife, actually do?"

I'm encouraged that you were able to vent some of your anger with pen in grip instead of glass in hand. Keep making progress.

Q: I am a 45-year-old woman. I recently stopped drinking. I have trouble with bloating, constipation, and weight gain even though I take dance classes regularly. I eat sparingly, drink a lot of water, and get plenty of rest. I have trouble falling asleep at night.

Are these "withdrawal" symptoms? How can I be more comfortable physically?

A: Rarely have I seen a person stop drinking, change nothing else in his life, and at the same time become physically and mentally comfortable. Your symptoms should not last more than one month. Adding dance classes may not be enough to change your life. Like almost all alcoholics, you need help from outside yourself through self-help groups (AA or counseling) so that family relationships, friendships, etc., will also change.

Right now you sound dry and tense instead of sober and serene. Any one of your present symptoms might be enough to "drive you to drink" again—which is often what happens.

Q: I'm a female alcoholic. I tried AA a few times, but I dropped out because I came home from some meetings feeling worse about myself. Anyway, I don't like myself or my drinking.

I keep thinking that I should go to a hospital for drying out, but I have a great fear of being strapped down naked on a bed.

A: Your distorted ideas about how terrible alcoholism treatment might be are not unusual, nor is your fear of the unknown. Rehabilitation for alcoholism in a modern, hospital-based unit begins with "drying out" or detoxification, if you need it. We would use certain anti-convulsant and tranquilizing drugs for three or four days to make your drying out safe. After that you'd go through rehabilitation for three or four weeks involving group therapy, individual counseling, lectures, movies, patient community meetings, physical exercise, AA, and a few other things.

The treatment is on a voluntary basis. The facilities are wide open, with no locked wards, and with no one strapped naked to beds or anything of that sort.

Any good treatment center will be more than willing to have you come in as a visitor, show you through the entire facility, and answer all of your questions. You then have a chance to make up your own mind about entering treatment. Nobody can force you or commit you into a locked facility unless you have deteriorated to the point where you have become a danger to yourself or others.

Right now, you sound like an ideal treatment candidate. I hope you will get treatment quickly.

Q: After my alcoholic husband left me for another woman, he filed for a divorce. I tried to get the courts to make me his conservator so I could get him into treatment. I thought that I would give him the divorce after treatment. After all, he was a sick man, and I had taken vows "for better or for worse, in sickness and in health, till death do us part."

I believe in God. My religion says that I'm not free to marry until he does. So—don't tell me to look for another man.

A: Regardless of whether your husband's problem is chronic alcoholism or something else, you cannot become his conservator unless psychiatrists are willing to say that he is a danger to himself or others. Go to an alcoholism treatment facility and, with the help of qualified counselors, make one final attempt to do an intervention in your alcoholic husband's life.

Regardless of whether it succeeds or fails (and even if you don't do anything else), the tone of your letter tells me that you need help for yourself. You are suffering the maladjusted lifestyle of the untreated spouse. Start by getting some outpatient treatment. Also, since religion seems to be important in your life, get some counseling from a clergyman who understands alcoholism. Your counselor and your minister very likely will have seen marriages in which real life events seem to have added another phrase to the vows: "Till booze do us part."

Q: The letter from the woman whose husband drank a fifth of vodka every day while still being able to function on the job hit me like a bolt.

My husband was on the job until a week before he died. He never called in sick and he was never fired. As a matter of fact, he never really lost anything except his life.

He also drank a fifth of vodka a day. He started doing that at age 53 and died at age 57.

All my doctor ever did was give him pills, although I now know that he had all the classic symptoms of alcoholism. Today I feel very bitter toward the medical profession. Why did nobody ever suggest Alcoholics Anonymous or Al-anon? That seems to be the answer.

A: Your letter is typical of many I receive. Yes, AA and Al-anon are two of the best answers, and also the most widely available. You seem to have learned in Al-anon about yourself and alcoholism as a family disease. I hope your children have learned something as well because they have a predisposition to becoming alcoholic, or marrying alcoholics.

Also, you may benefit from reading a fine resource book called *Another Chance, Hope and Health for the Alcoholic Family* by Sharon Wegscheider (Science and Behavior Book Publishers).

You have one problem remaining, however, and that is that you are still "very bitter toward the medical profession." You now have to integrate those feelings and memories. You need to defuse this anger by using your sponsor in Al-anon or a therapist in an alcohol center. It may be hard for you to understand that your husband's doctor got as much useful information in medical school about alcoholism as you got in high school. Medical schools generally teach nothing about early diagnosis, intervention, or recovery.

Q: I am 25 years old and an attractive woman. I have been drinking at least six or more drinks a day for over six years. Three months ago I quit drinking because I had a rude awakening: I noticed several large, broken blood vessels around my nose and eyes. Then I found a couple more around my collar bones. (Fortunately, they are low enough on my chest that they are covered up when I wear a dress.)

I am horrified by what I have done to myself. I am now taking vitamins, eating lots of vegetables, drinking only mineral water and avoiding exposure to the sun. Will these blood vessels go away if I never drink again? Can a dermatologist help?

A: A daily habit of six drinks or more is heavy drinking. Have a doctor who understands alcoholism evaluate your liver function status by blood tests so that you can find out how sick you have really become. The doctor will also confirm whether the dilated blood vessels are spider angiomata, a common finding in chronic alcoholism.

If you never drink again, and if you leave your skin problem alone, it will improve only slightly. A plastic surgeon can do electrodessication under local anesthesia for the blood vessels in your face so that you can look beautiful again.

However, it is much more important that you come to understand the nature of your drinking problem. Most people who have quit on a dare, a scare, or out of vanity sooner or later return to drinking again. Get some extra insurance by going to some AA meetings or by getting some counseling so you will understand what is the matter with you.

Q: My wife is a severe alcoholic. She has refused help for years. She has finally agreed to see an internist, but she would not enter the hospital. She is very malnourished. The doctor put her on two vitamins and a special diet. In passing he said that she's been getting half her energy from drinking. What does that mean, and what is her prognosis?

A: Many alcoholics get much of their energy from drinking. Alcohol contains 100 calories per ounce of alcohol. Thus, a pint of 86-proof bourbon, Scotch, etc., has in it about 1,600 calories, which is about half of the energy the average person needs per day.

However, these calories are "empty" calories, which means that they contain no vitamins or minerals. It's like pouring very low-octane, watered-down gasoline into your car engine. Add to this the appetite-spoiling effect of heavy drinking, and the impaired absorption of what little food your wife has been eating, and you can understand how and why she is so ill.

Q: My wife has a drinking problem. The funny thing is that she admits it—but she refuses to seek any kind of help. We have two children (ages 3 and 6). She insists that her drinking is not bothering the children or me. She says she is hurting only herself. But in the past three months it's gotten worse. She now drinks from noon until night every day. How can I prove to her that she needs help?

A: For her to admit that she has a drinking problem, but then refuse help, is only a cop-out. It's like saying that she has tuberculosis but she doesn't need any medicine.

Unless you have a serious mental problem—and your letter doesn't suggest anything like that—you must be quite aware that her drinking is definitely harming your two children. It's not possible for her to drink alcohol from noon until night every day and be a competent mother. Although you didn't say it, I'm sure that you and her mother or a neighbor or others are heavily involved in raising your children.

You alone can't prove to her she needs help. You must immediately contact a treatment center and arrange for an intervention, using a qualified counselor who can help you. Furthermore, you must involve the very people who are enabling your wife to stay away from help, namely, yourself and the others who are taking care of your children. Together you can get her into treatment.

Q: I grew up watching my father's alcoholism at its worst. He broke his promises, frightened me, called me terrible names, and abused me. When he died, I was old enough to realize he was sick. I loved him very much.

I don't drink at all. But I have problems with people who love drinking. Once in a great while my husband has one beer or mixed drink, and it really bothers me. I think it's a stupid thing to do. It alters your behavior and destroys brain cells. I am afraid someday he will be an alcoholic.

A: Your husband doesn't have a drinking problem, but you most certainly do. The societal custom of drinking alcohol is ruining your life because of the many unresolved personal problems and childhood recollections you have that are intertwined with your father's alcoholism. Stop talking to your husband about his drinking, and start talking to a therapist about your fears and your thoughts about his drinking. You need counseling by a therapist who understands alcoholism. Ask your husband to attend a couple of sessions with you. Your reaction and suffering are not unusual for the children of alcoholic families.

Q: My father has always been a social drinker and my mother has been hard to live with because she is moody and temperamental. Now that they are over 60, I notice that my father has increased his drinking. My theory is that he is doing it to help him live with the strain caused by her personality. I am hesitant to say anything about my thoughts for fear that it will get a mixed reaction.

A: Your theory is almost certainly correct. As people get older, they unfortunately don't just "mellow," they also become "more so" (grumpy, complaining, suspicious, etc.). Chances are your mother is probably becoming more difficult to live with, and your father is "self-medicating" his nervous system to drown her out. (He may always have used alcohol to make the world around him more tolerable. One might successfully argue that he may not exactly have been a social drinker all along.)

In any case, if a man over 50 begins to drink more than he has in the past, he has to be made aware of it because the increased drinking will impair his functioning and damage his health. Your dad may be harming his liver to preserve his marriage. To avoid a mixed reaction, talk to him privately first. Don't call him an alcoholic. Tell him honestly and lovingly—what you see and what you fear is happening.

Chances are very good that he will be relieved, grateful, and responsive to your suggestions about cutting back on his drinking and substituting some healthy hobbies, interests, and friends, some of which may give him some time away from her.

Q: My mother, 64, lives in a posh retirement home. Because we are a "very proper" family, we hid my mother's drinking problem for 15 years. I now know that she had alcoholism. Shortly before moving her to the retirement home, we made a clumsy effort at confronting her, but with her iron will, she just simply quit drinking and refused treatment.

For the past six months the doctor who visits the retirement home has been giving her Dalmane pills to take for sleep. But she seems drowsy to us in the daytime, too. We are worried about her when she drives her car.

A: Pills or booze for senior citizens seems to be society's answer to the retirement problem. But as in the case of your mother, it usually doesn't work. Dalmane is a "long-acting" benzodiazapine drug and the most frequently prescribed sleeping pill today. It has a half-life of more than 24 hours. It means that the drug accumulates in her system because the body destroys it slower than she is taking it. As a result, there may be slurred speech and a slowing of hand-to-eye coordination. In older people it can also mimic senility or confusion.

People who have a past history of addiction should not be given sleeping pills except for a short time and under unusual circumstances. Tell the doctor about your mother's past alcoholism because she may already be overusing the Dalmane. She may also be sneaking drinks. Suggest that he alter her treatment plan. I would also recommend more human contact, walking, and hot baths.

Q: My husband and I go to AA and Al-anon, respectively. Since he has stopped drinking, we have grown a lot emotionally and we are much closer than we were in the past, but we no longer have any kind of sex life. I'm too embarrassed to discuss this in AA and Al-anon meetings. Is his lack of interest due to his sobriety?

We are both young. I have trouble dealing with this. Where can we get help?

A: Early in treatment about half of my patients have unsatisfactory sex lives manifested by impotence, frigidity, or just plain lack of interest in becoming sexy.

Because of emotional as well as endocrinological, hormonal changes which are taking place during the first six months, it is best not to make a big issue of decrease or lack of sexual activity during this period. However, if the problem persists beyond six months, then I recommend that an evaluation be done by a sexual dysfunction clinic. To be comprehensive, this should include an evaluation by an M.D. who is not only knowledgeable in sexual dysfunction but also in addictive diseases. For best results this should be coordinated closely with whoever is doing the after-care follow-ups from the alcoholic program.

Another source of help is a good book by Theresa Crenshaw, M.D., *Bedside Manners, Your Guide to Better Sex* (McGraw Hill).

Q: Some time ago I was treated for alcoholism the second time. This time I'm convinced I will be successful. I'm attending AA five times a week, and actively participating. I am also on Antabuse which gives me a feeling of security. I feel good about myself.

I'm 65 years old. I'm vigorous in all ways except for my sex life. I can achieve an erection, but cannot maintain it long enough. Is this physical or could it be caused by anxiety? I also take megavitamins, zinc, eat well, and get plenty of fresh air and exercise.

A: This time around you're doing the right things and you have a good prognosis. Your sexual dysfunction is almost certainly due to anxiety and attitudinal problems that are left over from your drinking days.

The primary danger is that if you consult a physician who is well qualified but does not understand alcoholism, he will almost certainly ask you to stop taking Antabuse on the assumption that your sexual dysfunction is a side effect of the Antabuse. This is a widely held misconception. Consult an alcoholism treatment center in your area or ask for a referral to a sexual dysfunction clinic, and don't stop taking Antabuse.

Q: I think my lover and I have developed a sexual problem which is due to alcohol. During the week, our sex life is sometimes even more active than I want it to be, but on weekends he often gets impotent. The only thing I can relate this to is his heavy drinking on Friday night and Saturday. Could this be psychological? Can it also be that he's getting tired of me?

A: Normal or frequent sexual intercourse during the week, alternating with intermittent impotence and heavy drinking on weekends, almost certainly means that the alcohol is causing your lover's problems. The fact that he is comfortable discussing it is also not typical of emotionally caused impotence.

Dr. David Van Thiel from the University of Pittsburgh reports that even non-alcoholic males suffer impotence after a one-night drinking bout. This is caused by a lowering of the testosterone level, a hormone which controls erection. Discuss this with your lover. Have him cut down on his drinking and together conduct your own experiment. You should see the results very quickly.

If he's unable to change his drinking life for the sake of your sexual life, you both need counseling. Otherwise, he will end up a chronic alcoholic and you a total abstainer (from sex, that is).

Q: I'm worried about our sex life. My wife is 28. When we first met, we literally had beautiful chemistry. Social drinking even seemed to make things better at times.

Now we have a serious sex problem which parallels her heavy increase in drinking. In recent months sexual intercourse has become painful for her and unpleasant for me because she seems to have no vaginal lubrication. I read somewhere that lack of lubrication means she is losing her love for me. When I tried to discuss it with her, she got angry but she agreed to ask her gynecologist about it on her next visit. Is there anything I can do?

A: The physiological problem may be your wife's, but the mechanical problem is mutual. Scientific research has repeatedly documented that excessive drinking in a female will cause reduction in vaginal lubrication, lack of interest in sexual intercourse, and eventual failure to have orgasm. Once there is little or no lubrication, the other problems obviously are not far behind and inevitable.

Since sex is important to both of you, offer to accompany your wife to the gynecologist for a joint consultation. The only alternatives are to break up the marriage right now, or to drift apart emotionally and physically in a more gradual way. (Incidentally, breaking up right now would only solve your problem. At her present rate of drinking, your wife will have the same problem with future sex partners.) Another reason you need a joint consultation is that decrease in vaginal lubrication also is frequently caused by an emotional estrangement and "falling out of love." Whichever the cause, in order to solve the problem— you both have to be involved in the solution.

Alcohol is a far greater killer than all opiates. You can buy alcohol on any street corner throughout the world. It gets your brain, your liver. It destroys your morals, destroys your vitality, kills your sexual potential, and you become sluggish. Drinker that I am, I think essentially I am the victim of an addiction that is here in the world, revealed to all, exposed to all. As one of the hardiest drinkers in the world, I speak with a voice of authority.

My Wicked, Wicked Ways
Errol Flynn

4

When Alcohol or Drug Use Damages Your Health

When I was in medical school thirty years ago we learned that alcoholism or drug addiction was a hopeless dilemma: annoying for the doctors, heartbreaking for the patients' families, and eventually fatal for the patients themselves. By contrast we saw that coronary patients, surgical patients, and ulcer patients usually recovered; and we learned that hypertensives, diabetics, and other chronically ill patients—given proper treatment and education—could also recover.

The contrast was a glaring lesson: we never saw alcoholic patients recover. As a matter of fact, we never even heard of any such thing; the term "recovering alcoholic" would have been a contradiction in terms, much like a "living cadaver." Although one or two of our professors mentioned Alcoholics Anonymous as a possible solution, nobody we met—patients or faculty—had ever been to an AA meeting. As a result we came out as clinical pessimists. By the end of our internships and residencies we had funneled hundreds of alcoholics and addicts from the emergency room through the intensive care unit into the morgue. In the process we'd learned to deal with them without ever really seeing them; *we always felt their livers, but we never touched their lives.*

Although physicians today are more aware of the existence of addictive diseases in our population, most of them still don't know how to help such patients. A recent poll showed that although 90 percent of practicing physicians see alcohol abuse as a major national problem, only 27 percent feel competent to treat alcoholism.*

In their daily encounters with alcoholics and addicts, physicians manifest this lack of competency in various ways. They tend to prescribe inappropriate doses of the wrong drugs for the wrong symptoms because they are not aware of the interaction between alcohol and other drugs. More specifically, most physicians have never heard of "sedativism" (a term coined by Dr. Stanley E. Gitlow to show that addiction-prone patients can use alcohol or any other sedative-hypnotic with equal facility); and they are slow to accept empirical evidence which shows that for many patients, minor tranquilizers are as addicting as alcohol.

Since alcohol and other drug abuse affects every organ system in the body, physicians keep busy patching up various symptoms and problems until the patient develops terminal complications, (usually liver, cardiovascular, or brain pathology).

The underlying reason for this kind of medical mismanagement is that most physicians don't know how to recognize and deal with earlier signs and symptoms of addictive disease. Their lack of effectiveness stems from three causes: (1) lack of proper training in medical schools, (2) reluctance to learn from the experience of their patients, and (3) lack of familiarity with newer treatment approaches (rehabilitation facilities) that *are* effective.

I know from personal experience that this unhappy state of affairs can be changed. From 1974 through 1980 I was personally involved in training over 1,600 physicians. The idea was to help these doctors become more effective in the diagnosis and treatment of alcohol/drug dependent patients. In groups of twenty, for two weeks at a time, these doctors worked with my staff at the

*The poll was conducted by the American Medical Association Center for Health Policy Research, as reported in the *American Medical News*, June 29, 1984.

Alcohol/Drug Rehab Service in the Long Beach Naval Hospital. Through direct all-day contact with recovering patients, these doctors struggled . . . and fought . . . and learned . . . and gradually changed. In the process they lost their defenses and their prejudices; and they gained hope, skill, and knowledge. Today these physicians are in civilian practice all over the country, but now they are dealing as effectively with chemically dependent patients as they deal with diabetics, cardiacs, and others.

Admittedly, the above approach is not a solution to the problem on a national level, that is, putting 300,000 practicing physicians through this kind of training experience is not practical. However, something on this scale early in medical school would go a very long way toward increasing physician effectiveness. In my travels across the country I find an occasional doctor here or there who has "somehow" become effective with chemially dependent patients. The "somehow" invariably relates to a breakthrough in the doctor's personal awareness. The breakthrough was usually caused by the recovery of a chemically dependent relative, friend, or patient, which then spurred the doctor on to gain additional knowledge and experience through his own efforts. It seems that in all of medicine—but particularly in diseases of lifestyle—our patients are our best teachers.

Incidentally, there was an unexpected by-product of the two-week training program. Regardless of the physician trainee's age, sex, specialty or medical school background, 9.2 percent turned themselves in for treatment even though they had come to us for training. As a result of their daily group interaction with patients and their open give-and-take discussions with the staff, these physician-trainees became aware that they, too, were chemically dependent, and that their environment back home—nurses, colleagues, professors, families—had covered up for them, usually for a long time.

The Doctor Doesn't Always Know Best

The judgment of the American people is extraordinarily sound.
The public is almost always ahead of its leaders.

George Gallup

Although Mr. Gallup was referring to the public's political savvy,
two recent polls suggest that when it comes to diagnosing
alcoholism, the public is also ahead of its medical leaders.

One of the polls (Gallup, 1982) shows that 79 percent of the
lay public feel that "alcoholism is a disease and should be treated
as such in a hospital." By contrast, a recent poll of physicians
done by the AMA's Center for Health Policy Research shows that
only 21 percent of the physicians think that "alcoholism is a
disease," and 57 percent see it as a "combination of a disease
and symptomatic of a psychiatric disorder."

These numbers show graphically what happens to alcoholic
people in the clinical world and in the real world. Dealing with an
alcoholic patient puts the average physician in a clinical-ethical
pickle. He feels that this is not a disease and that treatment won't
work, but as a compassionate doctor he feels that he has to do
something for the patient. So he prescribes tranquilizers and
refers the patient for psychotherapy on the chance that the
problem could be symptomatic of a psychiatric disorder.

Unfortunately, even if the alcoholic accepts this advice—he
will probably accept only the pills—his situation will not improve
because the psychotherapist went to the same schools and therefore has the same attitudes as the referring physician, i.e., he is
skeptical about treatment success, but he also feels that he has to
do something for the patient. So he keeps the patient on
tranquilizers and tries to involve him in psychotherapy.

What happens next? Sooner or later the patient slides back
(often literally) into the laps of the lay people (namely his family,
his friends, his lawyer, his clergyman and his employer) who are

already perplexed by his illness and getting tired of covering up his problems. They can see that when the alcoholic isn't drinking, he is no more "psychiatric" than they are. They can also see that he likes being "in therapy" because it gets them off his back, and because he can stay drunk on pills as easily as he can on booze.

As time goes on and the alcoholic gets sicker with further psychosocial, legal and job deterioration, until one of the following happens: (1) he ends up in the morgue; (2) he becomes sick enough to be in a hospital with organ disease; or (3) one of the lay people literally takes charge of the diagnostic process and "refers," i.e., physically takes the patient to an alcohol rehab hospital for treatment.

Fortunately for us all, solution 3 is becoming more and more the usual outcome. Those of us who work in the field can see on a daily basis that less than 10 percent of the patients in alcoholism treatment hospitals are there as a result of physician referrals. This is another way of saying that 9 out of 10 alcoholics who are getting effective treatment (75 percent success rate) were "diagnosed" and "referred" not by health-care professionals but by the judge, the family, the employer, AA members, friends, etc.

In defense of doctors, it should be said that the early symptoms of alcoholism are more obvious to the people who live with the patient than they are to the doctor.

Probably the most important statistic of the physician survey is this: 85 percent of the doctors said that "special training was required to treat alcoholism properly," but they disagreed on when and how such training should be done. Thus, until some realistic changes take place in medical training, help for alcoholics and other addicts will have to come from what Mr. Gallup called the "extraordinarily sound" judgment of the public.

Doctors Need to Intervene Sooner

To call alcoholism a disease is correct, but it is also a mixed blessing. It can be misinterpreted to mean that alcoholism is a disease of the body only. For many people, alcoholism is synonymous with cirrhosis of the liver, i.e., that you have to have cirrhosis of the liver before you are considered an alcoholic.

The facts are that by the time a patient has cirrhosis, his or her alcoholism is terminal. In any case, only 11 percent of all alcoholics ever get cirrhosis; all the others die with beautiful livers.

Early effects of excessive drinking are on the mind, the personality, and the quality of life. Very soon there is damage to the patient's family, his friends, and his job. Heavy drinking does this by affecting the patient's judgment, his behavior, his performance, and his health—in that order. Notice—his health is the last to go.

The early effects on judgment and behavior are manifest when the patient gets drunk more and more often and makes a fool of himself; or when he causes embarrassment, pain, or injury to others. That's when we say, "John was not acting like himself Saturday night."

After about five to fifteen years, the cumulative effects of alcohol on John's personality and mood, together with attendant social and legal problems for his family, friends, and associates, will impair his job performance, although he still passes the company physical.

To view alcoholism as strictly a physical disease encourages John and others around him to dismiss the above consequences of his drinking by saying, "The doctor gave me a clean bill of health," or "I couldn't be an alcoholic—it isn't affecting my health."

Actually, there are clinical indicators other than health problems by which the diagnosis of alcoholism can be established earlier, but doctors have been taught to focus on organ damage.

Thus, it might be better to call alcoholism a psychological disease with terminal physical consequences. In that way we can diagnose alcoholism earlier by getting input from John's family, his friends, and his employer, because they see the eroding effects on his judgment, behavior, and performance. To wait for the doctor to diagnose alcoholism without this kind of input is usually fatal.

Chances are that with his physical health still "pretty fair," John will be forced to resign from the board of directors. And after he dies from a fall down the basement steps, we might hear the following conversation at his funeral:

Out-of-town cousin, puzzled: "How come John died so suddenly?"

Brother-in-law, whispering: "His drinking problem got him, you know."

Out-of-town cousin, still puzzled but now also whispering: "Did he ever try Alcoholics Anonymous?"

Brother-in-law, eyebrows raised but still whispering: "No, according to the doctor he never got that bad!"

Update Your Liver Portfolio

Have you ever wondered just how your drinking affects your liver? Clinical data shows that 15 percent of "normal" drinkers have fatty metamorphosis which is the first stage of alcoholic liver disease that eventually becomes cirrhosis. Thus, if you are a drinker of any kind, it is smart to periodically get a liver function test. (It's a simple blood test and costs less than a case of Scotch.)

Unfortunately, getting an alcohol liver test from your doctor is not as simple as getting a financial report from your broker. My mail is full of complaints about doctors who are vague about such tests when they do routine physicals; and many patients with terminal cirrhosis claim that they had only a mild warning or two from doctors over the years.

Why would a doctor be so reluctant? Well, the doctor may not be interested in alcoholism or know much about it. If your test is mildly abnormal, he may hint "nothing really serious yet—just watch your drinking"; or he might say nothing at all because he fears your anger, and he doesn't want to get a reputation as an alcohol zealot. Worst of all, he may have a booze problem himself.

(In their defense, however, many doctors claim that some patients, when told the truth about the damage alcohol is doing to their livers, just go and find another doctor, probably because they don't want to change their drinking.)

So, if you really want to know the truth, take your liver in your own hands. Ask your doctor to check your liver specifically for damage due to alcohol by doing an SMA-20 and a GGTP. On your return visit ask him to explain each abnormal finding on the computer printout and compare it with previous tests. He'll be pleased that you really want to know.

If he shows reluctance, you must remember that all of us— doctors included—are victims of alcoholism in that we suffer from varying degrees of "dis-ease" and denial when it comes to even talking about it. That's why some doctors need your "permission" or reassurance before they can be on the level about your liver.

You'll also have to stop denying the part that you yourself play when you meekly accept such vague reports as "mild" abnormalities from your doctor. If your broker said, "Well, you're losing a little money here and there, but it's nothing really serious yet. . ." would you heave a sigh of relief and thank him?

The bottom line is this: If you're a drinker, your liver performance should be as important to you as your investment portfolio. If there are early signs that you're buying the wrong kind of stock or drinking too much booze, you'll want to know it so that you can vary your investment pattern or change your drinking habits.

The problem with not knowing your physical condition is that sooner or later you'll be needing a new liver; and when that time comes, your liver broker will tell you that there are none on the market right now, and you'll have only yourself to blame.

Drinks Cause (and Hide) Nerve Damage

If you are a drinker and your feet or hands are growing numb, you may have peripheral neuritis (peripheral neuropathy). It means that you are developing nerve damage in your legs and arms. If the condition remains untreated, it ends with muscle wasting and paralysis.

George, age 52, was a typical case. When his daughter brought him to the hospital, he looked chronically ill with dull, old-looking eyes, and palsied hands struggling with a kleenex. Altogether, he seemed like a very old 52-year-old man.

"Doctor," his daughter said, "we thought it was arthritis and maybe the drinking. I got him to quit drinking last month, but now he is starting to have pain again."

"Tell me about the problem."

"He is not a drunk—just a daily drinker. Lately he has pains in his legs, like burning, or pins and needles, and he stumbles and falls, even without drinking."

I started to examine him. His knee and ankle reflexes were gone. I used a hypodermic needle to test his legs for numbness. He watched the needle break the skin, but he felt no pain below the knees. He watched more intently as I held a vibrating tuning fork to his ankle bone, then to his kneecap. He looked alarmed. "Doctor, how come I feel the buzzing on my knee, but not on my ankle?" I asked him to close his eyes. When I moved his big toe with my fingers, he couldn't tell if the toe was pointing up, down, right or left. And when I squeezed his calf muscle gently, he winced with pain.

"George," I said, "let's see you walk." He gingerly got off the table, planted his feet squarely on the floor and with a broad-

based gait slowly shuffled, one hand patting the wall to help his
balance. He looked pained, as if he were walking on pins and
needles. Watching all this his daughter thought, "Oh, my God,
he's dying from the feet up."

I mentally tallied the positive findings so far: pain, tenderness,
numbness, absent reflexes with impaired vibratory and position
sense, early muscle weakness and atrophy (muscle wasting).
Blood tests and other checks would later confirm the diagnosis of
peripheral neuritis and chronic alcoholism.

His daughter seemed puzzled. "How come he never complained about pain until this week?" she asked.

"Because his daily drinking covered up his symptoms. Alcohol
is a sedative drug, a painkiller, you know. You might say he was
'feeling no pain' until you made him quit drinking. Now he needs
treatment, and you need education."

While he was in the hospital, they both learned about alcoholism, vitamins and nutrition; and while she went to Al-anon, he
got physical therapy. Four weeks later George went home. He felt
better and he looked better, but he still walked close to the wall
for added security. After six months of daily vitamins, after-care
meetings and Alcoholics Anonymous meetings, he looked like a
changed man. He was smiling and walked straight down the
middle of the hallway like any 52-year-old would.

His sense of humor had also come back. "You know, Doc,"
he said with a sly grin, "I now realize that the booze was killing
me. My head no longer knew what my feet were doing. No
wonder I was stumbling and walking into things."

How Do Many Spell Relief? Sedativism

Life, as we find it, is too hard for us; it entails too much pain,
too many disappointments, impossible tasks. We cannot do
without palliative remedies. There are perhaps three of these
means: powerful diversions of interest which lead us to care little

about our miseries; substitutive gratifications that lessen it; and intoxicating substances which make us insensitive to it. Something of this kind is indispensable.

Sigmund Freud

Life was probably no different in the Stone Age or the Renaissance than it is in the Computer Age. Such "diversions" as painting on the cave walls or graffiti on cement walls; or "substitute gratifications" as Christians vs. lions in the Coliseum, or the Raiders vs. the Eagles in the Super Bowl, were and are never the real answer to relief from the stresses of life. The closest thing to a panacea always has been the use of "intoxicating substances."

Alcohol has been around from the beginning, but the ideal remedy (the tranquilizer) was designed to treat the "age of anxiety." And that's how we got sedativism.

What is sedativism? It is a term coined by Dr. Gitlow. It means that a troubled person ("Life, as we find it, is too hard for us") initially gets relief (from "too much pain, too many disappointments, impossible tasks") by taking sedative-hypnotic drugs. But soon, he gets less and less relief and needs more and more of the drug just to feel normal. It may take months or years for him to get there, but when that point is reached, the patient is hooked. He now has sedativism.

Sedative-hypnotic drugs are alcohol, the barbiturates, minor tranquilizers, most pain pills, and sleeping pills. They all work in the same area of the brain. As a matter of fact, the brain can't tell one from the other, which is why doctors can prescribe them interchangeably when they treat patients; and addicts can do the same when they have to. As a former patient of Gitlow's said, "Valium is a dry martini—*very dry*."

Unfortunately, an important feature of these drugs is that they not only sedate—but they also stimulate. The problem is that the sedative action is fairly intense—but short in duration, while the stimulating or agitating effect is less intense but lasts 10 times longer. (That's why the Friday-night heavy drinker wakes early Saturday morning with the "Big Eye," even though he was planning to sleep in.) When a patient begins to take these drugs on a long-term basis, the sedative effect wears off rather quickly. As the agitation accumulates, the patient will notice decreased ambition and attention span, trembling hands, insomnia, poor appetite, and nervousness.

If the patient tries to cut down on his drinking or drug use, the symptoms will get worse. Also, he now seems to need the drug for life's problems in general, even though the anxiety-provoking incident for which he started taking the pills in the first place might be long forgotten. Actually, he now has to continue taking the drug to ward off the symptoms that come from having taken the previous dose.

As a result, there is only one thing to do—take another dose to avoid feeling bad. Life has become a Valium deficiency—the patient has a new disease called sedativism. He can interchange any of the sedative-hypnotic drugs, including alcohol; he can take them singly or in combination, but he can no longer feel normal and not take any of them.

He—or she—now needs to go to an alcohol/drug rehabilitation facility to be detoxified and rehabilitated. It is very dangerous for the patient to stop this medication on his own—"cold turkey"—because the prolonged use of booze or drugs has lowered his seizure threshhold, which means he could have grand mal epileptic convulsions if he stops the medication or the booze. Also, combining sedative-hypnotic drugs with alcohol can easily lead to an accidental overdose or suicide.

Why are these drugs called sedative-hypnotics? *Because if you take one dose—you'll be tranquilized; if you take several—you'll be hypnotized; and if you take a handful—you'll be eulogized.*

A Pill for Every Ill

The desire to take medication is perhaps the greatest feature
that distinguishes man from the animals.

Sir William Osler

Dr. Osler's observation applies equally to Alice in Wonderland,
psychedelic Haight-Ashbury kids, the chronically anxious housewife, and the migraine-ridden Nobel Prize winner.

The notion that there is a pill for every ill and that it's okay to
take non-addictive medications off and on is dangerous. Even the
placebo is not harmless. When a physician prescribes a placebo,
he is, in fact, saying to the patient, "You are inadequate. You
can't handle life without some kind of drug."

I saw a patient named Dick who was on 40 milligrams of
Valium daily because of job-related nervousness. When his
stomach acted up and the X-rays showed no ulcer, he was given
Donnatal extend tabs twice daily. (Dick didn't know that each
tablet contains 50 milligrams of phenobarbital.)

A few weeks later when his headaches came back he got
Fiorinal, one pill four times daily, from another doctor. (He was
unaware that each contains 50 milligrams of barbiturate.) And
when he sprained his ankle at the bowling alley, probably because
he was unsteady from all the pills, the emergency room intern
prescribed Darvon. And since Darvon is also good for arthritis,
Dick began to take it frequently for shoulder pain.

From time to time, because of his smoker's bronchitis, he
would also take Tedral S.A. four times daily, each containing 25
milligrams of phenobarbital.

Because of his fear that there might still be something wrong
with his stomach, he had trouble sleeping, which is how he got on
Seconal—100 milligrams nightly. And when one of those drugs
caused a rash, he started taking an occasional 50-milligram
Benadryl capsule of which his daughter had a good supply

because of her allergy problems.

Many patients like Dick are put on pills by conscientious, busy, naive physicians who don't ask specific questions. Naturally, Dick contributed his share by not candidly voicing his own suspicions that he shouldn't be taking that many pills.

Since all but one of the pills Dick was taking have an addiction potential, he would eventually need medically supervised detoxification in a hospital.

Who is to blame for this state of affairs? The patients or the doctors?

The answer? Yes!

In the final analysis, the best person to reverse this trend is the patient. Since he is hiring the doctor as a health maintenance consultant, he should be honest with the doctor and insist that the doctor be explicit with him. That way, the patient will play a responsible role in maintaining his own health. If, on the other hand, he wants to remain passive and play the game by Dick's rules, he will probably become a chemical gourmet and maybe a sedative addict, or worse.

Dear Doc...

Question: I am angry. During my husband's annual physical examination, I overheard the radiologist tell a technician, "Here is a chest film on a chronic alcoholic," simply because there was a healed rib fracture on my husband's chest X-ray. When I told my daughter about it, she just smiled and said, "Of course Daddy is alcoholic." I think the doctor is a quack, and my daughter is a brat. What's your opinion?

Answer: If the radiologist was discussing your husband's X-ray in the off-hand, cavalier manner which your letter suggests, it definitely sounds as if he has a poor bedside (or darkroom) manner, and you should discuss it with him. As for your husband's health, the more serious problem is this: The most common cause of silent rib fractures in seemingly healthy people is chronic alcohol or drug overuse. Radiologists see them often. It is odd that neither the radiologist nor your family physician mentioned the rib fracture to you or your husband. Could it be that they sense your anger?

Talk to your husband's doctor and to your daughter. The quack and the brat may be on to something.

Q: I have enjoyed drinking heavily for several years. For the past two years, I have had sleeping problems. I wake up at 3 a.m. covered with sweat, and my heart is beating faster than usual. When I stopped drinking for awhile, these problems went away. I have also found if I have a highball or Scotch on the rocks during the night, those troubles go away.

Are these problems related to liver or heart disease? I have had a mild heart attack in the past.

I'm most curious to know what is happening. Also, is it

possible that in time I might again be able to enjoy a pre-dinner Scotch and a post-dinner brandy. I'm 63 years old.

A: You are now addicted to alcohol. Although, as your letter says, you are a decent, self-respecting, middle-class man, you have a disease. Your body cells now process alcohol differently than they used to. The sweating and rapid heartbeat and sleeping problems at 3 a.m. are withdrawal symptoms. They wake you up because your body needs another fix. In the same way that the jumpy, jangling heroin addict feels better when he gets a fix, your body now responds with relief when it gets a fix of alcohol, which is what your "high ball or Scotch on the rocks during the night" is.

As for your hope that someday you'll be able to "enjoy" a pre-dinner Scotch or post-dinner brandy, that's no more likely than it is for a heroin addict to someday "enjoy" or "chip socially" again with occasional heroin.

You need treatment in a hospital. Since you are physically addicted to alcohol, and in view of your past history of a heart problem, it is dangerous for you to try and quit drinking cold turkey on your own. Up to 15 percent of alcoholics die while in alcohol withdrawal, especially if they have a history of heart disease. Your treatment should begin with detoxification and should take place in a medically supervised hospital environment.

Q: What chance is there for my husband, a man in his 60s, who is diagnosed as having advanced alcohol liver disease? On the proper diet, with vitamins and complete abstinence, he has shown marked improvement. General outlook so far is encouraging. Is the condition totally irreversible or is there hope? My hopes are high, but are they false?

A: No, your hopes are not false. When an alcoholic manages to stop drinking completely, there is always some improvement in terms of appearance and functioning, no matter how sick he was when he was still drinking.

Recently, I saw a patient whom I treated two years ago when he was 79. At that time, he had diabetes, heart disease, had suffered his second stroke, had high blood pressure and several minor problems, such as skin disease. Like your husband, with abstinence, diet and vitamins, this man continues to improve.

What he also has is a loving, supporting wife who helps him to get occasional encouragement from other alcoholics and their spouses and good medical support from a physician who understands alcoholism and doesn't prescribe tranquilizers.

Q: My wife doesn't like the taste of whiskey, but she drinks a lot of beer. In recent months she tends to get coughing spells and spits up bright red blood. She also has pain in her chest.

When I took her to the hospital the doctor said there was no blood in her stomach and that the blood was probably coming from her head. The doctor also said that it was not a bleeding ulcer.

I'm worried that my wife may have esophageal varices. What are the symptoms and how do you test it?

A: Your wife probably has blood coming from her lungs in view of the chest pains. It may also be coming from her sinuses. If she had esophageal varices, there would be traces of blood in her stomach and altered blood in her stool. Esophageal varices usually cause no pain. The patient may vomit bright red blood or have black stools from blood that has gone through the digestive tract.

Esophageal varices are dilated, thin-walled, engorged veins, much like hemorrhoids or varicose veins. They result from liver disease which is usually caused by alcoholism. One method of diagnosis is through barium X-ray. Another method is the gastroscope which is a flexible tube which the doctor puts into the stomach through the mouth and esophagus. It enables the gastroenterologist to directly see the lining at the juncture of the esophagus and the stomach where the varices occur.

Q: In a recent column you said medical schools teach mostly about terminal complications of alcoholism, such as cirrhosis. Your column scared me, because I have cirrhosis. Do you mean anyone with cirrhosis of the liver will die from it? Will you please explain?

A: The intent of my column is not to scare but to educate and make it easier for people to accept help and treatment. Liver disease due to alcoholism usually progresses from fatty metamorphosis to alcoholic hepatitis or cirrhosis. This process in many patients takes 15 or more years. Both fatty metamorphosis as well as hepatitis improve when the patient stops drinking even temporarily.

Cirrhosis, on the other hand, is often referred to as a terminal complication because it is generally not reversible to any significant extent. The reason is that more and more liver cells end up as scar tissue, which means more and more of the liver is converted into a non-functioning organ. This creates a number of medical complications that are aggravated by the fact that the patient by then is usually so deeply entrenched in the alcoholic lifestyle that he responds poorly to rehabilitation. As a result, most alcoholics who die because of organ damage die from cirrhosis. Nevertheless, there is always hope for liver function to improve to some extent if you remain abstinent.

Q: I'm not an alcoholic, but I have bleeding veins in my esophagus. My doctor calls them esophageal varices. The last time I was in the hospital, he got mad because I drank again. He said I'd be dead in 12 months. How can that be if I feel good? Was he trying to scare me?

A: You have one of the most serious, terminal complications of alcoholism. I don't think your doctor was trying to scare you. He was probably referring to the fact that 50 percent of the patients with esophageal varices are dead in six months. The reason is that they drink again and bleed to death.

Q: I am probably an alcoholic. I want to stop drinking, but I will not go to a hospital. It takes too long. Besides, I don't want anybody to know about this problem. What withdrawal troubles can I expect, and how long will they last?

A: Withdrawal symptoms depend on the severity of your drinking problem. Within 8 to 12 hours after stopping, there may be nervousness, trembling hands, sweating, fast heart beat, temperature elevation, and thirst. It may stop there, but it may not. Within 24 to 48 hours, you may not be able to sleep. You might feel agitated, pace back and forth, and become suspicious and paranoid; or you may see or hear things that are not really there. You can then make up your mind to go to a hospital because this is too much for you—but by then there isn't much mind left with which to make that kind of decision. You may also get sick enough with mental derangement (delirium), exhaustion, very high temperature and heart blockage and die.

How far along this spectrum of symptoms you will go depends on the severity of your alcohol addiction. If you've been taking other drugs with the booze (tranquilizers, pain pills, etc.), the situation is more dangerous, and the symptoms will last for weeks. Only somebody who is out of his mind will try to do this at home on his own. Maybe that is what is meant by the insanity of the disease of alcoholism.

Q: Is it possible for a person who has suffered pancreatitis ever to drink alcoholic beverages in moderation?

A: In the Western world, almost all cases of pancreatitis are due to the effects of alcohol excess on pancreatic tissue. A very small percentage of patients with pancreatitis have this disease because of primary biliary (bile duct or gall bladder) disease. Patients who have blockage of a common duct tumor or gallstones, for example, may have this problem corrected by surgery, such as a cholecystectomy (excision of the gall bladder). A very careful study of such a case may hold open the possibility of light drinking on occasion.

Internists in general advise against any consumption of alcohol if a patient has had pancreatitis. There are even some patients who have what is called chronic, relapsing attacks of pancreatitis even after years of abstinence.

Q: What is the relationship between heavy drinking and puffy eyes and swelling of the eyelids?

A: Heavy drinking in most people causes fluid retention. It is most prominently seen in the face, especially around the eyelids where the skin is very thin. Many alcoholics, after being dried out for several months, are told by friends that even their facial bones seem to have changed. That's because the non-drinking alcoholic has only a normal amount of fluid in the tissues; he no longer has a water-logged head and finally looks the way he was meant to look.

Q: I am probably a heavy drinker. On my annual physical my blood pressure is always high; but it was lower on a casual reading at a shopping mall mobile unit. Any explanation?

A: Heavy drinkers/alcoholics usually stop or cut down the night before they see their doctor, hoping to hide their drinking problem. However, when the doctor takes the blood pressure the next morning, the pressure is often sky high. Why? Because high blood pressure is one of the symptoms of alcoholic withdrawal, and when you stop drinking, you manifest withdrawal symptoms after eight or more hours of abstinence. My guess would be that your "casual reading" at the mobile unit was done during the daytime when you were drinking as usual. This could mean that you were getting the "medicine" (namely, alcohol) which your body has come to look upon as a necessity. To get a correct answer to your problem, you will have to become honest with your doctor and ask him to help you figure out whether, for you, life has become an alcohol deficiency.

Q: My husband is an everyday drinking alcoholic. We've been married for nine years. I didn't want to accept the fact that he has alcoholism.

He now gets lightheaded, is sick to his stomach in the morning and has chills. Could this be cirrhosis? How can I help him?

A: Yes, this could be cirrhosis, but it is more likely that he's having withdrawal symptoms and that he will soon have to start drinking earlier in the day. In short, he probably has moderately far-advanced alcoholism.

Insist that he go to a doctor. And you go too, so you can provide the history to the doctor because your husband, like all alcoholics, will down-play the actual extent of his drinking. A busy doctor who gets an incomplete history might prescribe Maalox for the stomach, which would mean that your husband would switch from Scotch and soda to Scotch and Maalox.

Q: I am a moderate drinker with "essential hypertension." My doctor suggested I cut down on my drinking to see if we can cut down on my high blood pressure medicine. Is my doctor too tough?

A: No. Your doctor is not tough enough. Drinking is the number one cause of high blood pressure. More than 90 percent of high blood pressure patients don't need medication after they have stopped drinking. "Essential hypertension" means that nobody knows what causes it. Therefore, in most cases it means that it is "essential" for the patient to take high blood pressure medicine so that he can keep on drinking.

If you're unwilling to stop drinking, say for two months, to see the effects on your blood pressure, it means you are willing to have a "sickness" (high blood pressure) and take pills as the price for drinking. If your doctor told you that stopping your intake of broccoli might cure your hypertension, would you insist on being at least a social broccoli eater? Not unless you really are a "broccoliholic."

Q: My doctor told me that I might have gout because my uric acid level is elevated. I didn't tell him that I drink a half a fifth of liquor a day. Could the drinking be causing this problem?

A: Alcohol causes metabolic changes in the liver of some drinkers so that the breakdown of fat and carbohydrate foods leads to high uric acid levels. This happens especially to people who have a family history or predisposition to gout. The danger is that high levels of uric acid may cause gouty arthritis or kidney stones.

Fifteen percent of patients in alcohol treatment programs have elevated uric acid levels. If after one week of no drinking the level goes to normal, it means you have a predisposition to gout, not gout itself. You then have to cut your drinking down low enough to where the uric acid level stays normal. You might feel that drinking at such a reduced rate is a nuisance—and decide to quit drinking altogether.

If your uric acid level stays up even after you quit drinking, you have gout and will need to take a drug like Allopurinal for the rest of your life. In any case, give your doctor the facts. As long as you're secretly playing with half a fifth, your doctor is playing with only half a deck—but you are losing the poker game.

Q: Do pre-dinner drinks really stimulate appetite? If so, do they cause weight gain?

A: Alcohol taken with food, especially starches, will increase the rate of insulin production from the pancreas. This will, in turn, increase your appetite. Since sherry, sweet wines and beer contain starches, you have the ideal combination for increased insulin and appetite. Most mixes also contain small amounts of starches.

That's why you get similar results from drinking mixed drinks before meals.

Q: Sometimes on the last night of a drinking bout I feel fairly good; but the next morning, even after eating a good meal, I feel dizzy, nervous, perhaps even paranoid. I find myself pacing, almost "passing out," yet remaining conscious.

On my last attack I was diagnosed as "imminent D.T.'s." I was paranoid, restless, fearful, and had high blood pressure. I quit drinking for good. Is this life-threatening?

A: It sounds as if you are physically addicted to alcohol because you have withdrawal symptoms. "Imminent D.T.'s" means that the clinician sees early signs that indicate you might be approaching D.T.'s.

Twelve percent to 15 percent of people in D.T.'s die. But even if you avoid full-blown DTs, you could die of some other complication of alcoholism. Get some help now because people who are physically addicted and successfully "quit for good"— without help—are extremely rare.

Q: My husband stopped drinking four years ago because he was retired with a diagnosis of brain atrophy. However, he now drinks near beer. He feels it's safe. I'm worried because it gives him the same symptoms as alcoholic beer: slurred speech, staggering, and bad breath. Is near beer harmful to recovering alcoholics?

A: Brain atrophy (shrinking of the brain) is a serious defect. Your husband should use no mind-altering drugs unless they are life-saving.

Near beer is made by taking regular beer and distilling the alcohol out of it down to .5 percent. If your husband drinks enough of it, he will get enough alcohol to make him drunk because his brain capacity is already limited.

Since alcoholics are clever rascals, it may be that unbeknown to you, he is adding real vodka to his near beer. In any case, with brain atrophy he should not drink even near beer. If he gives you an argument about that, he's probably more than a "near-alcoholic," and you'll have to take your case to his doctor or to a nearby treatment center.

Q: My daughter, age 27, is a heavy drinker. When she stayed with us over the weekend, I heard her fall during the night. I also noticed bruises on her hips, probably from previous falls. When I confronted her about any possible connection between her drink-ing, the falling and the bruises, she listened politely and brushed me aside by saying that she had seen her doctor and nothing was wrong except "a little anemia, probably due to my period." She admitted that she had not told her doctor about her drinking.

A: Alcohol, even in moderate doses, has a direct poisoning effect on bone marrow, where the blood constituents are made. In some studies, as many as 80 percent of chronic alcoholics have decreased numbers of red cells, which means anemia and abnor-mal blood counts. This kind of blood picture leads to prolonged bleeding and clotting time and easy bruising, among other things.

If she can stop drinking, eat a regular diet and take prescribed vitamins, her blood picture will return to normal in about four weeks. She has to be honest with her doctor, however, because there are several other (rare) conditions that also can cause this picture.

Q: In a recent column you said that alcoholics have a shorter life expectancy than other people. My husband calls me a denying alcoholic. He cites your column as evidence that I have probably damaged my health already. I admit that I sometimes drink too much, but his scare technique makes me angry. Tell me how I can dispute him.

A: Actuarial tables from insurance companies show that an alcoholic's life expectancy is shortened by 12 years. This is due to the damaging effects of heavy drinking on the vital organs (liver, pancreas, heart, blood vessels, brain, bone marrow and kidneys) and due to the impairment of the body's ability to fight infections and other diseases.

Here is how you can dispute your husband: (1) Ask any life insurance agent about the statistics. (2) Have your organ functions appraised by a physician at an alcohol treatment center. (This can be done by a physical examination and simple blood tests.) (3) Having gotten the facts, act as the intelligent person you say you are.

Q: My grandfather drinks at least six to eight beers every night. Although he does not have all the symptoms you described (blackouts, violent incidents, etc.) he now vomits almost every morning, although he still manages to eat his meals. Is this a physical problem or is it alcoholism?

A: You sound very concerned for your grandfather, and well you might be. Throwing up every morning soon becomes a physical problem, regardless of what causes it. Gastrointestinal disturbances, including gastritis or upset stomach, are the number one physical manifestation of problem drinkers.

The fact that he drinks up to eight beer a night—even though he knows he is going to vomit in the morning—suggests that your grandfather feels he cannot get along without alcohol. Alcoholics feel that throwing up is the price they pay for drinking.

Get him to see your family doctor immediately to rule out other conditions that could be causing the vomiting. Daily vomiting, especially in older people, quickly leads to life-threatening problems because of failure to absorb nutrients and because of fluid loss that causes dehydration and electrolyte imbalance.

Q: Is foot trouble part of an alcoholic problem? My husband has a 20-year drinking history. About one year ago, his feet began to feel cold, so he started wearing his socks to bed. Over the ensuing months his feet began to tingle, hurt or feel as though there were needles pricking his toes. When his sleep became disturbed, our doctor put him on 1 milligram of Prolixin three times a day and 100 milligrams of Amitriptyline at bedtime. Combined with the alcohol, the medication restored his sleep and the feet seemed to improve. Now that the medication is stopped, the feet are as bad as before.

Are these symptoms associated with alcoholism?

A: The symptoms you describe are classical for peripheral neuropathy, also known as polyneuropathy. It is an inflammation of the nerves. It frequently occurs in middle- or late-stage alcoholics. Prolixin (major tranquilizer) and Amitryptyline (anti-depressant) have no beneficial effect on inflamed nerves.

Tell the doctor about your husband's drinking. I'm sure the doctor will agree that the treatment for polyneuropathy is (1) no more drinking, (2) heavy doses of B vitamins and (3) a normal diet. Incidentally, if the drinking continues, your husband's condition will get worse regardless of any other treatment he might be getting.

Q: I get angry when I read about do-gooders and politicians wanting to get health insurance companies to pay for treating alcoholics because they have a "disease." Alcoholism is a self-inflicted bad habit, and the treatment should not be paid for by the premiums of people like me who can control their own drinking. Also, I don't think alcoholics should be on the public dole or get free treatment in state-supported facilities.

A: If we treat alcoholics for the disease of alcoholism, a high percentage get well and become self-supporting again. Calling alcoholism a self-inflicted bad habit and denying health care coverage for its treatment ends up costing a lot more in the long run. The reason is that alcoholics gradually develop serious physical and mental problems.

If no insurance for "alcoholism" is provided, the treatment becomes very expensive because it is provided in medical, surgical, and mental hospitals under such face-saving diagnoses as ulcers, heart disease, accidents or depression; and people like you are paying for it.

Eventually, when insurance coverage runs out and the alcoholic's relatives' funds run dry, the alcoholic ends up exactly where you don't want him, namely, on the public dole or in a state-supported facility, and people like you will continue to pay for it until he finally ends up in the morgue.

Q: My doctor says I have high tolerance because I can drink a lot of booze and not show it. What puzzles me is this: By Saturday night my blood alcohol must be very high—and yet I feel good; but the next morning I feel terrible (nausea, nervousness, shaking) even though my blood alcohol is probably zero. How can I feel good when I have a high blood-alcohol level, and feel terrible when there is no alcohol in my blood? If alcohol is poison, shouldn't I feel the other way around?

A: You feel better as long as you are drinking and your blood-alcohol level is rising. When it starts to drop, bad feelings (withdrawal symptoms) begin, and six to eight hours later they are undeniable. That's why alcoholics drink again and why "hair of the dog" is so widely known as a remedy.

Alcohol is a poison. The destructive effect on liver cells, brain cells, etc., is highest when the blood alcohol is high. Thus, when you're feeling the best, your body organs are suffering the worst.

Q: I quit drinking three weeks ago for good. Now, instead of drinking 12 beers a day, I have that many colas. It upsets my stomach. Could this much soda be harmful?

A: Abstinent drinkers often switch to excessive coffee or cola drinking early in their recovery. The danger is due to the caffeine contained in those drinks: A cup of coffee contains 125 milligrams and a 12-ounce cola about 50. It's a stimulant that can cause a number of symptoms including increased gastric acidity.

Taper off over a three-week period to avoid sudden withdrawal symptoms. The best solution is to switch to decaffeinated coffee. It contains only five milligrams per cup.

Q: Can drinking cause heart attacks? My father, 56, drinks daily and very heavily on weekends. Two years ago he had a heart attack, but he said it was more of an irregular heartbeat problem. He won't tell the family exactly what the doctors said about this.

Now and again, he complains and clutches his chest. When he lies down and rests for a while, he feels better. Is this just an effect of heavy drinking?

A: Alcohol in heavy doses is a poison to cells in the heart muscle as well as the nerve centers that regulate heartbeat. Some drinkers develop irregular heart rhythms while others experience destruction of the heart muscle. In either case, the heart becomes less efficient and eventually that leads to failure.

Your father may have a combination of these. He may also have angina pectoris. All of these conditions are made much worse by heavy drinking and will shorten his life expectancy.

Q: In a recent statement you were quoted as saying that a high percentage of patients with high blood pressure end up with normal blood pressure if they quit drinking. Can you elaborate on that?

A: When patients with high blood pressure come into alcoholism treatment, we take many of them off all high blood pressure medication. By the time they leave the hospital four weeks later, up to 90 percent have normal blood pressure even though they are no longer taking medication of any kind. All of them had a diagnosis of "essential hypertension" or functional high blood pressure for several years before they came into our hospital. All of them were drinking because (1) they were not told anything about their drinking, (2) they were admonished to "cut down" on their drinking, or (3) they flagrantly disregarded their doctors' advice to stop drinking.

It leads me to the conclusion that if all patient with high blood pressure were asked to stop drinking, we would find a high number of "dramatic" cures.

Q: I am a recovering alcoholic with a lot of liver damage. I had a choice of either quitting drinking or letting liver failure do it for me (by killing me). I decided to quit. My doctor said, "You are one of those unlucky drinkers whose liver just can't handle alcohol. You have destroyed your liver in 13 years of heavy drinking."

One thing you might tell your readers is that age has nothing to do with it. I'm 27 years old.

A: You have a wise doctor. Age, indeed, has nothing to do with it, and nobody knows why. The good news is that if you never drink again, your liver will recover substantially.

Q: On a recent hunting trip our guide told us that the best way to ward off getting cold or frostbitten is to drink at least one or two stiff drinks every hour because "Alcohol keeps you warm by dilating the blood vessels."

I'd heard that theory before. I couldn't help but notice, however, that our tour guide stuck to the same theory even when all of us had been indoors for quite a while. I'm now suspicious. Does drinking really help preserve body heat?

A: Alcohol produces the sensation of body warmth because it dilates the blood vessels of the skin. Unfortunately, that causes a loss of body heat. Incidentally, drinking on hunting trips or when handling guns in any setting is not a good idea because drinking, especially drinking excessively, causes euphoria, carelessness, and may bring out aggressive feelings which often lead to accidental shooting of other hunters or to other kinds of violence.

Q: I can't sleep without taking a pill. But I'm afraid to get addicted, so then I try alcohol, which sometimes puts me to sleep, but at other times leaves me wide-eyed. I am 50. I work at a stress job. Sometimes I come to work with only two or three hours of sleep and a hangover. I have thought about going to AA, but then I wonder if I don't have to get rid of my pill habit first.

A: You have "sedativism," which means that you need alcohol or other sedative-hypnotic medications to help you make it through the night. About 60 percent of the patients in alcohol treatment units have the same problem as you do. Check in to such a facility to get off both pills and alcohol under medical supervision. The counselors will help you find AA groups that will accept you with open arms.

Q: I am a 58-year-old social drinker. I also have taken Deprol every day since 1955. Is this harmful?

A: Each Deprol pill contains 400 milligrams of meprobamate (also known as Miltown or Equanil). It is a tranquilizer with abuse and addiction potential. Alcohol is also a drug with abuse and addiction potential. Keep your physician apprised of any change in the amount or frequency of drinking or pill use. An increase would mean abuse or dependence.

Don't stop this drug suddenly on your own even though you've been taking it in a low dose. You can have serious physical withdrawal symptoms even from low doses of tranquilizers, especially if you've taken them for a long time.

Ask your doctor why you've been taking this drug for almost 30 years. Chances are the reason for starting it is no longer a "crisis" and you should consider discontinuing its use.

Q: My husband has been a heavy drinker for 35 years. Three months ago when I started going to Al-anon, he decided to quit drinking on his own. He was also taking some tranquilizers which he quit taking sometime later. His only problem now is that he sleeps poorly. Is this a part of his withdrawal and is it dangerous?

A: Heavy drinking ordinarily initiates sleep by knocking you out, but it disturbs the quality of sleep by causing disruptive brain-wave activity. Some alcoholics do not regain normal sleeping patterns for as long as six months after they have completely detoxified. In the case of alcoholics who also took tranquilizers or sleeping pills, the disruptive sleep pattern is more accentuated and may last for as long as nine months.

Tell your husband he was fortunate that he was able to quit drinking without having any more serious withdrawal symptoms, such as seizures or convulsions. The real danger now is that his disturbed sleep pattern may drive him back to drinking on the rationalization that "if I'm this miserable without drinking I might as well drink." Obviously, he is well on his way to winning the battle, at least in the daytime. Going back to drinking or taking pills would only get him back to ground zero.

Q: I've been taking 30 milligrams of Valium a day. The prescription is automatically renewed each month by our doctor. He says I need it because of chronic anxiety. I started on the Valium two years ago because I was nervous when I smashed up my husband's car.

Lately I've been hearing about Valium addiction. When I stop taking the Valium for a couple of days, I get nervous, my stomach cramps and I get headaches. When I go back to the Valium, I feel okay again. Does this mean I'm becoming addicted? My doctor says not to worry; the dose I'm taking is normal, and the only people who become addicted are people who overdo it. Somehow, I still feel I should get off the drug.

A: In light of present-day knowledge of Valium addiction, you already are addicted because when you stop the drug you get withdrawal symptoms (nervous, stomach cramps, headaches) that are relieved when you go back on the drug.

We used to think that only abnormally high doses caused addiction, but that is no longer so. According to a study by Dr. Carl Rickels from the University of Pennsylvania, 43 percent of patients who were taking up to 40 milligrams of Valium a day showed withdrawal symptoms. Ask your doctor to reduce the Valium gradually. For patients on your dose, this can be done safely over a four- to six-week period.

Q: Why do I continue to read statements made by medical authorities that "Valium is one of the safest drugs on the market today"? How can it be safe when you also read a lot about Valium addiction and abuse? Is it not true that Valium is also involved in a lot of emergency room visits by people who take it inappropriately?

A: The statement that Valium is "one of the safest drugs on the market today" refers to the fact that the lethal dose of Valium is so high that it is practically impossible for anyone to commit suicide by taking Valium alone. Thus, in comparison to many other drugs with which people commit suicide by overdoses, Valium is safe.

Your reference to Valium being a frequent drug involved in emergency room visits for the past several years is correct. Such visits are usually made by people who mix Valium with alcohol or with other drugs.

Q: About three years ago, I underwent drying out and alcoholic rehabilitation. Because I had high blood pressure when I started treatment, I was placed on a medication called Salutensin.

After discharge from the hospital, I continued to have the same reactions and behavior problems that I had when I was drinking. About two years later, I went to a physician specializing in alcoholism. He took me off the high blood pressure medication because it contained Reserpine.

A short time later I was beginning to feel like a changed person, and I have enjoyed happy sobriety since. Was the second doctor correct, or did I get better because I am imagining things?

A: The medication you were taking does contain Reserpine, which is not only an anti-hypertensive medication, but also a sedative that has been known to cause depressive symptoms. Alcoholics should not be placed on any sedative medication because alcohol is just another sedative.

In terms of hypertensive patients in general, it is best to take all alcoholics who enter rehabilitation off their anti-hypertensive medication. Up to 90 percent of such patients are able to maintain normal blood pressure subsequent to their rehabilitation, even when they no longer take any kind of anti-hypertensive medication.

Patients must be sure, however, not to do this on their own but only under medical supervision.

Q: What is the half-life of a drug?

A: The half-life of a drug is the amount of time that is required for the human body to detoxify (get rid of, or neutralize) one-half of the dose that was taken. This is important in understanding the action of drugs. For example, if a drug has a half-life of 24 hours, and you start taking 50 milligrams daily, it means that on the second day, even though you took only 50 milligrams (the prescribed dose), you actually have 75 milligrams in your body because your body got rid of only one-half of yesterday's dose (25 milligrams). On the third day, the working dose in your body is higher still, and so on.

Some commonly taken drugs such as Valium and Librium have a half-life of about 100 hours. This is part of the reason that detoxification and rehabilitation of patients dependent on such drugs are usually longer and more complicated than for "pure alcoholics," who are dependent on beverage alcohol only.

Q: I am a recovering alcoholic. Recently I was told that some cough syrups contain alcohol. Is that true?

A: Most cough syrups and many other medications in liquid form are dispensed in a solution which contains alcohol. For example, Donnatal elixir, a commonly prescribed stomach sedative, contains 23 percent alcohol. ("Proof" of any beverage is double the percentage of alcohol it contains, which means that Donnatal elixir is really 46 proof.) Phenobarbital elixir, a common way of prescribing a barbiturate, is 14 percent alcohol, or 28 proof. Nyquil cough syrup is 25 percent alcohol (50 proof), and Terpin Hydrate elixir is 42 percent alcohol, or 84 proof. Most popular mouthwashes are 25 percent alcohol, or 50 proof.

Recovering alcoholics can easily become dependent on high alcohol-content medicines and go back to uncontrolled drinking. If they are taking Antabuse and use any of these preparations, they will become sick with the Antabuse-alcohol reaction. Ask your physician or pharmacist for a list of non-alcoholic cough syrups.

Q: Is it true that alcoholics should not take aspirin?

A: Aspirin, even when used alone, will cause some irritation and bleeding from the lining of the stomach and duodenum. Alcohol alone has the same effect, and when alcohol and aspirin are used together, the effects are exaggerated. Taking three or four aspirins before going to sleep after a heavy drinking bout is not a good way to avoid or to minimize the next morning's hangover. This is a particularly dangerous practice which can lead to fatal gastrointestinal hemorrhage.

Q: My husband is an alcoholic who keeps going on benders, and he tends to become weak and dizzy. He is also taking high blood pressure medicine, but he keeps his drinking a secret from the doctor. Is it dangerous for him to take these pills?

A: Certain high blood pressure medications, including Reserpine, Aldomet, and Apresoline, will have an exaggerated effect if the patient is also drinking alcohol. It means that if the patient stands up, he can momentarily feel lightheaded or lose consciousness. You or your husband should tell his doctor about the drinking. It is highly likely that your husband's high blood pressure would be normal if he stopped drinking.

Q: My husband is a chronic, but moderate to heavy drinker. I have never accused him of being an alcoholic, but on one or two occasions when I implied it, he didn't argue the point.

The problem I'm facing now is this: Even though my husband has been put on antibiotics for an infection, he merrily goes on drinking. When I suggested that he should stop drinking, or at least cut down until he is finished with the antibiotics, he dismissed my suggestion as not scientific. When I called our doctor about it, the doctor was too busy to talk to me, and the pharmacist refused to get involved, saying that it is not his province to comment on the subject.

A: Your question raises a very important point. It is clear that most antibiotics are less effective when the patient is a chronic drinker. This is due to the fact that the enzymes in the liver which normally break down antibiotics work more effectively in the presence of alcohol. As a result, the antibiotic is eliminated from the body in a shorter time, which means that the infecting microorganisms are in contact with the antibiotic for a shorter time.

If your husband is not honest with his doctor about the heavy drinking (or if his doctor is unaware of the things I have just described), the doctor will mistakenly conclude that the antibiotic is ineffective against the particular type or organism which is causing your husband's infection. His doctor will probably react to this by switching your husband to another antibiotic. Naturally, valuable time is lost. Furthermore, the next antibiotic he puts him on will also be less effective than it would be under ideal circumstances, the ideal circumstances being abstinence.

An added problem is that a number of antibiotics react with alcohol like Antabuse does, causing nausea, vomiting, headaches and other symptoms. The physician who assumes that the patient is abstinent (when in fact he is drinking) will mistakenly conclude that the symptoms are side-effects of the antibiotic. Again, the doctor's reaction to this problem is to switch the patient to another antibiotic in order to avoid the side-effects. But the next antibiotic will usually have similar side-effects because the alcohol is the real culprit.

A third complication is that if there are significant amounts of alcohol in the stomach or intestines, there will be a marked decrease in the rate of absorption of antibiotics from the bowel into the body. As a result, the patient ends up with a lower concentration of antibiotics in his system because most of the medication is being lost from the body through feces.

Clinically speaking, the drinker who is on antibiotics is not getting his money's worth because he is absorbing less of the antibiotic than he should; and whatever he does absorb is destroyed before it can work. Most important of all, the consequences of the patient's drinking are giving the doctor a confusing clinical picture. If it's true that the patient who treats himself has a fool for a doctor, then the patient who drinks while on antibiotics most certainly has a fool for a doctor.

Q: My husband is an alcoholic who recently went through rehabilitation. He has also been an epileptic for a number of years and has taken Dilantin without ever giving it any thought. However, since he's out of the hospital, the doctors keep checking his blood to see how much Dilantin he is carrying. They have never done that before, and I am puzzled. He is doing well, is going to AA and is taking Antabuse.

A: The probable reason for periodically checking your husband's Dilantin blood levels is that he is now taking Antabuse. Antabuse tends to decrease the rate at which the human body normally breaks down the drug Dilantin. In other words, Dilantin stays active in the body longer because of the actions of Antabuse. As a result of this, Dilantin levels may increase and lead to Dilantin toxicity (overdose effects) even though your husband is still taking the dose he used to take before he was on Antabuse. This kind of reaction can be managed by decreasing the Antabuse dosage, the Dilantin dosage, or both. But in order to be able to do the right thing, the doctors have to know what's going on, and that's why they are now checking the Dilantin level.

All in all, it sounds like your husband is on the right track with his recovery. It also sounds like he has good doctors managing his case.

Q: My sister-in-law is a professional person. Although an alcoholic, she consistently refuses treatment. In a very condescending way, she recently told me that a scientific breakthrough is imminent. It involves a chemical called TIQ. She says it will show that alcoholism is due to neurochemical and biological causes.

What is TIQ? Is there anything to her statements, or is this just another one of her delaying tactics?

A: TIQ stands for tetrahydroisoquinolines. TIQs are substances formed in the human body as a result of chemical reactions between aldehydes and neurotransmitters.

When TIQs are injected directly into the brains of rats or monkeys (animals who previously chose not to drink alcohol when given a choice of water or alcohol), these animals then showed a preference for alcohol. TIQs also are found in higher concentrations in the cerebrospinal fluids of people who are drunk. Also, in toxic people TIQs remain at a high concentration for about a week, even after detoxification.

All this is very fascinating research, but much of it is unconfirmed and fraught with contradiction. Experts in the field agree that no breakthrough is imminent. For the foreseeable future (years), the treatment of alcoholism and drug addiction will begin with total abstinence for the patient and will require a change in lifestyle for the patient as well as his family and friends.

Effective treatment for alcoholism is available now. For your sister-in-law to keep on drinking while she is waiting for a "breakthrough" makes about as much sense as for a person with lung cancer to keep on smoking while refusing surgery because a "breakthrough" in cancer research might be imminent.

Q: I read somewhere that the brain can produce its own morphine. Is there any connection between alcohol and morphine effects in the brain?

A: Possibly. Alcohol, much like morphine, can produce euphoria (feeling good) and analgesia (killing pain), depending on the dose. Brain research shows that in response to exercise, stress or pain, the brain normally produces its own endorphins (morphine-like substances). Animal studies show that endorphins can also be produced when alcohol interacts with normally occurring brain chemicals. Thus, there may be a connection.

Q: My husband is a heavy drinker with high blood pressure. His doctor prescribed Apresazide, Ativan and a two-mile walk daily. He drinks three doubles as a nightcap, then wakes up at 2 a.m. and takes his Ativan. While on vacation, he drank more and walked less—so his doctor said the blood pressure was up because he skipped the walk.

I have two problems—my husband's drinking and his doctor's ignorance. I have written the doctor a personal letter. No response. I believe the doctor has the same problem as my husband. Is there anything else I can do?

A: Apresazide is a powerful combination of an anti-hypertensive drug and a diuretic. Ativan is a Valium-like tranquilizer. With these drugs, there should be no drinking at all, let alone heavy drinking.

As I see it, there are three possibilities: (1) the doctor never got your letter; (2) the doctor warned your husband about this, which means your husband is an alcoholic because he drinks in spite of medical warnings; and (3) the doctor got your letter but didn't warn your husband, which probably means that the doctor is not up to date on modern treatment or—as you suspect—has a chemical problem himself.

Make an appointment to see the doctor about your own problem, which is living with a heavy drinker on medication. If the doctor never got your letter, he will appreciate your information and will change his approach and treatment. Very likely, your husband has been less than candid with the doctor.

In any case, the present course of action is dangerous. Prescribing a two-mile walk for a patient with high blood pressure so he can keep drinking is like prescribing milk for a patient with ulcers so he can keep eating hot peppers. The first thing to do is stop the drinking and the peppers. If your husband's doctor can't understand that, or if he refuses to see you, you need another doctor for your own problem.

Q: Sometimes your column sounds critical of doctors. In my case the doctor did everything just right, and I want your readers to know about it. I tried to stop drinking for years on my own and through the church, but I never made it for longer than a month or two. About a year ago when I had minor surgery, my doctor discovered my alcoholism because my blood test showed bone marrow poisoning due to alcohol. He confronted me, prescribed Antabuse, and sent me to an alcohol rehab unit.

I accepted his advice because I had faith in him, but deep inside I was angry for what he did to me. Now I realize that he actually did a wonderful thing for me. I still see him for my other medical needs. He is a fine surgeon, but he referred me to the alcohol ward because he did not feel competent to treat my alcoholism. I think he did everything just right.

A: You are fortunate to have such a fine doctor. The aim of medical education as regards alcoholism today is to teach physicians to do exactly what your doctor did. Even the best doctor doesn't have the expertise or time to give definite treatment for tumors, diabetes, depression, etc., but every doctor does know how to correctly diagnose and properly refer patients with these conditions to appropriate treatment resources.

I heartily agree that your doctor did everything just right; and so did you—by telling our readers about it.

The ravages of alcohol were beginning to make themselves felt. I heard him (W. C. Fields) ask Eddie Sutherland if Eddie got pleasure from drinking. Eddie answered in the affirmative, and said, "Don't you, Bill?"

"No," he (W. C. Fields) returned sadly. "It's medicine for me now."

W. C. Fields and Me
Carlotta Monti

5

Nobody Ever Wants
to Get Hooked

In my view, chemical dependency is a community illness. Since the patient's early symptoms are played out in the family, the community, and the work place, the disease is usually detectable long before it is diagnosable. Regardless of whether the patient is an early alcoholic, a periodic drug abuser, a closet (secret) alcoholic, or an obvious (skid row) addict, *somebody knows about it*. Thus the crucial diagnostic question seems to be: When does an alcoholic or drug addict need help with his problem? The answer is very simple: When his use of drinks or drugs is causing harm to himself or others, yet he is unable to stop or cut down with any degree of consistency.

What complicates matters is that by the time the patient reaches that point, you yourself (spouse, friend, colleague, boss) have already become part of his illness. Therefore, the real question becomes "How much are *you* willing to tolerate before you decide that help is needed?" The answer to the question "How much is too much?" will therefore depend on how healthy or how sick, that is, how tolerant the community is of the chemically dependent patient's behavior and malfunction.

Most usually the community reaction is to look the other way and hope that "somebody else" will get the patient to stop drinking and using. Unfortunately, that usually doesn't work: the wife wonders why the lawyer keeps getting him off; the lawyer

wonders how long the wife will tolerate the abuse; the boss waits
for the doctor to diagnose him; and the doctor waits for the boss
to fire him. Needless to say, the patient almost never diagnoses
himself.

So what's to be done? An impulsive confrontation by somebody who "can't stand this anymore" is not the solution. Such
"Dutch uncle" talk may work wonders for a "reasonable"
person (i.e., somebody who is not chemically dependent) because
such a person can and usually will respond positively when faced
with the facts. A chemically dependent person, on the other
hand, will respond to such a confrontation by taking his habit
underground long enough for the confronters to get off his back,
but soon after that, he or she will be off and running again.

Instead of further covering up or impulsive confrontations,
what the patient needs is an *intervention*. An intervention is most
likely to be successful if the patient's family, friends, doctor, and
boss can all agree that there is a problem, and if he or she is
healthy enough to cooperate with the intervention counselor.

When is the intervention a success? When the patient agrees to
accept help. Months or years later when he is recovered, the
patient (your friend) will have regained what Norman Cousins
described as "a feeling of genuine pride in belonging to the
human species," and he will always remember that you were the
person who got him headed in the right direction.

What Causes Addiction?

There is no known single cause for alcoholism except excessive
drinking. Nevertheless, I see patients every day who are positive
about what they think caused their alcoholism.

One such favorite cause is pain. However, in the course of
rehabilitation it becomes clear that the drinker was using alcohol
or pills as a self-prescribed remedy, not for the apparent cause

(the pain of an ulcer, a fracture, etc.); rather he was treating the pain behind the pain, that is, the fears and feelings caused by an injury or chronic illness.

Here is a clinical example. Sue Jones, a 37-year-old, unmarried woman, was an excellent bookkeeper but also a very private person. She was told by her doctor that she had a duodenal ulcer. Shortly after that, her drinking increased markedly. Two years later, I saw her in consultation. The ulcer was not healing and she was about to be fired from her job because she had become addicted to alcohol. (By now her drinking was a major reason for the ulcer not healing.)

In our sessions we uncovered the "reason" for her drinking. Sue had a secret fear that she really had cancer, not just a peptic ulcer. But her fear prevented her from talking to the doctor about her symptoms in more detail so that when her doctor casually assured her that "all you have is an ulcer," Sue eagerly accepted this reassurance, but continued to worry that she might have cancer. To hold herself together, she began drinking more and more and kept clinging to her "pain" by drowning it.

We further learned that Sue's father had died of alcoholism and that Sue's brother had recovered from alcoholism 4 years ago. Also, over the years, Sue had been engaged three times, but each of her fiances had broken off their engagement because of her drinking.

Thus, Sue had been a chronic alcoholic for a number of years, and her current drinking was only a way of dealing with her emotional pain (fear of cancer), just as her previous drinking episodes had helped her deal with the pain and strain of engagements, work problems, etc. The only difference was that now she had finally become physiologically addicted to alcohol.

A similar case was Ray, a 29-year-old mechanic who, after having a few drinks, drove his car into a tree. In the accident he killed his wife and her six-month-old infant. (The infant had been fathered by his wife's former boyfriend.) Ray initially remained in the hospital where he was being treated for two broken ribs and cuts and scrapes. About six weeks later as an outpatient, he continued to demand more and more pain pills, until his doctor became alarmed and referred him to me for psychiatric evaluation. Meanwhile, unbeknownst to the referring doctor, Ray had increased his drinking markedly because he felt depressed and needed alcohol (on top of the pills) to get to sleep.

When I saw Ray in the initial session his ribs were well healed. I also learned that while he was in the Army, Ray had been drinking up to a fifth a day and quit for a three-year period because, while drunk, he'd almost beaten a friend to death.

As a result of the psychiatric consultation he entered an alcohol rehabilitation facility where he finally dealt with his emotional pain: his love for his wife; his anger surrounding the imaginary rivalry with her previous lover (whom he had never met); and his irrational belief that in the auto accident he had killed her infant on purpose. Previously, he couldn't even think about these feelings and events consciously—let alone talk about them out loud—because in his own mind it made him appear like a jealous coward and a murderer. The booze and pills helped him keep the lid on these emotions: but the drinking and pill-taking made him look, feel and act like a zombie and function like an alcoholic.

In rehabilitation patients like Sue and Ray learn to deal with the facts and feelings surrounding their pain, illness or injury, and they learn to understand their alcoholism as a way of drowning fears and feelings. They also learn to live the life of the recovering alcoholic; and after sobriety is established, they can get whatever additional psychotherapy they need.

When an alcohol abuser happens to get drunk and injured, he may be "feeling no pain" simply because of the sedative-hypnotic effect of alcohol. *But when an alcoholic is drinking or using pills on a chronic basis he is "feeling no feelings."* That's why alcohol, pain pills, or tranquilizers don't solve the alcoholic's (or the neurotic's) problems. Rehabilitation is needed to learn how to deal with feelings and how to accept reality without the use of mood-altering drugs and alcohol.

A Blood Test for Drinking Problems

Some drinkers actually want to know if they have a drinking problem, although rationalizations—some positive and some negative—abound. Here is what they say:

Family man: "My mother died of it. It runs in families. I owe it to my children to get a test on myself."

Businessman: "I want to know—but I don't want the company to know."

Practical man: "I want a scientific test, not a psychiatric analysis."

Middlescent type: "I'm approaching middle age. Let's see if it's time to cut down."

Physical fitness buff: "My body is the temple of my soul, and I want to keep it fit."

Harassed husband: "I'm sick and tired of being nagged about my drinking. I wish there were a simple blood test so I could prove to her—once and for all—that I don't have a problem."

Well, there is such a blood test. For about thirty-five dollars your doctor can do a GGTP (gamma-glutamyl-transpeptidase) test of your liver. Normal is up to 40 international units per liter. In 90 percent of heavy drinkers, it is elevated because alcohol destroys liver cells. (It is also positive in non-drinkers who have liver cancer or viral infection of the liver; and in people who take prescription drugs such as tranquilizers, Dilantin, and certain antibiotics.)

An elevated GGTP means that some two dozen vital functions which your liver normally performs are being performed at a substandard level because your liver cells are dying.

Since your bone marrow is also sensitive to alcohol, have your doctor do a complete blood count (CBC). If it shows a low red cell, white cell or platelet count and an increase of the mean corpuscular value of your red cells, it means you are drinking enough booze to poison your bone marrow. That's why your blood cells are poor in quality and quantity.

In practical terms, your heart and lungs have to work harder just to keep you alive. Needless to say, your ability to play tennis, to jog and perform other strenuous activities slowly goes by the wayside because you are in effect living with "poor blood" or "tired blood" (blood is what carries the oxygen to all the muscles with which you exercise).

The low white blood cell count makes you more susceptible to infections of all kinds; and the low number of platelets impairs your blood-clotting ability, regardless of whether you nicked yourself shaving or whether you're bleeding to death from internal injuries while trapped inside a wrecked auto, or lying alone on the floor of your hotel room after a fall caused by excessive drinking.

In short, your drinking is damaging your health. If you stop drinking, these values will return to normal in about six weeks. You then have to make a decision. You can stay stopped for good or you can resume drinking and slowly increase the amount to whatever degree of damage you want to live with.

Actually, not all drinkers really want to know. They naively feel that "what you don't know, won't hurt you." That may be true in affairs of the heart. But when it comes to your health, what you don't know—does, in fact, hurt you, if what you're doing is harmful. Of course, if you don't know it, you won't have to do anything about it.

I recently saw a patient who was less than enthusiastic about his laboratory results. Here's how the conversation went.

Doctor: "Well, Charlie, now you know what the damage is.

The good news is that if you stop drinking, your alcoholic
hepatitis and anemia will clear up."

Patient: "You mean it's all gonna be normal?"

Doctor: "Yes."

Patient: "Well, on second thought, what's a little hepatitis,
anyway? You know, Doc, that could be from the shellfish I ate in
Malta." (Actually, Charlie was in Malta as a corporal with the
Army in 1944.) "As for the anemia, I'm not planning to go into
combat, or climb the Himalayas, or run a marathon, anyway. So,
I'll just cut down on my drinking for awhile."

Charlie seemed in a hurry to leave. "Anyhow, Doc, I'm sure
glad I don't have a real serious drinking problem."

"Listen, Charlie, you may not have a drinking problem, but
your liver does."

"To be honest with you, Doc, I don't want to stop drinking
completely just yet."

"Charlie, you may not want to stop drinking, but medically it
is important that your liver stop drinking. So, just check your
liver into the hospital here, and come and see us in about four
weeks, and we'll tell you how your liver is doing."

"All right, Doc, I get the point. No drinking for four weeks,
then we'll repeat the tests."

Actually, if you're like Charlie, you probably didn't read this
column anyway. But—have no fear. Your wife, or somebody else
who really loves you, did read it. That's how this book ended up
on your desk. And that's why you're reading it now.

Also, now you know why your friendly bartender always says,
"Name your poison, Charlie."

Detectable Before Diagnosable

Once the alcoholic is in treatment, I hear angry complaints from
him and his family because his doctor didn't make the diagnosis.
The anger, only partly justified, is usually not the whole story.

The reasons why the doctor failed to make a diagnosis are many. A malpractice-conscious doctor fears a libel suit. The "society doctor" doesn't want to become known as an alcoholism zealot because some of his elite patients are high-class drunks. The specialist depends on referrals from other doctors; he doesn't want to lose their good will. The family doctor could lose the patient—and the whole family—to another doctor. The doctor who is a "meticulous scientist" has to disprove all other possible diagnoses before considering alcoholism. And the doctor who is alcoholic himself is reluctant to have the pot call the kettle drunk.

Any of the above may be true, but judging from my daily practice, the main reasons for avoiding the diagnosis are (1) all of us (doctors included) still see alcoholism as something to be ashamed of or as a weakness rather than a disease, and (2) we're afraid to face the alcoholic's anger.

Early treatment of any disease improves the prognosis. To get the alcoholic into treatment sooner, we have to accept two facts:

1. Early signs and symptoms are evident to a number of people besides the doctor, i.e., the disease is *detectable* (by many people) long before it is *diagnosable* (by the doctor).

2. Somebody other than the alcoholic will have to make the first move to get the diagnostic process rolling. *To wait until the alcoholic asks for help is to help him die.*

The most helpful thing I tell audiences is that if you think there is a problem, then there is one. And invariably it has been a problem for some time. When two concerned people sit down to helpfully discuss an "early" sign of a drinking problem which they've seen in a friend or in somebody they care about, it only takes a few minutes before they both realize that their friend's problem is more serious than they thought. Each had only one or two pieces of the puzzle because the alcoholic, in order to hid the problem, has kept them in the dark.

A recent case is Joe. When his drinking increased, his wife Mary got worried, but said nothing. When he developed blackouts—in the morning he couldn't remember what he had said the night before—she hinted that he might have a problem. He denied it angrily, defending his right to drink. This marked a personality change.

She tried to forget it. She agonized for weeks. Finally she asked herself: If Joe had some other disease, would I stand by idly? Surely, I would be able to talk about it with my sister. Still uneasy, she dropped a telephone hint to her sister who lives in another city. To her surprise her sister expressed relief and was eager to talk.

Both her sister and her husband had been worried about Joe. On a recent business trip, Joe was their house guest. They noticed his heavy drinking, personality change and memory blanks. When they tried to talk to him about it, Joe made an ugly scene. "Don't stick your nose in other people's business!" he yelled and moved to a hotel. After he left they both talked about it some more but decided to drop it because it might hurt his job. A week later they discovered that he had a drunk-driving charge in a rental car that same night that he'd moved to the hotel.

Now Mary was really worried. She asked Joe to see the company doctor, but he threw another fit and refused to go. Puzzled and frightened, she casually told the family doctor that Joe might have a problem. The doctor glanced up alarmed but quickly regrouped himself. "Mary," he said reassuringly, "sometimes work pressures cause a person to drink a little more."

Sensing that there was more to it, Mary became insistent. The doctor then gladly agreed to arrange a joint visit. With both Joe and Mary present, he explained some abnormalities on Joe's last physical exam: high blood pressure, a slight heartbeat irregularity, and early signs of liver damage. "This kind of damage," the doctor said, "usually goes away if you deal with your drinking."

At this point Mary began to wonder if maybe she was overreacting; maybe Joe wasn't really that bad yet. But with the information she had provided, the doctor was able to diagnose an early or moderate-stage problem and point to the good prognosis which goes with early treatment. Through outpatient counseling for Joe, his wife and their teen-age daughter, the case was successfully resolved.

Each of the actors in this drama had seen a number of easily detectable, early signs of a problem, but nobody wanted to talk because of stigma and fear of Joe's anger. (Incidentally, Joe's boss had seen him come to work late at times, obviously hung over and offending customers at lunch. The boss had wondered if "somebody shouldn't say something to Joe.")

Fears of witch-hunting are not justified. If anything, I see daily evidence of our tendency to go overboard to protect a man's right to drink even when he is dying of alcoholism. Mistakes in making the diagnosis are not likely because you can't make a social drinker into a nasty alcoholic, any more than you can make a silk purse into a sow's ear.

The other stumbling block, namely Joe's anger, should not frighten us. When we face his problem squarely, it turns out that most of Joe's anger is really his anger at himself. Deep down, he knows that he's losing control; he would never drink like this if he could help it. But he doesn't know what else to do.

Incidentally, what kind of a guy was Joe? He was a promising junior executive, a devoted family man, a Little League coach and a Sunday school teacher. Clearly, he was a man who doesn't lie, cheat or get drunk just for the hell of it. He had a disease called alcoholism.

Addiction—The ABC's of Avoidance

If you know a drinker who has begun to avoid what he previously accepted or even sought after, look behind his excuses. If alcohol is the common denominator for his avoidances, he is headed for alcoholism.

Mrs. J.'s letter is a case in point. "Three weeks ago," she writes, "my husband decided that two couples—close friends for 20 years—are boring. Now he refuses to see them. I was puzzled. When I mentioned this to my sister she hinted that it might be due to my husband's drinking problem.

"I was shocked and angry that she could say such a thing about my husband. But then I realized that our friends are practically teetotalers. Does this mean my husband is an alcoholic?"

Dear Mrs. J.: I can't tell whether your husband is an alcoholic because you didn't tell me enough about his drinking. But here are some ideas on what else to look for and some guidelines on how you might resolve your problem.

One of the early signs of alcoholism is a newly developed tendency to avoid certain people, places and situations. The drinker begins to avoid them because they remind him that he's losing control of his drinking, or that he is no longer comfortable in places where alcohol is not available. It's not unusual for him to begin avoiding old friends because they are light drinkers, because they have quit drinking, or because they have joined AA. If your husband says that such friends have "suddenly" become boring, or that they espouse the wrong politics, cheat at golf, or have annoying mannerisms—check it out. It is not normal to "suddenly" discover these kinds of things about old friends.

Usually these friends are as puzzled by your husband's reaction as you are, but it's also possible that they are quite clear about what's really going on with your husband. Maybe there was a "scene," or maybe some unpleasant words about your husband's drinking were passed around, but you were not told about it. Your friends may be avoiding the "problem" because they are embarrassed, and your husband avoids the "problem" because he's angry.

Of course, a wife's drinking problem may also create confusing behavior. Avoidance of certain places or situations is common; for example, a certain restaurant which used to be a family favorite. "It takes too long to get waited on," she gripes, or "they must have hired a new chef," she complains. Again, you are puzzled. You didn't notice any of these changes; but you also didn't notice that they stopped serving alcohol. But she did notice—for obvious reasons. For similar reasons, church socials, school concerts and PTA meetings have gotten on your wife's avoidance list.

However, avoidance is not the drinker's monopoly. Think about it! Why did your sister avoid telling you (or your husband) about this before? Why did you avoid asking her to elaborate when she did start to tell you? Why did you avoid asking your "old friends" about the "problem"? Are you afraid that your husband's problem is common knowledge? Are you avoiding more bad news?

If you're getting anxious or angry just reading this now, imagine how those drinkers must feel. All you are avoiding is being embarrassed. If our speculations are correct, imagine what they are avoiding. They are full of pain because of what they are doing to themselves, full of guilt because of what they are doing to the people they love, and confused because they can't understand it—or change it. Now there is something worth avoiding.

Are Alcoholics Born That Way?

Are alcoholics born that way or do they become alcoholic after years of social drinking? The answer is simple: Some drank alcoholically from the first drink on while others seemed to have crossed into alcoholism gradually. If you want to know which kind of alcoholic you're living with, here's how: (1) define alcoholism as the kind of drinking which causes problems in the drinker's life and (2) compare the consequences of the earliest drinking episodes with the problems of the recent drinking episodes.

Jim, a 47-year-old alcoholic, is a case in point. He had his first drink of alcohol as a 17-year-old sailor in a saloon with three other sailors. They drank whiskey, told a few sea stories and had "a heck of a time." Several hours later his buddies had returned to the ship but Jim stayed on, had some more drinks and got into a fight with seven Marines.

It was a short fight. He regained consciousness in jail at 10 o'clock the next morning. He had a hangover, a broken hand and was charged with being drunk, disorderly and assaulting a policeman. He couldn't remember anything that happened after his buddies had left him at the saloon. To add to his trouble, his ship had sailed at 7:00 a.m. and he was officially AWOL. Three similar episodes later he was discharged from the Navy.

Over the next 30 years Jim drank his way through two marriages, several physical injuries, three drunk-driving charges and two psychiatric hospitalizations for "depressive reaction." Because he never drank in the morning and was able to periodically go on the wagon, the people in his life felt that he had not yet crossed the line from social drinking into alcoholism.

By age 47 he had liver problems and alcohol addiction but was still a good welder. One morning on his way to work he stopped at a bar for an eye-opener. By 10 o'clock he was still in the bar, unable to make himself go to work. Ashamed and depressed he phoned his boss and described his dilemma. The boss said emphatically "For heaven's sake—stay where you are! I'm sending Mike to get you right away."

Jim ordered himself another drink and waited. When Mike arrived, Jim easily persuaded him to "have at least one drink with me while I explain this whole situation to you." An hour and a half later Jim was back on the phone. "Boss, this is Jim again;

I'm real sorry, but now Mike and I are both drunk. I guess the bartender served us doubles every time."

Now, for the answer to our quiz: Was Jim a born alcoholic or did he gradually cross that invisible line from social drinking? The answer is that Jim was a born alcoholic because his first drunk at 17 and his last drunk at 47 were practically identical in their consequences. In both instances—and in many binges in between—he alienated other people (friends or family), got into legal problems (jail or drunk-driving), and caused damage to his physical health (broken hand or cirrhosis), his mental health (memory loss or depression), and his work record (AWOL or absenteeism). That's *not* social drinking!

If you look at drinking consequences objectively, you'll find that most alcoholics are either born alcoholics or they crossed over from social drinking long ago. For many a Monday morning—the handwriting was on the wall, but nobody was willing to read it. Aside from the drinking itself, the alcoholic's major problem is the "willingness" of the people around him to wait until *their* cup runneth over.

Drinks, Drugs, and Doctors

It is hard to escape the impression that there are doctors making their daily rounds 'high' on alcohol or other drugs—their clinical judgments clouded, and their patients at risk of misdiagnosis, serious injury, or perhaps even death.

The *Journal*, April 1, 1984

The above quote from the Addiction Research Foundation *Journal* highlights a recent symposium on "Drinks, Drugs and Doctors." Here are some conclusions from this lengthy symposium:

The extent of alcohol and drug problems among physicians is not clear. Dr. Edward Senay, professor of psychiatry, University of Chicago, says doctors "probably have a little bit more" than other people "and the only reason for that would be availability." But Dr. David Smith, Haight-Ashbury Free Medical Clinic says: "Prescription-narcotic addiction (among doctors) is four to six times the national average."

Do doctors have special stresses that drive them to drugs or drink? "No," says Dr. Senay. "Physicians have the same kinds of life crises as anyone else: their wives or their husbands have problems; there are money problems and status problems and all the stresses that anybody else has."

Dr. Donald Goodwin, University of Kansas psychiatrist, agrees: "There appears to be no connection between stress and use of drugs. Many people under a great amount of stress don't use drugs, while people who appear to have very little stress, such as youth in the 1960s, can use very large amounts."

Next to alcohol, the most frequently abused drug is Demerol (a morphine-like synthetic). Besides availability, Dr. Senay says, there are also pharmacological reasons for the high abuse rate of this drug among doctors. "Demerol is just stimulating enough so that they don't get the down effect one would get from being hooked on other narcotics . . . . Those doing surgery or things like that would not be able to be very effective if they were using other drugs that would cause them to nod off."

As in the rest of society, the abuse picture in general is changing among doctors, too. Dr. Douglas Talbott of the Ridgeview Institute says older physicians still prefer alcohol, but drug abuse is more common in young physicians because drug use "has been a part of their way of life." Smith specifically points to "a rising use of cocaine among young physicians."

Surprisingly, the experts agreed that physician-addicts are able to function professionally with very little impairment of their intellectual judgment. You might be puzzled by this conclusion, especially since the subject of this symposium was "the impaired physician."

Actually, it is understandable that doctors would come to this kind of conclusion about doctors. Group loyalties incline all of us to protect ourselves by speaking well of our own kind. Could it be that the experts were rationalizing just a little? Probably. The reason I think so is that every alcoholic pilot, lawyer or priest I have ever treated took great pains to assure me that his addiction never affected a passenger, a client, or a parishioner.

Mulling over this report brought to mind F. Scott Fitzgerald's remark about people of wealth. He said, "The rich are different from you and me," to which Hemingway replied, "Yeah, they have more money." In the same way, perhaps doctor addicts are different from other addicts—they use better stuff, like Demerol. What this really means is that doctor addicts should be treated like other addicts, but also that special attention should be paid to their prescribing habits, both before and after treatment.

Treatment Program for Addicted Doctors

> We got Bob home and into bed, and right then we made an alarming discovery. He had to perform a certain operation that only he could do. The deadline was just three days away; he simply had to do the job himself; here he was, shaking like a leaf. Could we get him sober in time?
>
> *Alcoholics Anonymous Comes of Age*

Alcoholism or drug addiction is stigmatizing. That's why patients with that disease don't ask for help at the drop of a hint.

As a matter of fact, the higher the patient's station in life the more likely he is to go on with his disease and get sicker until he is finally disabled.

While this applies to VIPs in general, it is even more true for the practitioner of medicine who is in solo practice.

Why? Because VIPs such as movie stars, athletes, politicians or executives live by checks and balances, namely, the business agent, the fans, the voters, or the boss. In other words, the patient's growing disability sooner or later makes him unmarketable.

The solo practitioner of medicine, on the other hand, has a career which is tailor made for self-destruction through addiction. He is self-employed, has no deadlines to meet, no public appearances to show up for, no annual relicensing requirements, a high income and no mandatory retirement age. Also, he can eventually work out of his own office—alone—under the overprotective eye of a loyal nurse or family members.

Getting addicted doctors into treatment was practically impossible until the 1970s at which time the doctors began to take care of their own. Today more than 40 states have programs that provide guidelines for the detection and diagnosis of impaired physicians, as well as specific procedures for getting them into treatment.

By the way, in case you are wondering about Bob, the surgeon at the beginning of this section, yes, he did perform the operation on June 10, 1935 as scheduled. The operation was a double success: the patient lived, and the doctor recovered. And the doctor never had a drink of alcohol again for the rest of his life. How can we be sure? Because he was Dr. Bob Smith, one of the two co-founders of Alcoholics Anonymous.

Dear Doc...

Question: In a recent column you made the statement that "getting the same feeling of drunkenness from less alcohol is alarming because it means a loss of tolerance and possibly a late stage of alcoholism." That's happening to me now, and I am worried.

I'm only 40 years old. For years I've had both emotional problems and a drinking problem. Also, for the last two years I've been seeing a therapist. He is giving me Serax and Norpramin.

Answer: For most people tolerance for alcohol decreases when they become 40 or 50 years of age. In your case, the problem is more likely the result of a synergistic (additive effect) which is due to the fact that you are combining both alcohol and pills. Serax is a minor tranquilizer which is very much like Valium, and Norpramin is an anti-depressant medication. Together they markedly increase the depressing effects of alcohol. Thus, you are, in effect, taking in a greater amount of tranquilizing medicine than you did formerly when you drank only alcohol.

Discuss this with your therapist. If your life is so stressful that you need psychotherapy, Serax, and Norpramin, then you should not drink alcohol at all until your problems are cleared up and until you are able to stay off the pills. If you can't quit drinking for the duration of your therapy, then you have a problem; and if your therapist is afraid to tell you to quit drinking, then he or she has a problem.

Also, your past history of a "drinking problem" suggests that you may have alcoholism. Perhaps you should stop for good. In any case, as long as you're drinking enough to get feelings of drunkenness, you are not getting your money's worth out of psychotherapy.

Q: Our son is in the Air Force and is constantly getting into trouble because of his drinking. I believe he may have had an alcohol problem even before he entered the service, but now that he's out of our reach so to speak, I don't know what to do.

A: The Air Force, as well as the other branches of the armed services—Army, Navy, and Marines—have excellent alcohol and drug programs. Have your son contact the chaplain on the base where he's stationed. The chaplain will see that he gets into the rehab program. And if your son won't take this first step, you can take it for him by calling the chaplain on the base nearest your home. Tell him the situation and he'll make the necessary contacts so your son can get help.

Q: My husband and I frequently argue about his drinking. He insists that an alcoholic is somebody who misses a lot of work or calls in sick or is unable to function properly on the job because of drinking.

I'm worried about my husband because regardless of what's happening at his work, he drinks a quart of vodka daily, starting first thing in the morning, and drinking into the night. He is 52.

What are some of the symptoms I should notice regarding his health, due to this much drinking? I worry about his liver.

A: Every alcoholic can find justifiable reasons or arguments for drinking the way he does. Your husband is using the "work" argument to throw you off the track. He is, in effect, saying that a diabetic is not somebody who has high blood sugar, or sugar in his urine. Instead, he's saying that a diabetic is somebody who is unable to function properly on the job, misses a lot of work, or calls in sick because of diabetes. Obviously, a person who has that kind of diabetes is a far-advanced diabetic who should have gone to treatment long ago.

The same applies to your husband in terms of drinking and his health. As long as he drinks a quart of vodka daily, I would worry about his liver, too. I would also worry about his pancreas, his stomach, his heart muscle, his bone marrow, and a number of other things. Undoubtedly, one or more of these organs is already affected.

To get his attention, ask him to go with you to a doctor who understands alcoholism so that his organ functions can be checked out. It can be done on an outpatient basis. This would also serve as a diagnostic test because if your husband refuses to go, he is telling you that he wants to continue drinking the way he does because he cannot face his disease right now. That would mean that you would have to take care of your own problem, namely your problem of living with him and suffering with him. Start by going to a few Al-anon meetings, listed in your local telephone directory.

Q: My husband must be a beeraholic. Once he starts, he can't stop. I never know when he might come home drunk, and sometimes he's drunk for two or three days continuously. Also, his whole personality changes when he's drunk.

We have been to AA, but the speakers talked only about whiskey, which made my husband say he wasn't as bad as them because, after all, he "only drinks beer."

A: I have treated many alcoholics who drank only beer. I have also treated many upper-class wineaholics. Your husband sounds like a classic alcoholic who has loss of control, personality changes, family problems and job impairment (absenteeism). The only difference between your husband and a whiskeyholic is that your husband has to make more frequent trips to the liquor store and to the bathroom.

Go with him to an alcoholic treatment facility, get a consultation, and ask to talk to some recovering beeraholics. It may help him to get a better look at himself. If he refuses to go, it may mean that he already knows what's really going on. You will then have to ask the therapist to help you arrange for an intervention.

Q: I am 32 years old. My drinking has grown worse through the years. I seldom drink liquor, but I drink two six-packs of beer a day. My body is taking a beating, and I don't get enough exercise to burn up the calories.

Is this alcoholism, and what remedy would be most successful?

A: Twenty drinks or more per week is heavy drinking, and you are drinking much more than that. Of course, your body is taking a beating, and you're too lethargic for exercise.

To realize that you may need help is the first step. If you can stop drinking without having withdrawal symptoms (hands trembling, sweating, agitation, or convulsions), then stop drinking at once and join Alcoholics Anonymous. If you don't want to do that, then go to an outpatient clinic for counseling. If you can't stop drinking without withdrawal symptoms, you need to enter a hospital for safe detoxification and rehabilitation.

Q: I heard of the "two-drinks-a-day test of alcoholism." It's supposed to prove whether or not you have a drinking problem. Can you explain that?

A: This test is like any other test. What it will show depends on how honest you are when you take the test and on who grades the test. The danger is that some alcoholics I have known are able to pass this test through sheer determination and a one-day-at-a-time will power struggle. But they do it at considerable emotional expense to themselves and others, then lapse into problem drinking soon thereafter. The test is a fairly good instrument for signs of early dependency.

Here's how the test works: Have two regular, bar-sized drinks every day for 60 days—no more, no less—regardless of whether you get promoted or fired, whether the Dodgers win or lose, or whether your kid is valedictorian or hangs himself in the garage.

What happens to your mood, your behavior, and your attitude about drinking during those 60 days will indicate whether you can take life and its ups and downs without alcohol, or whether alcohol has become your crutch or your tranquilizer.

The test should be graded on a weekly basis by somebody who cares about you, someone who sees you almost daily and is willing to discuss with you your preoccupations and your behavior. (Of course, you have to be honest enough to tell that person about your preoccupations.)

Here are some of the things which might happen while you're taking the test: You practically inhale your two-drink daily quota during the first 20 minutes of a party, then brood and sulk for the rest of the evening because you can't drink any more, or you get furious when the ball game goes into extra innings, because it means that you need more beer now that the game is getting good. Another response might be to want to increase your daily booze quota because you caught the flu, and you always treat the flu with brandy, or you come home tipsy from happy hour and explain to your wife, "The boss was buying—and you just don't refuse the boss." Then perhaps you offer to skip your daily quota for a week because you want to keep on schedule, but you also want to drink a whole bottle of wine tonight because it's your wedding anniversary.

By the second week you want to stop the test altogether and try it again "the right way" after New Year's Day. And when your wife stops you from doing that, you start counting your two drinks a day like a prison inmate marks his calendar. And on the final day of your test, you're so relieved to have proven your point that you celebrate the event by getting smashed at the club, totaling your car, and ending up in jail.

(P.S. Be sure the person who grades you is not also your drinking buddy. If you're both in jail, the test is still valid. It means your glass crutch broke again, and both you and your buddy need help to cope with your drinking problem.)

Q: I wonder if I'm an alcoholic. I'm a 32-year-old man, and I've been drinking for 10 years. I started with one or two beers a day, and now I am up to 6 to 10 beers a day. I drink because I like it. The drinking doesn't seem to affect me except it makes me irritable and gives me temper flares. My friends say they don't mind my behavior, however.

A: You are well on your way to being an alcoholic because you're showing the early signs of addiction: tolerance, which means that you need increasingly larger amounts of alcohol to feel the effects, and personality change, namely, irritability and loss of impulse control which you describe as temper flares. The fact that your friends don't object to your behavior is no reassurance. At your stage of alcoholism it is likely that you have begun to surround yourself with hard-drinking friends only.

The most positive thing is that you are still able to wonder about whether or not you have a problem. It means that your denial is not yet set in concrete. Now is the time to act: (1) Ask some friends or family members how they feel about your behavior when you're not drinking (be sure they are not drinking buddies). (2) Go to at least 12 Alcoholics Anonymous meetings and see if anything you hear sounds familiar. If nothing sounds familiar, or if you don't like what you hear because it sounds too familiar—but you also don't want to join AA. Then (3) go back to drinking two beers a day and see how you feel about what's happening.

A note to Quaalude users: I recently hospitalized an executive who had decided to get treatment for his cocaine addiction. When he told me that his cocaine use had been "at least half-safe," I asked him to explain. He said he'd known all along that the cocaine was black-market imported and often cut with garage-manufactured impurities, but at least the come-down was safe. He elaborated in junkie jargon: "I never had to worry too much about being screwed up on God only knows what and unable to go to sleep at 2 a.m. because I knew that my come-down vehicle was safe. You see," he went on to explain, "I always used Quaaludes. Regardless of whether I bought them on the street or from the coke dealer, I knew that the 'Ludes' were made by American know-how, by a reputable manufacturer, with quality control, and in accordance with FDA specifications."

Well, if you are using Quaaludes in that manner, I have bad news and I have good news. The bad news is that your quality controlled, parachute-safe come-down is now a thing of the past. Last month the manufacturer of Quaaludes (Lemmon Pharmaceutical Co.) withdrew Quaaludes permanently from the U.S. market because of "unjustified negative publicity." Henceforth, any Quaaludes you buy will probably be black-market imports, just like the cocaine.

The good news is that this bad news may help you to come to the conclusion that you need to stop using cocaine. You see, the fact that you need a come-down at all means that you are overdosing on cocaine. And if you are overdosing, you are obviously not a recreational or social user, which in turn means that your habit is going to get worse—not better.

Q: My 30-year-old brother lives with my husband and me. He has lost several jobs in the last year because of drinking on the job or getting drunk during lunch. He now works for my husband doing yard work, landscaping and other handy work. Occasionally he still drinks on the job. We have repeatedly warned him about this. He is a very good worker when he's not hung-over. We have been putting up with his work habits and his slips because we want him to feel worthwhile by having employment. Maybe we are too sentimental. What do you think?

A: Drinking on the job is a most serious sign of alcoholism, especially if the employee is a skilled person who has deteriorated to the level where he is doing menial work. Your repeated warnings only reinforce your brother's sick notion, the notion that for him it is okay to go on drinking while he is working.

You and your husband are mistaken if you think that you are making your brother feel worthwhile by giving him a job. Deep down your brother knows that most of the time he is actually impersonating an employee, and that the quality of his workmanship is poor.

Look at it this way. Your husband is actually your brother's employer. That means boss. Your husband needs to do exactly what any responsible employer today would do if he has an alcoholic employee who drinks on the job: offer him a chance at rehabilitation right now—and terminate him if he refuses to go through with it. Anything else is a grave disservice to your brother.

The phrase "he's the best man we've got when he's sober" usually means that we are talking about a moderately far-advanced alcoholic. The good news is that after successful treatment, he will be the best man you have all the time—because he'll be sober all the time.

Q: My husband is a 62-year-old alcoholic who drinks a fifth of bourbon daily. Two years ago he was told that he had cirrhosis. He stopped drinking for six months, but now he's worse than ever.

Our family doctor says my husband has to want help before we can do anything for him. But his mental condition is bad; he's a menace to himself and others. The family's future is in jeopardy financially and medically.

Is it possible to do anything for him without his consent? Your statement in a recent column about giving him "tough love" gave me new hope.

A: Waiting for an alcoholic to ask for help is an old idea. It has killed many people. See your nearest alcoholism treatment center and ask them to help you with an intervention. They will invite your doctor to participate. This method helps alcoholics recover long before they hit bottom. Your husband being "a menace to himself and others" and "jeopardizing" the family could mean that he is so sick that you may need a psychiatric evaluation and perhaps even a brief commitment to get him into treatment.

Q: I have been in AA and Al-anon for 15 years. My husband admits his alcoholism and stops drinking at times but refuses to do anything else. He is close to getting in trouble even though he is an executive. He drinks himself to sleep every night. Our children see his alcoholism, but one married daughter says it's my fault. She says he drinks because we argue so much.

I think he is an alcoholic not because of me but because he drank too much for too long. How can I convince my daughter that I'm not responsible for his drinking?

A: You can't convince her, probably because she has personal reasons for clinging to her own denial. You have to decide whether you want to get him into treatment or continue as the wife of an intermittent, periodic alcoholic executive.

Get professional help from a treatment center to help you set up an intervention. Be sure your daughter is not on the intervention team. She would be destructive at this time. She will probably see the light after your husband is recovered and shares with her what was really going on during his drinking days. This will happen during the family week of his treatment or sometime in his early recovery.

Q: A woman friend of mine spends more time drunk and hung over than she spends sober. She also has ulcers, bladder problems (including incontinence) and swollen ankles. I told her that drinking makes these problems worse, but she says she "has to drink." She sees a psychiatrist regularly, but I don't think the psychiatrist knows how much she drinks. Her only living relative is an uncle.

You keep saying in your column that an alcoholic doesn't have to "hit bottom." If you see any way in which I can help, please let me know.

A: Your letter describes a lonely woman whose compulsive drinking is harming her physically and mentally. She will get much sicker if she continues drinking.

I'm impressed by your concern and willingness to help your friend. Unfortunately, in order to help her, you will first have to do some things that will make you uncomfortable.

First, speak to her uncle and one or two friends or neighbors about how bad her situation really is. Second, tell her psychiatrist by phone (or write him a letter) about the extent of her drinking. Don't worry about a negative reaction from the psychiatrist. If he is a good physician, he will welcome your "intrusion" because he will be able to use your information in his work with her, and he will keep your information confidential if you ask him to. Your information will prompt him to get laboratory tests which will then enable him to put her in a hospital, where he can start treating not only her emotions but also her alcoholism.

Once she is actually in a hospital bed, you can ask him to coordinate a joint meeting with your friend's uncle, neighbors, yourself and the psychiatrist to do an intervention.

Q: Your advice on intervention is always given to people who have a legal right to do it, such as a wife. I have a friend whose family lives in another state. They wouldn't help with the intervention even if they were here. As a matter of fact, my friend moved away from them. Now his drinking is getting much worse. My problem is that unless he moves away from here, I won't be able to get away from him. He admits that he has a serious drinking problem, but he says that he can stop on his own. But he never does.

A: An intervention is not a legal maneuver. It is a loving, therapeutic act. It can be done in any relationship such as marriage, living together, working together, being tennis buddies, bridge partners, etc. The intervention is usually started by somebody like you (spouse, friend, co-worker) who suffers along with the alcoholic. It is best done with the help of a counselor, doctor or clergyman who knows how to do interventions.

The idea is that since your alcoholic cannot quit on his own, he will have to accept help. If he refuses, you will have to sever your relationship with him because you have come to the conclusion that you won't go on spending your life with a drinking alcoholic because it hurts too much. Very likely your friend lost his family and moved away from them because they put some of their pressure on him, but didn't know how to do an intervention.

In your particular case it sounds as if your boyfriend is doing with you what he did with his family: He will stay with you as long as you put up with him the way he is.

Besides doing an intervention, you have other options: You can plunge into your job and become a workaholic; you can let your hobbies consume you; you can go into psychoanalysis; you can join a self-help group; you can ask your doctor for nerve pills; you can start prescribing drugs for yourself (cocaine, marijuana, etc.); you can become psychosomatically ill; etc. The point is you either do an intervention to get your alcoholic to change *now*, or you use any of these other methods to live with the situation until you can no longer stand it, or until he "somehow" changes, or until he dies.

Q: My mother is a chronic alcoholic. Although she can still get around, she drinks throughout the day, every day. I moved out when I was 18 because of her drinking. My younger brothers are still living at home. On the advice of our pastor I am going to Al-anon. I have also made an appointment with an intervention counselor because I can no longer sit by and watch her drink herself to death.

The problem is that my stepfather has avoided Al-anon. He admits that my mother needs treatment, and he wants her to get help, but he's afraid to do anything like an intervention. Am I doing the right thing? I feel helpless and impatient.

A: To get a better handle on your impatience, keep going to Al-anon. As for your helplessness, part of the reason is your stepfather's hesitancy to confront your mother even though he knows that she needs intervention and treatment. I would suggest several group discussions involving your brothers, the pastor and your stepfather, under the guidance of the counselor. During these pre-intervention sessions, your stepfather will gain the necessary strength and insight so he can help all of you help your mother. Good luck!

Q: Your column entitled "Success Doesn't Help Alcoholics" is my husband's story exactly. He and I talked openly about his disease. By now I have learned enough about alcoholism so that I no longer feel that I caused it. I also accept it as a disease, and I see my husband's defenses as rationalizations. Nevertheless, he is still an alcoholic who is destroying himself and refuses to go for help. I need to know how I can help him or influence him to get help. Intervention through work is not possible because he is a self-employed professional.

A: Even in a case where you can't use the threat of job loss (because there is no boss), intervention usually works if it is done with an intervention team and counselor who is trained to help. The intervention team will have to have one or several sessions with a counselor to prepare them for the intervention. The team should consist of three or more of the following: you, his children, a parent, a trusted friend, a family or business attorney, his doctor, psychologist, clergyman, and one or two of his trusted professional associates, e.g., a client, a colleague, partner, supplier, adviser, personal secretary, etc.

The secret of success is that you have to make up your mind to let your secret out and with professional help involve other people who can help you do the job.

What motivates the self-employed professional to accept help is his love for you and his children, the affection and concern shown by his friends, his own pride as a professional, and his need for respect from colleagues and subordinates. In the intervention, these are the emotions he will come to feel, and they will make the difference.

The only other alternative is for you to get help for your own emotional pain so that you become strong enough to leave him or to more comfortably live with him until he has destroyed himself or until he decides to get help on his own. Unfortunately, the prospects for the latter possibility are remote.

Q: I have the quality of family life I have always wanted. I'm happily married and have three lovely children. I have recovered through Al-anon, Adult Children of Alcoholics and individual therapy. But every holiday season my parents come to visit—and they create chaos.

My father quit drinking six years ago but refuses Alcoholics Anonymous ("I don't need it"); and my mother is a classic co-alcoholic who refuses Al-anon. Your column often talks about doing interventions on drinking alcoholics. My question: Is there an equivalent of an intervention which can be done on the ill-tempered, authoritarian, negativistic, non-drinking alcoholic?

A: Basically, an intervention is a well thought-out, dispassionate, loving but firm statement which you make to an alcoholic whom you love. During the intervention you point out how the drinking behavior is causing harm to him, to you and to other people. You also explain how this can be changed (usually by treatment); and you make a commitment to get help or treatment for yourself to whatever extent is appropriate.

Looking at your family problem from that vantage point, both of your parents need help—your mother is a martyr, and your father is a dry drunk. Arrange a meeting between yourself, your husband and your children. With their help, confront your parents with the fact that they are repeatedly and predictably destroying the holidays for your family. In a loving, dispassionate way, tell him that this is harming you, that it is harming them, that there is help available (AA, Al-anon and treatment), and that you have already started getting help for yourself.

If after the intervention your parents are unwilling to start making some changes, then you can no longer go on with your "relationship," even though it is a family relationship. Your situation today is no different from what it was six years ago when your father was an abusive drinker and your mother a silent martyr. The reason you still have a problem is that your parents took the easiest way out, namely, your father gave up drinking. The easiest part of solving an alcoholic's problem is for him to give up drinking (that's why alcoholics do it so often). But that's only the first step.

Lest your anger blind you to the real issues involved—and thereby lead you to destroy rather than create—remember this: neither your father nor your mother deep down really wants, or likes, what is going on right now.

Q: How do I handle an intervention? My husband is an Air Force captain with 12 years of active duty. He thinks nobody at his office knows about his problem. (They'd have to be blind not to see it, because he often comes to work several hours late with a hangover.) He tried counseling two years ago but stayed sober only three months.

I can't continue to live with this situation. Al-anon has helped me feel better, but I'm not content to wait until he hits bottom. The only other option I see is to leave this marriage, much as it pains me to think about that.

A: You sound fed up, scared and desperate, but still loving. Rather than packing up and leaving your husband now, you can have a confrontation with him and insist that he get help for his drinking, along with counseling for both of you. If you're sure you have the guts to carry it through, you can also tell him that if he refuses help, you will inform his superior officer. Getting a divorce without trying the other options first would be a cop-out on your part. Your husband may be angry at first, but later he will thank you for saving his life. If it doesn't work out, you can still get your divorce. You will not have lost any more than you are losing right now.

Q: While going to Al-anon, I saw an alcohol counselor. With his help, my family and I did an intervention on my alcoholic husband. He admitted to being an alcoholic. I offered the ultimatum: Go for treatment to a hospital, go to AA, or I would file for legal separation. He refused help.

Now he appears to have stopped drinking. He keeps asking me when he's getting the legal separation papers. I just ignore him. I feel like a failure because I didn't go through with the separation. The papers are in the attorney's office, but I just don't have the courage to do it. Meanwhile, my alcoholic is verbally abusive.

A: Your intervention is not complete because you did not follow through on your promise. Your husband's drinking problem still is in charge of your life. It is clear now that he needs treatment because he is the kind of alcoholic who becomes angry and verbally abusive when he doesn't drink.

You have in effect traded a drinking, emotionally absent husband for a dry one who is angry and verbally abusive. You have to decide whether you want to live with this situation and wait for the other shoe to drop, i.e., for him to drink again, or whether you want to proceed with the legal separation. (He may also be waiting for you to actually get the separation before he finally goes for help.)

Q: I'm dating a college-age alcoholic and have begun to educate myself about his disease and how to do an intervention.

I'm going to try to help him. Even if it fails, at least I will be able to say I tried before I had to say goodbye. We are both 23. Am I on the right track?

A: You are on the right track, but you should be more optimistic. Be sure you have a trained counselor help with the intervention. Also, your intervention team should include at least one recovering alcoholic who is educated and in your friend's age bracket.

The tone of your letter suggests that you are still not sure about whether you are playing fair with your friend. I have seen many alcoholics go through treatment and recover simply because somebody cared as much, and was willing to risk as much as you do.

Q: My husband is a physician with a busy practice. He has finally accepted the idea that he is an alcoholic. He is able to stay dry, but it obviously requires tremendous psychological effort for him to do so. I can tell from his actions and from what he tells me that he is deeply ashamed of his alcoholism. Deep down he feels that it is some kind of weakness. Also, he seems convinced that he is the only physician in the world who has this disease, maybe because we've never known nor heard of any other alcoholic doctors. Is there anything I can do to help him?

A: Alcoholic physicians are among the most guilt-ridden of alcoholics. This is especially true for those physicians who, since their early childhood, had a need for being strong, responsible and always be able to help others. "How can you be considered strong and help others if you yourself are a weak alcoholic?'' they ask themselves.

Ironically, physicians have the highest incidence of alcoholism. You can help your husband by having him write to International Doctors in Alcoholics Anonymous (IDAA). It is a fellowship that was founded in 1948 and now has about 3,000 members. All of them are recovering alcoholic physicians. They have annual and regional medical conventions with scientific as well as recovery sessions in the scheduled program.

Families also participate. If you and your husband attend such a convention, your husband will run into not only medical school classmates but even one or two faculty members of his medical school or admired teachers from his residency program. Your husband's contact with IDAA will remain strictly confidential, and there are no dues or fees for membership. The address is IDAA, 1950 Volney Road, Youngstown, OH 44511.

My little binge lasted only three days, and I haven't had a drop since. There was one other in September, likewise three days. Save for that, I haven't had a drop since a year ago last January. Isn't it awful that we reformed alcoholics have to preface everything by explaining exactly how we stand on that question?

Letters of F. Scott Fitzgerald
Andrew Turnbull

6

Recovering Addicts Are Weller Than Well

To accept the idea that they have a problem and that they can improve their lives by accepting help from others is the beginning of wisdom for chemically dependent patients. *Recovery means switching from pills and booze to people and feelings.* It's a process that takes from two to three years.

For most recovering patients the first six to twelve months after rehab are more in the nature of relapse prevention. From day to day the patient may still be hurting and worrying. In some cases he may drink or use again; he may even go to the hospital once more. But as the sober periods get longer, he slowly gets a handle on life. As he waits for the urges to diminish, and while people around him wait for the other shoe to drop, the chemical fog is slowly lifting. Then—one day at a time—he looks better, feels better, and functions better. He still has some ups and downs—as all of us do—but instead of drinking about them, he can talk about them; instead of getting high with addicts, he shares with friends.

Day by day he is a little more comfortable. Formerly willful, he now becomes willing. From having been essentially unconscious, he grows to being self-conscious and eventually self-confident.

Soon he is so busy with living—growing, realizing and understanding—that the urge to use or drink is not conscious for days at a time. He is now recovering, and most people around him can tell. On the job he used to be "the best employee we got when he's sober"; now he's consistently a good employee because he's always sober. He no longer visits doctors except for routine problems or annual physicals. *He's on his way to becoming weller than well.*

Starting Down the Road to Trouble

There's an old saying that "If an alcoholic takes even one drink, he's off and running." Now, that is not literally true. It doesn't mean that after one drink he'll keep right on drinking until he's drunk again.

If you're living with an alcoholic, you already know that. What you are probably wondering about is, "Can he go back to drinking without sooner or later getting into trouble again?" The answer is no. His drinking may appear normal for a while, but over the long haul it'll get him into trouble again.

When you study your alcoholic's drinking pattern with the objectivity and hindsight of a therapist, you'll finally understand the true meaning of "off and running." You'll see the self-deception, the rationalization, the magical thinking, the trickery, the theatrics and the chicanery that the drinker has to use in order to make his controlled and troubled drinking appear casual. You'll also hear the verbal sleights of hand which he uses to weave you into the "off-and-running" process. Finally, you'll come to see the active role which you are playing as a seemingly innocent, but involved bystander.

Let's thumb through the file of a patient named Hank. Hank was on the wagon again because his wife Sue had been nagging. Then one night he had a beer. When Sue came home and saw the empty can she had a fit.

"Relax," Hank said firmly. "I drank that beer two hours ago. There are five cans in the fridge. They're left over from the six-pack I bought this noon. Now then," he raised a logical finger, "do you see me clawing my way through the kitchen door for another beer, huh? Well, so much for your mother's 'off-and-running' theory!"

The next evening Hank said, "Listen, if I was able to stop with one beer yesterday, I can stop with one beer today." Sue couldn't argue with that. So he drank a beer. Sue watched him nervously as he read the paper. Two hours later he grinned at her, "Honey, I'm going to bed. I'm tired of waiting for the 'off-and-running' Milwaukee bull to come crashing through the wall." Sue felt like a fool. "Actually, he's funny," she thought, grinning to herself. "Maybe I'm worried about nothing."

In any case, Hank was now back on his nightly beer. Two weeks later there was a farewell lunch for somebody at work. "What the heck," Hank rationalized. "I'll just have my nightly beer at lunch—that's all." But driving home that evening, he rationalized some more. "Anybody who can stop with one beer a day can stop with two beers a day," he assured himself. So he sneaked in the back door and quickly got a beer before Sue could smell him. "I like the taste of that first beer," he toasted her with his second beer when she walked into the kitchen. (Already he was back into lying and "stinking thinking"; maybe not yet off and running, but certainly jogging.)

After supper her brother came by unexpectedly. "Hank," he said, "let's have a beer and settle that Little League problem." Sue made a face and went into the kitchen. Hank followed her. "I gotta have a beer with him," Hank pleaded with her. "You know what a gossip he is. Anyway," he added logically, "if I can control one beer, I can control two. It's no big deal. How about it?"

Well, she thought, Hank was certainly right about her brother's big mouth. "All right," she gave in, "you can have two—but just this once."

And now they were both "off and jogging" because she already knew in a preconscious sense that tomorrow Hank will say, "I handled two beers yesterday—I can handle two beers today," and she will have to agree. And Hank already knew that tomorrow he'll have one beer at lunch; and if she smells him as he comes into the house, he'll say, "Honey, I had one of my two beers at work." But, if she doesn't smell him, he'll have one at work and two at home, because if you can stop with two, you can stop with three. And she'll agree.

Then they'll both be off and running.

Stopping Drinking Is a Series of Decisions

A sincere desire to stop drinking is not a snap decision; it's more a process of mini-decisions. It usually comes about in a setting that promotes emotional growth, for example, an alcohol rehab center or Alcoholics Anonymous.

Here's a scenario of the mental changes an alcoholic goes through during a month of rehabilitation. When Bob Jones first arrives for treatment—usually because someone close to him is fed up with him—he will be in a cautious, guarded mood. During his first week in treatment his attitude will be a reflection of his personality style: he may be overly confident, arrogant, brash, and even cynical; or he may be quiet, aloof, obsequious, or downright passive.

One kind of alcoholic will meekly tell his counselor, "I'm a real alcoholic. I'm glad I'm here. I'll do whatever you tell me to." Another type of alcoholic may literally blow up and yell, "Okay—I'll play your stupid game for 28 days, but I don't really have a problem. It's true that I drink a little too much at parties, but I'm not an alcoholic. If you want a real alcoholic, you ought to have my boss here—now there is a lush for you."

During his second week, having sat through a number of counseling sessions, AA meetings, training films, lectures, etc., the alcoholic patient is subdued, maybe even a little depressed. Why? Because he is talking less and listening more than he did during his pseudo-confident or manipulatively compliant first week.

Some early cracks appear in his wall of denial; he is having some quiet thoughts. "Boy," he is saying to himself, "it's amazing what alcoholism can do. It's a real disease. These patients I'm seeing here have experienced a lot of damage. If I drank like some of these folks—I'd quit too. In any case, I'm gonna have to cut down on my drinking after I leave here. In a way, I'm glad I'm here," he rationalizes. "If I keep my eyes and ears open, this course will make me into a better manager in my business."

In order to play the game and to keep the counselor off his back, he will stand up in an AA meeting, intending to say, "My name is Bob, and I'm an alcoholic." But instead he may end up stammering, "My name is Bob, and I'm ah, ah, alco . . . I am ah, ah, al . . . " With a superhuman effort, he'll finally spit out the word *alcoholic*.

(I remember this sort of thing happening to an alcoholic who was earning his living as a rather well-known speech therapist. At his first AA meeting he stuttered and stammered. With an embarrassed laugh and a sheepish grin, he finally looked around the meeting room and said, "For some reason I just can't pronounce the word right now. Come on, you guys, you all know what I mean." And he was right. They all did know how he was feeling.)

In the third week Bob's mood is brightening. He is beginning to see that a number of the things which other patients have done in their own lives, he too has done, but his style had been to pretend that these things didn't happen, or he usually put the blame for doing them on other people. With each passing day in treatment, he becomes more comfortable and involved because he can see that it's safe to talk in this environment. He even laughs at some of the funny things that made him frown during his self-righteous first week.

His thoughts are now something like this. "Boy, I'm sure glad I'm here. I'm also glad I'm not a real *sick* alcoholic like some of these other people are. If the whole truth about my drinking had been known all along, I could, at times, have been diagnosed as an early, potential, mild alcoholic—in an early stage. Obviously, some of my drinking buddies are sicker than I thought they were. I now understand the psychological truth behind our barroom jokes, for example Tom shouting 'How do you spell relief?' and the gang, with glasses raised, cheering, 'D-R-I-N-K.' "

By the end of the third week, Bob no longer feels like he is a visitor. He is beginning to believe that he's an alcoholic. He is undergoing some changes in his feelings toward you and the others who helped get him into treatment.

And during his final week he will telephone you and say something like, "Good morning, boss, this is Bob. I've come to the conclusion that some of the things I said to you when you sent me to treatment were the product of my illness. I was angry and afraid. I want to apologize for how I acted. I also want to thank you for saving my life. I will always be grateful to you because you were honest and helpful with my problem." There will be a catch in his throat because he is feeling everything he's saying.

For years to come, the most meaningful Christmas card in the bushel basket on your coffee table will be the one from Bob because it conveys warmth, real gratitude, and true spirituality.

So, how do you motivate an alcoholic to want help? You don't. You just get him into treatment any way you can. Real motivation comes from the patient's interaction with other patients and from the treatment environment. They help him to become honest and to realize that he needed to change his way of life. But that kind of life–changing transformation cannot come about until you, or somebody like you, has done the things that are necessary to get the alcoholic into a treatment situation.

The Beneficial Uses of Antabuse

There are many kinds of drugs that alcoholics use in order to help them combat their disease. Most are useless or even harmful. The most potentially useful, without a doubt, is called Antabuse, also known as Disulfiram. It is a pill which, when taken in proper doses, has no significant effects unless the patient drinks alcohol, in which case the effect is quite significant: he will experience the alcohol Antabuse reaction, known to doctors as the ethanol-disulfiram reaction or EDR. And therein lies the therapeutic usefulness of Antabuse.

Antabuse was discovered accidentally by Jacobsen and Hald in Denmark in 1947. While searching for a drug that would kill intestinal parasites without causing harm to the patient, they came across this compound. As a part of their research, they both took the drug without any effect.

However, several days later at a cocktail party, Jacobsen got sick after only one drink. His face was flushed, he began breathing rapidly, his heart was pounding, and he was feeling anxious and faint. He knew there was something wrong. He then vomited, slept for a couple of hours and felt normal again.

Since Hald had an identical reaction, they concluded that the alcohol-Antabuse combination had produced the reaction. Maybe it could be tried on alcoholics.

In 1948, Dr. Ruth Fox began to prescribe Antabuse in the United States. Since then, it has been used by thousands of alcoholics without adverse effects. During my service as a Navy doctor, I saw it used successfully with 22,000 alcoholic patients every year, year after year, also without adverse effects.

Here is how it works. Normally, when you drink alcohol, your liver changes the alcohol into carbon dioxide and water. One of the intermediate breakdown products, called acetaldehyde, is a very toxic substance. However, since acetaldehyde under normal conditions is rapidly destroyed, it never causes the drinker any unpleasant symptoms. Well, Antabuse works by blocking the breakdown of acetaldehyde, thereby causing it to accumulate in the body. Acetaldehyde then causes the symptoms that Hald and Jacobsen experienced.

Fox described Antabuse as a "chemical fence." Others have called it an insurance policy against drinking, a chemical deterrent, or outpatient aversive therapy. It is frequently prescribed for the patient who has poor impulse control. It also helps the drinker who is obsessed with craving for a drink all day long to the extent that he or she can't concentrate on anything else. A special circumstance, like the stress of having to appear in court, is a good reason for taking Antabuse for a week or two. Of course, the alcoholic who has tried everything else and still gets drunk may find sobriety with the help of Antabuse.

An occasional alcoholic takes Antabuse so that his family will worry less about him drinking again. I have one patient who takes it every year around Thanksgiving because his very annoying son-in-law comes to visit. He doesn't like this son-in-law, but he also doesn't want to get drunk about it.

When others criticize him for his attitude or for taking the Antabuse, he says, "Don't knock it. When it comes to making a choice between getting drunk again, breaking up a marriage or committing murder—this pill is a godsend. So after Thanksgiving when my son-in-law has gone, I am off the pill again and still sober."

I also prescribe it for another type of patient. This is the kind who, you would think, won't need it because he has a lot of self-discipline, moral integrity, will power, obsessive-compulsive psychological defenses, and lives a very orderly life. He also has a strong need to have a hand in his own treatment and says that he doesn't need Antabuse.

How do I motivate him to take the pill? By hooking into his need to have a hand in his own treatment. I make him realize that it is he, in effect, who is prescribing the Antabuse; that I as the doctor am only making the drug available to him. In short, when he takes his Antabuse first thing in the morning he is, in effect, saying, "I, John Doe, am going to will this pill into me because it will increase my chances for not drinking today. I'm not doing this for Dr. Pursch, for my family, for the boss or for anybody else. I'm doing this because I, John, don't want to drink today. To that extent my treatment is in my own hands."

This leaves him free to use his energy, imagination, brain power, integrity, etc., to work on his own lifestyle, on his AA program, in psychotherapy, and on his recovery in general. He no longer has to put any energy into controlling his craving or impulse drinking. After he's taken his morning pill, he may well have the kind of day we're all familiar with: he breaks his shoelace, his wife burns his toast, and the boss chews him out unfairly. Well, he will have a whole range of options to respond to these catastrophes—he can buy loafers, divorce his wife, or quit his job.

But, because of the Antabuse commitment he made with himself that morning, the one option not open to him is to drink alcohol. Usually, by noon of the same day, especially if he has had a conversation with his AA sponsor or his therapist, all of these minor irritations will have lost their sting. He will be terribly grateful to himself for having taken the pill which helped him preserve his sobriety so that he can work some more on his real problems. For, as one of the most respected speakers in Alcoholics Anonymous is fond of saying, *"Alcoholics don't have a drinking problem—they have a living problem."*

Antabuse: Pill Power for His Will Power

Ron, 38, an accountant, was 10 minutes early for his appointment. His firm handshake was moist. He frowned at my untidy desk. After stiffly waiting for me to sit down first, he came right to the point.

"Doctor, I need more will power so I can stop drinking."

"Are you sure you have a drinking problem?"

"Yes. I'm an alcoholic. I often drink more than I want to. It changes my personality, and makes me less efficient after lunch. Also," and this really seemed to bother him, "I embarrass my clients. My doctor agrees with my diagnosis."

He searched my face for clues. "Some mornings," he went on, "I can't recall exactly what I did or said the previous night. I can't stand to have any part of my life out of control."

Ron looked exasperated. I watched him line up the corner of my briefcase with the edge of my desk. His glasses were as highly polished as his speech; not a dangling participle anywhere. Clearly, he was an obsessive-compulsive personality type alcoholic with controlled anxiety, covert hostility, ambition, and secret doubts. He also had too much moral integrity, pride of accomplishment, will power, and a need to be perfect.

For many years he had successfully controlled these conflicting emotions by being punctual, proper, polite and superficially friendly, but in recent months, it took more and more alcohol to keep the facade from cracking. (Not hard-core boozing or even happy-hour socializing, but rather disciplined, self-medicating, civil kind of imbibing.)

Compulsive people also are sensitive, superconscientious workaholics. I probed gently. "I suppose it's only a question of time before your boss finds out?"

He gave me a stern look. He felt slandered. "My drinking has *never* affected my job. My boss already knows about it because I told him. It wouldn't be fair for me to hide it. What makes me drink is the fact that other people are so inefficient. They just don't do things right!"

To stimulate more insight, I said, "Overachieving perfectionists like you often get frustrated by people who are average or merely competent."

He seemed pleased. "That's it exactly! Some days I have to decide again and again to go without a drink; but it's hard—with so many screw-ups around."

Ron's character traits undoubtedly made him a good employee, but they also made him resistive to conventional therapy. He seemed to be reading my mind. "I've tried AA, group therapy, and the church. It's all too nonspecific, too inexact. But now I'm desperate. Is there anything you can do to increase my will power?"

Now was the time to close in, I sensed; this was about as close as this guy was going to get all day. "No," I said firmly, "there is nothing I can do. But there is something *you* can do. You can take Antabuse. It's a pill to increase your will."

His face fell. He saw me as just another screw-up. "I've heard about that pill. If you drink on it, you get sick and vomit. I don't need that. It's a chemical crutch. I . . . ."

"It beats the glass crutch you've been using," I countered sharply. "Antabuse puts you in control of your drinking urges. Every morning when you take the pill, you are in effect saying, 'I am going to will this pill into my body because it will help me not to drink today. I am in charge of this part of my treatment.

He was cautious, but listening. The word "control" had gotten his attention. "Ron, it is you, in effect, who is in charge of the Antabuse; I only write the prescription. Your will and determination administer the pill."

He was all ears. I pressed on. "With the help of this pill your decision to drink or not to drink has to be faced only once a day. Taking the pill frees your imagination, your brain power and your determination to work on your living problems, your AA program and your recovery in general. You'll learn more about changing your lifestyle as you get further away from drinking. Also, the pill prevents impulse drinking."

I could see that he was really pumping adrenaline. "Doctor, that's another reason I drink. Some mornings the kids are fighting, I get stuck in traffic, then my computer's down . . . Boy, on such days I can hardly wait till lunch to get a drink." His face lit up. "Hey, I just figured out something. With Antabuse in my gut, I won't be able to drink about all those screw-ups. Right?"

He looked better, but still bothered by something. "Doctor, in other words, I am not being treated for a weakness."

"On the contrary. If anything, you're too strong. You're too good for your own good. As you learn to control your drinking, the treatment sessions will lessen your need to manage the world."

He felt relieved. "Doctor, now that I have a way of controlling my drinking, the idea of therapy is beginning to make sense." His defenses seemed reinforced—but on a new track.

"I'll see you next week, Ron. Good luck with that pill for your will."

He was halfway out the door. "Doctor, to be exact, it's 'your pill power for my will power.' "

Ron was gone before I could reply. That's another thing about compulsives. They always like to have the last word.

Profile of a Recovering Alcoholic

"Exactly what is a recovering alcoholic?" I was challenged by the talk-show host. "How can you tell he is not just biding his time?"

The answer to this question is very simple. A recovering alcoholic is a person who no longer drinks alcohol in any form for any reason. Maybe for many years he was unable to live comfortably without alcohol, and he probably tried many "easier, softer ways." But then came the turning point. He finally experienced a lifestyle change, usually through treatment and self-help groups. As a result of his changed outlook, he now lives comfortable, happily, and productively without using alcohol. Also, he uses no other mood-altering drugs unless they're essential to his mental health and prescribed and monitored by a psychiatrist who understands addiction.

He—or she—has switched from booze (or pills) to people—without making sick substitutions. That means he has not substituted an eating disorder (obesity, bulimia, or anorexia) or compulsive gambling to cope with the ups and downs of everyday life; nor has he become a psychosomatic patient who is addicted to doctors, allergy medicines, physiotherapy, etc.

He no longer is angry toward the people who coerced him into treatment. On the contrary, he is grateful to them because they had the courage and the compassion to be honest with him. He no longer feels like a victim. He doesn't ask, "Why did God do this to me?" nor does he agonize over the cause ("Were the alcoholic genes on my father's side or on my mother's side?"). He doesn't scrutinize the daily papers to see whether a pill has been developed which would enable him to drink without getting drunk. (He now knows that he usually drank in order to get drunk, and that if such a pill were invented, he wouldn't take it.)

He no longer is ashamed of his alcoholism any more than he would be if he had diabetes. On the contrary, he is glad that he has an illness which forced him to become "weller than well." He can see that he is a better person today than he was even before his drinking became a noticeable problem. He has told his family, his friends and other significant people about it. True, he doesn't advertise it, and he doesn't pester other people with his abstinence; but he does share insights from his recovery freely, dispassionately, and optimistically when appropriate, or when it would help others.

If he is in psychotherapy (and he may well be, just as you or I might be), the focus is on "here and now" living problems; on how he can make his life better, more successful and serene by coming to understand how some of the past events in his life still cause him to behave in a maladaptive way today. Most importantly, his therapy is not aimed at "strengthening his defenses" so that he can become a controlled social drinker again.

Finally, his sense of humor has returned. He no longer takes himself or others too seriously. He has also learned the difference between being assertive or being aggressive. As a result he is no longer a doormat or a dictator.

Actually, it's easy to spot a recovering alcoholic when you see one. You will recognize him by his solid step, friendly smile, firm handshake, good eye contact, healthy self-concept, and an almost palpable inner peace which is seldom seen in other people.

Life of the Party—and Cold Sober

Most people don't know what to say or do in the presence of a recovering alcoholic. Even if they're nice people they're usually embarrassed because of the stigma and because they don't know what a recovering alcoholic is really like.

Bob and Mary had such a problem one night. They were going through last-minute preparations for their cocktail party. The guests would be arriving any minute now.

"Oh, my God," Mary said. "I just realized that Dick and Jane are coming to the party. Didn't Dick just come back from one of those alcoholic treatment farms?"

"Hey, you're right," Bob said. "What will we serve him? And what are we going to tell the other guests?"

"Let's just not say anything."

"What? I should just pretend I didn't notice he was gone from the office for six weeks?"

"Just say 'condolences,'" Mary snapped. Somehow that didn't sound like a good solution to either one of them, so Bob suggested, "Let's just quietly tell him he can only have beer."

"No," Mary said. "I heard somewhere that these kind of people definitely can't drink anything at all."

Bob was taken aback. "What do you mean, 'these kind of people?' Dick has always been a friend of ours. And he was such a nice guy, too."

Now it was Mary's turn to look surprised. "He might just still be a nice guy, you know. I think we're both acting crazy because we think it's going to be embarrassing."

"I got it," Bob said. "Let's tell him to just stick to the punch only."

"Not the way you spiked that punch—we *can't*," Mary chided. "And you better protect him from Harry Booze. Harry always gets tipsy and sooner or later does the lampshade-on-his-head dance. He probably won't like Dick anymore."

"And what about Dick's wife, Jane?" Bob wondered. "Poor Jane, maybe she had to quit drinking too for his sake."

"Oh, I don't know what we're gonna do." Mary was exasperated. "Quickly, mix a bowl of virgin punch."

"Too late! There's the doorbell."

"Oh, I give up," Mary groaned. "Let's just say, 'Dick, what would you like to drink?'"

Twenty minutes later they were both relieved when Dick ordered ginger ale. But later in the evening when Dick said he would like another ginger ale, Harry Booze stepped in front of him. "What do you mean, ginger ale—aren't you gonna have a real drink?"

"No, I'm not drinking today," Dick said calmly.

"Well, then have one for tomorrow—and one for yesterday. Ha, ha, ha, that will make it a double." Harry was sounding pretty jovial. A small circle of embarrassed guests was forming around them.

Dick realized that he would have to be more definite. Harry, like most drinking alcoholics, wasn't getting the message. "No thanks, Harry, I don't drink because I'm an alcoholic."

"What do you mean—you're an alcoholic?" Harry looked puzzled. "You don't look like a drunk to me."

"Oh, I'm not a drunk because I don't drink anymore."

"Oh, I get it. You are a reformed alcoholic."

"Oh, no! Orthodox, Harry."

By now people were getting more relaxed and laughing at Dick's sense of humor. But Harry was still struggling. "I knew an alcoholic once," Harry went on. "He drinks only wine nowadays. I guess that makes him an ex-alcoholic."

"Harry," Dick explained, "an ex-alcoholic is like an ex-virgin. I am a *recovering* alcoholic."

One of the ladies, sipping white wine, came to the rescue. "Dick, it sounds to me like you're describing an illness. I've heard of it as a form of allergy."

"Yes," Dick said pleasantly. "You might say that."

Harry's face lit up. "Hey, now you're talking, pardner. An allergy I can understand. I'm allergic myself. Penicillin allergy. When I take that stuff I have a reaction. I break out in spots. What happens to you?"

"The same thing," Dick said with a grin. "I too break out in spots. I break out in Chicago. I break out in Atlanta. Boy, during our last sales convention in Honolulu, I really broke out. But that was before I quit drinking."

Amid general laughter Harry was about to make his standard remark, "I'll drink to that," when their hostess Mary cut into the conversation. "Dick, you've just taught all of us a lesson. You can be a guest at our house any time. With your sense of humor, you're a real addition to the party. Also," with a meaningful glance at Harry, "you can drive the others home."

Dick raised his glass of ginger ale and said, "I always did drive the other guys home before. But now I would actually know where we're going."

Later that night after all the guests had left, John said, "Mary, the party was a success. I'm simply amazed at how well Dick handled the whole thing. He is a man of great charm and tact."

"He always was when he wasn't drinking," Mary pointed out.

"Yeah," Bob added, "and tonight even without booze he was still the life of the party. I guess from now on we'll know what to do about a recovering alcoholic. You just treat him like a person—just like anybody else."

Naltrexone—New Hope for Narcotic Addicts

Heroin and other opiate drug addiction has always been a difficult problem to treat. Methadone, the only drug available to clinicians, has not worked satisfactorily for a variety of reasons. Early this year the Food and Drug Administration approved a new drug which so far sounds very promising.

The drug is naltrexone. Marketed as Trexan, it is a synthetic, long-acting antagonist or blocking agent. What this means in plain English is that if an addict takes naltrexone and then takes heroin (or any other opiate drug), he will feel no effect no matter how large a dose of opiate he takes and regardless of the method of administration (needle, smoke, or swallow). Naltrexone continues to exert this blocking effect for up to 72 hours.

There are many advantages to this new drug. For example, naltrexone taken by itself has no mental or physical effect. It is not addicting and therefore the patient experiences no effect when the drug is discontinued; it can be given to anybody except those patients who are in liver failure or have acute hepatitis; and a week's supply costs less than $20.

Naltrexone seems to work best with patients for whom continued addiction would mean that they're going to lose their families, their jobs, or their freedom (jail). It seems especially effective with addicted executives or physicians. Of course, naltrexone is not a wonder drug, a complete answer or a painless solution to daily difficulties. Although it enables the addict to continue his work or career, he (or she) still has to work on changing his lifestyle and personality problems which were at one time alleviated by the use and abuse of narcotics.

A good example is Steve, a middle-aged dentist who was addicted to narcotics for three and a half years. He is now on naltrexone. "I look at the drug as insurance because I'm around drugs all day and I can write myself a prescription for a narcotic at any time. When I first went on naltrexone, I took the pill in the presence of my wife. For the first two weeks I encouraged her to look in my mouth and make sure that I had actually swallowed the pill because it made her feel more secure. Although my wife still considers naltrexone as a security blanket for herself, she has also learned in group therapy with me that she really has no control over me or anybody else."

And what has Steve learned in therapy? "I used to say, 'I'm just a dentist,' like some women say, 'I'm just a housewife.' It showed my low self-esteem. I now realize that I've always wanted to be a brain surgeon. I'm slowly becoming comfortable with what I am. I've also discovered that in a behavioral sense, I've been my wife's fourth child. And I'm learning not to let people walk all over me. Most of all, I've discovered there is more to life than getting high; and I'm proud because I'm able to accomplish a difficult thing like conquering an addiction."

Dear Doc...

Question: In a recent column you described alcoholism as an illness which forces the patient to become "weller than well." I find that hard to believe.

I have never heard of any other disease from which you can get that healthy. To me, a disease is something you are better off not to have, especially if it's alcoholism.

Answer: After successful treatment, and especially if he works the Twelve Steps of Alcoholics Anonymous, the recovering alcoholic no longer uses alcohol or other mood-altering drugs, becomes honest with himself (which reduces psychological stress), and changes his lifestyle (work, eating, exercise, hobbies, etc.) which also reduces living stress.

In that sense, recovery "forces" him to become a more ethical and healthier human being than he would have been had he not had alcoholism. That's what I mean by "weller than well."

To a lesser extent, the same thing applies to other diseases. Properly treated, a patient who had a mild heart attack, a "cancer scare" or similar experiences may change his lifestyle so dramatically that he is better off than he would have been without the illness.

Q: For years my husband was a bad drinker: drunk at parties, fights, embarrassments, not remembering things the next day, and abusive with me. But sometimes his drinking was a lot of fun for me, too.

When he stopped drinking for six months, I was delighted because I thought he had cured himself. I was happy for him when he started to drink socially again, but he was back to bad drinking in no time. I have always defended him against friends and family who thought he had alcoholism. What do you think?

A: His friends thought he had alcohol*ism*, and you thought he had alcohol*wasm*. It's clear now that your friends were right. The "ism" doesn't go away with a six-month ride on the water wagon. Talk to his family, his friends and his doctor and get some treatment for both of you.

Q: I am a recovering alcoholic two years sober. I heard of an alcoholic who shampooed his hair with an alcohol-containing product and absorbed enough alcohol through his scalp to "set him off" drinking again. Are alcohol-containing colognes, after-shave lotions, etc., dangerous? I use cologne and a skin toner daily. Both contain alcohol, but I feel no urge to return to drinking. What's your opinion?

A: Alcohol-containing shampoo, after-shave lotion, etc., are very dangerous—especially for alcoholics—if you drink them. As long as you use them the way they were intended to be used, there is no danger of being "set off" to drinking again.

Q: I heard about a study called the Rand Report that showed that alcoholics can drink again. Is that true?

A: Yes, alcoholics can drink again—and usually do. That's what makes alcoholism a relapsing, chronic illness. Clinical experience shows that alcoholics cannot drink again without causing problems for themselves or others. The only thing the Rand Report proved conclusively is that when alcoholics drink again they tend to get drunk again and end up worse than before. No sensible therapist in the field today recommends "controlled drinking" as a treatment goal for alcoholics. For most people, there is no easy way to handle a drinking problem. *As long as there are fat, alcoholic, bald doctors, you can be sure that there is no easy way to lose weight, control alcoholic drinking, or grow hair on a bald head.*

Q: My husband grudgingly stopped drinking but refuses to go to AA or spend his "hard-earned" money for treatment. He says he's doing it all on will power. His father was also an alcoholic.

In my Al-anon meetings they say I can't trust him until he goes to AA. Of course, I have kept my Al-anon meetings secret from him.

A: Changing the alcoholic way of life is not a matter of will power. Very few alcoholics can quit on their own and have serenity and meaning in their lives. Your husband sounds like a good man who is trying to do what most alcoholics try initially, which is to deal with shame and pain by denial and stubbornness.

Be honest. Tell him that you're in Al-anon. Admit that you also have an alcoholism problem (this is a family disease) and you are getting help for yourself. Lovingly, but firmly, insist that he now take a look at his part of your joint alcoholism problem by going with you for an evaluation to a treatment facility.

The "hard-earned" money line is just more denial. He has spent much more money on booze than treatment will ever cost. Without being insulting or challenging, offer to spend some of your part of the "hard-earned" money (you say you've been married 20 years) to explore treatment alternatives that include a variety of things other than AA. The outcome of this kind of discussion will tell you both whether your husband really objects to AA and to spending money or whether he still refuses to admit that he has a problem.

Q: My husband says he doesn't have an alcohol problem because he can take it or leave it. Although he sometimes doesn't drink for weeks or months, he doesn't seem to know how to stop drinking at social events. When there is beer, liquor and people, he drinks until he can't walk straight and his speech is slurred. He looks foolish and acts foolish. He often passes out in bed fully clothed and doesn't remember events the next day. Of course, I'm embarrassed and humiliated.

A: Your husband has chronic alcoholism with loss of control over his drinking, overdosing (getting drunk), inappropriate behavior, blackouts and severe denial.

Another problem he has is a loving, but destructive co-alcoholic—and that is you. You are lovingly helping him and protecting him, but at the same time you are "enabling" him to get sicker by going along with him with his style of drinking, and by enduring (and containing) your embarrassment and humiliation. (I hope that between his slurred speech at parties and passing out in bed at home, you don't also "enable" him by letting him drive you home.)

There are several things you must do. Tell him you will no longer go to parties with him until he gets help for his drinking. Offer to go with him for the evaluation. Start going to Al-anon, and tell him you did so. Talk to a trusted friend or family member about his problem to give you assurance that you are on the right track. Most of all, remember that if he could drink like other people, he would. He needs help so he can stop.

Q: What's the difference between an alcohol abuser and an alcoholic? Is the treatment any different? My 24-year-old brother-in-law is an "alcohol abuser." He doesn't drink every day, but when he does, he doesn't know how or when to stop.

A: The term "alcohol abuser" is something applied to a person who gets drunk about six or eight times a year but seems to control his drinking the rest of the time. Many such abusers can change their way of drinking through AA, counseling, or as a result of a family confrontation.

Your brother-in-law is not an alcohol abuser. When you don't know how to stop drinking once you've started, that's called loss of control. It is a cardinal sign of alcoholism. For him, the most effective treatment is approximately four weeks of in-patient rehabilitation combined with after care and AA attendance for at least two or three years.

Q: My husband has been drinking for more than 40 years. Since I'm going to Al-anon, I've been giving him articles about alcoholism to read. He finally quit "cold turkey" six months ago.

Now he tells me that he feels depressed about everything. Could it be he is depressed because the alcohol is no longer in his body?

A: Unless your husband still is drinking occasionally, the alcohol has been out of his system for some time. Most likely he feels depressed because he misses one of the best friends he ever had— namely, alcohol. It sounds also as if he didn't replace the alcohol with anything else.

There probably are AA meetings that run concurrently with your Al-anon meetings. Offer to go with him to some open meetings to introduce him to the ways and ideas of AA fellowship. Also, get into outpatient treatment with him as a couple.

If all this doesn't help, have him see a psychiatrist who knows how to treat alcoholic patients without prescribing tranquilizers. Continued depression and covert anger and loneliness eventually lead back to the bottle. Famous last words for many an alcoholic are: "If I feel this bad without drinking—I might as well be drinking."

Q: I heard you speak on a lecture tour. You said that recovering alcoholics often live longer than other people. Can you elaborate on how this might happen?

A: Specifically, I said that recovering alcoholics live longer than drinking alcoholics, including binge drinkers or intermittently abusive drinkers. The main reason is that they no longer damage their health through alcohol.

Equally important is the fact that through education and rehabilitation, the quality of their lifestyle improves. Heavy drinking impairs the drinker's judgment, which in turn impairs behavior, which in turn leads to neglect of the drinker's health in general. Specifically, the heavy drinker sleeps poorly, eats improperly, works in frenzied spurts (to make up for previous foul-ups), and doesn't do any exercise because of hangovers, weakness, weight loss or just plain lack of interest.

In the words of Oliver Wendell Holmes, a good formula for longevity is "Have a chronic disease and take care of it." That's why recovering alcoholics live longer. They become weller than well.

Q: I am a recovering alcoholic and drug addict. In the past I used Quaaludes at times because I needed something to help me come down when I got too wired.

What bugs me is that I am doing pretty good now, but my employer wants me to have urine tests once in a while to prove that I am not using again. And my parents agree with that idea. Why can't they trust me and believe me?

A: Look upon your employer's attitude as a sign that he really wants to help you. (Unless you have a very unique skill, it would be much simpler for him to let you go and hire somebody else.) Also, having occasional tests will help you to stay clean and sober.

A characteristic feature of the addict's lifestyle is that he becomes dishonest about his drug use and about the things he does (stealing, sneaking, etc.) to get more drugs or alcohol.

I am sure that before you had treatment, you often told people that you were not using—when in fact you were. Once you have this disease, the best way to convince others that you are clean is to show them—instead of tell them.

Q: I am 42 years old. Although I'm now 10 years sober and reasonably happy, the first five years of my sobriety were a difficult struggle with self-doubts, craving, depression and occasional flirtation with the idea that I may not be an alcoholic after all.

What puzzles me today is how different the process of recovery has been for a friend of mine. She is also 10 years sober but she had no trouble staying that way from her first day on. The only difference between us that I can see is that while I hit a number of so-called bottoms (financial trouble, losing a job, and two divorces), she hit only one bottom: She tried to commit suicide, but was found accidentally by total strangers who took her to a hospital.

Is there a rational explanation for the trouble-free sobriety she seems to have had ever since?

A: The answer to your very intriguing question came to me about 10 years ago when I reviewed the case histories of a number of patients whom I had treated. Several of the patients had smooth recoveries with no craving, slips or depression, much like your friend has. They also had in common a reasonably benign alcoholic history, as "bottoms" go.

But in every case, the final bottom was a singular devastating, almost fatal event. These patients were men and women who in connection with a drinking or drug-using episode had somehow survived an almost fatal extent of third-degree burns, shot themselves through the brain and somehow didn't die, were cut down after they had hanged themselves, or—especially those who were public figures or persons with high moral and ethical values—suffered a crushing, scandalizing, public humiliation.

In the course of their therapy with me these patients repeatedly used expressions such as, "I now feel that I've paid for everything I've done," "I feel the world is now even with me," "I think I've been to hell already and life has to be heaven from now on," or "God must be saving me for something better."

Other thought associations and parts of their histories suggested that they finally considered the reckoning to be complete, that they had tried their best to pay all they owed society, and that they were finally at peace with the world and their Creator.

This course of events also makes sense in accordance with psychoanalytic thinking, which says that alcoholism and other addictions are a chronic form of suicide, a form of self-punishment and atonement.

Q: After reading some of your columns, I have come to the conclusion that I am an alcoholic. Even though I still have a good job and jog every day, I can no longer deny that I should stop drinking.

I am alarmed by your statement that all the good hospital treatment programs seem to use Alcoholics Anonymous. I keep getting bogged down by the fact that I'm not a religious person. I am not immoral, but I am not openly religious either. I am uncomfortable with what I perceive to be the religious aspects of AA.

A: AA is not a religious program. It is a spiritual program of recovery. The 12 Steps that are the basis of the AA program are guidelines for living; and the only references to God are, "A Power greater than ourselves," and, "God as I understand Him."

In addition to AA, rehabilitation programs in hospital-based facilities involve group therapy, individual counseling and physical exercise, as well as education on nutrition, physiology, family relationships, and a number of other things. The total aim of rehabilitation is not to make you religious, but to help you achieve comfortable abstinence and a change in lifestyle.

Q: With my alcoholic husband, I'm living on a roller-coaster of highs and lows. He goes to AA meetings weekly but without enthusiasm. He also keeps drinking off and on. He refuses to go for treatment in a hospital because it "costs too much" and because "it takes too much time." Just what is next?

Could other counseling help? I may be near the "ultimatum stage" in our marriage; but this is my second marriage, and I don't want to get a divorce again.

A: AA helps many people, but, unfortunately, not all. Your husband is slipping and sliding. He should have an AA sponsor, he should attend 90 meetings in 90 days, and he should not drink alcohol. If he can't do that, he needs more intensive help.

Here are some options. He can take Antabuse prescribed by a doctor; it will help him to not drink while he gets a sponsor and becomes more active in the AA program. You can also both enroll for joint therapy in an out-patient program for joint therapy.

If these steps don't seem to work, then you will have to insist that he goes into an in-patient program for treatment. Time and cost factors don't make sense. If he keeps doing what he's doing now, you will both spend more money and time over the years—if he lives long enough—than you will in one intensive period of hospitalization.

If none of these is acceptable, then you really are at the "ultimatum stage." You will then have to decide whether you are going to continue to go on like this, or whether you are going to act firmly in your best interests and his.

Q: I have some of the symptoms your columns describe, but I'm afraid to go to AA. I've had a very genteel upbringing, and I'm very sensitive. I fear that the people in the AA system might convince me that I am an alcoholic—when there is a possibility that I'm really not.

A: Stop hesitating and start going to AA at once. Get yourself an AA sponsor who can help you understand the program and guide you, and at the same time, protect you and help you grow at your own pace.

As far as the people in AA mistakenly convincing you that you are an alcoholic—forget it! Even AA can't make a social drinker into an alcoholic. Unfortunately, they can't do the opposite, either.

Q: I am a recovering alcoholic. I've been sober for five years, but my nose still looks the way it did when I was drinking. Sometimes it's an embarrassment to me. Is there anything that can be done?

A: You did not describe the appearance of your nose in any way so I have to make some assumptions. You have one of several conditions. One such problem common in alcoholics is Rhinophyma, which is a hyperplasia (overdevelopment) of the sebaceous glands and thickening of the skin. Some dermatologists use electric cautery to shave off the thickness and restore the nose to normal.

There is another condition which is called acne rosacea. It consists essentially of acne-like pockmarks or even active acne over the area of the nose. It can be treated by dermatologists through the use of antibiotics or with antibiotic ointment applied directly. Finally, you may have prominently dilated, very noticeable blood vessels, often referred to as blue nose. For this, some plastic surgeons or dermatologists use desiccation through electric cautery.

In any case, you have a purely cosmetic problem which, although it occurs in many alcoholics, also occurs in people who have never had an alcohol problem. Any surgery or corrective measure will be strictly cosmetic and will mean nothing else.

Q: For 30 years I was so busy complaining about my alcoholic husband's drinking that I overlooked my own drinking which had become abnormal. I finally "consented" to go to Al-anon to learn about "his problem." Through the love, support, help and mild confrontation I had in Al-anon, I finally realized that I was in the wrong place. I joined AA. I am now a recovering alcoholic in my own right. I hope some readers who are in the same bind as I was will find this helpful.

A: A number of alcoholics find their way into AA through the "back door" as you did from Al-anon. In my practice about 30 percent of the spouses of alcoholics have a problem of their own with alcohol, drugs, food abuse, or doctor abuse (psychosomatic illness). You and your husband should attend AA meetings and Al-anon meetings (in a three-to-one ratio) because each of you is living with an alcoholic.

Q: Last week a friend of ours entered rehabilitation on his own initiative. How should we treat him when he returns? Do we hide all the alcohol in our house? Do we offer him a non-alcoholic beverage? Do we not drink at all when he's around?

We hope he will come to realize why he became an alcoholic, but how will we know when he's ready to talk about it? Should we avoid the subject? We would like your advice because we want to keep him as a friend.

A: Alcoholism is a treatable disease. Treat your friend accordingly, just as if he had diabetes or ulcers. Don't hide the alcohol in your house. When he is your guest, ask him what he would like to drink. Like any good host, you should have a variety of non-alcoholic beverages such as juices, soft drinks, coffee, etc., openly available. If you yourself choose to drink alcohol for social reasons, then you should not change your behavior because he is around.

The worst thing you can do is pretend that you don't know that he was gone, or why. That would be treating him as a non-person. He may never learn "why he became an alcoholic" (very few people ever do, and it is not important anyway); but he may well want to talk to you about his treatment. How will you know whether he is ready to talk about it, or what he prefers? Ask him, just as you would as if he were returning from a heart operation. If he refuses to talk about it, or if he wants to keep it a secret, that's his prerogative, although in the long run, it's not a good sign.

Q: Our 30-year-old son still lives with us at home. After years of pleading with him, he finally admitted himself to an alcoholism hospital for treatment. My husband and I were dismayed when the boy showed up at our doorstep three days later. He had left the hospital when he found out that his counselor is not a recovering alcoholic. He said it proves that they didn't know what they were doing because modern hospitals have only recovering alcoholic counselors. He also said the counselors did not want to speak to us because our son is over 21.

How can we find out whether this is really a good hospital? My husband and I are paying for the treatment.

A: Modern alcoholism hospitals employ counselors who have had special training in counseling techniques and are credentialed by state certification boards.

The treatment approach in such hospitals is based on the idea that alcoholism is a family disease. In the case of a 30-year-old who still lives at home, I can assure that the counselors would definitely want to talk to the parents.

Here are some possible answers. Your son is a typical, untreated alcoholic (immature, manipulative, scared, rationalizing and full of denial); or he is a conscienceless sociopath who will tell you anything to get you off his back so he can continue to be the way he is.

As for the quality of the hospital, you may be dealing with a modern hospital, or the hospital may actually be an antiquated drying-out farm. To find out whether the hospital is a good one, talk to the administrator yourself. After all, you're paying the bill.

Q: Although I spent three weeks in alcoholic rehabilitation recently, I could never admit that I was alcoholic. My wife and daughter both say that I am an alcoholic because I drink 10 or more cans of beer every day. I never missed work because of drinking. I admit I had many hangovers, but I always got over them.

While I was in treatment, I saw many films and heard many talks, but all the information we got was mental talks instead of telling us what real damage alcohol can do to the human body. I think more films should deal with what alcohol can do to the human body and forget these mental attempts at changing people. I personally think they don't work.

A: Most alcoholic rehabilitation centers strongly emphasize what you call the mental attempts to get through to the patient. The reason they do that is that alcoholics need a change in attitude and lifestyle. You see, most of them already know that alcohol damages their body, but the knowledge has not enabled them to stop drinking.

If you are an exception—and there are exceptions—the problem can be easily rectified. You and your wife and your daughter should go back to the treatment center and have the doctor there explain to all three of you briefly what the effects of 10 cans of beer daily are on body organs. Even the most liberal experts in the field of addiction don't recommend more than three drinks per day for anybody. At the same time, you can review with your doctor the blood tests and other examination results that are still in your chart. If after that, you return to drinking again, you are just an ordinary alcoholic and you will have to give the mental talks a fair hearing.

Q: What happens to the blood pressure when a problem drinker goes through rehabilitation? Recently, I was dried out in another part of the country and I am reluctant to tell my doctor that I don't need blood pressure medicine anymore.

A: Blood pressure is almost always high when alcoholics enter detoxification. Within one or two weeks it goes down to normal. Ninety percent of all patients are discharged three weeks later and no longer need anti-hypertensive drugs or even diuretics. Now that you have a new lifestyle tell your doctor the truth. He will understand. And if he doesn't understand, get a new doctor.

Q: My son is going into alcoholic rehabilitation by a court order. He has a history of getting infections, allergies and cold sores. I'm worried about what will happen to him. He is certainly not an alcoholic.

A: Don't worry. The doctors in the treatment center will deal with your son's medical problems. As for being there on a court order, your son has the same chance for complete recovery that voluntary patients do. If anything, the court order will discourage him from signing himself out before treatment is completed.

My biggest concern is you. Why do you think a judge or a court would order your son into treatment if he didn't have a drinking problem? Maybe, as a "good mother" you are consciously denying your son's illness. Try Al-anon. Also, talk to the treatment staff to help you understand his illness and your tendency to be overprotective. If he is old enough to have a drinking problem, he shouldn't need you to intercede with doctors.

Q: Last week a friend of mine who is a recovering alcoholic took me to an Alcoholics Anonymous meeting. When we first walked in, I felt strange. It wasn't what I expected. I was impressed by the high caliber of people who were at the meeting and by the politeness, the pleasant conversation and the warm friendships that many of them seemed to have for each other.

The speeches were also interesting. I even enjoyed it and learned some things. But there was one thing I did not understand—and I was too embarrassed to ask my friend about it. My question is why did several speakers refer to themselves as "grateful" recovering alcoholics? How can anyone be grateful to have that terrible disease?

A: Many alcoholics call themselves "grateful recovering alcoholics" because they feel that through their recovery from alcoholism they became better persons than they would be today had they not become alcoholic. They not only gained their freedom from alcohol, they also discovered a new spiritual meaning to life. As a result, their life is improved in all areas including relationships to family and friends, the quality of their work, and their attitude toward life's obligations in general.

When social drinkers or problem drinkers hear about a recovering alcoholic, they tend to unduly focus on the abstinence part of the recovery program. As they see it, recovery is a program of *losing* something, of giving something up, namely the right to continue drinking alcohol. Recovering alcoholics, on the other hand, focus on the things they *gained* through recovery, namely, a life enriched in areas in which they formerly didn't even know they had problems.

Q: For about seven years I tried to recover from alcoholism on my own. All of my friends in AA were supportive and accepting. But there were some who kept telling me to "put the plug in the jug." These same people were generally disparaging of hospital treatment programs.

Three months ago my children finally put me into an alcoholism hospital. The care, understanding and education I found there were just great. As part of the treatment program, the staff skillfully introduced me to the principles of Alcoholics Anonymous.

I now feel that although not everyone needs a treatment program, I did. I am also becoming aware that there are a number of people in my AA group—the same group in which I was "white-knuc-kling" it—who wish they had gone through a treatment program themselves. They seem to know that treatment makes sobriety much easier. I hope you can print this letter to admonish some of the hard-liners in AA.

A: It is not the purpose of this column to "admonish" anybody about anything. However, I'm glad to print your letter as an education tool. Even though I'm not an alcoholic myself, I've been to many AA meetings in the past 20 years. I see a definite rise in the number of people in the AA fellowship who know—either from their own experience or from the experience of others—that sobriety seems to come easier with treatment.

Regardless of philosophic considerations, as a clinician I have no doubt at all about the following: anybody who is "slipping and sliding" for five years should have been given a shot at treatment at least four years before now. Treatment is not an "easier, softer way." But it is faster and safer because in addition to saving time, treatment helps to preserve marriages, health and job.

Q: I have been going to Al-anon for three years. Their philosophy contradicts your idea of intervention. They say "live and let live," "detach," and let my husband hit bottom by himself.

When I read your column, I feel guilty for not doing anything. But when I go to Al-anon, I feel I'm doing the right thing. Should I try to intervene? I am confused and need an uncomplicated answer.

A: Al-anon came about as an answer to the frustrations of people like yourself. However, waiting for an alcoholic to "hit bottom" is an antiquated idea. Go to Al-anon for support, clarification and personal growth; and go to an alcohol rehab center for help on how to do an intervention. Intervention at an early stage of the alcoholic's disease is the best answer. More and more AA and Al-anon groups are accepting this idea.

Q: My husband died a year ago of cirrhosis. He was 35. For years I was concerned about his drinking, but neither of us realized that he had a disease until it was too late.

Now I want desperately to know what causes somebody to drink like that. Was I such a bad wife that he drank because of me? Could I be responsible for his death?

A: Nobody can make anybody else into an alcoholic, but it's easier for me to say it than it is for you to believe it. You need a brief period of intensive outpatient counseling in an alcohol center to teach you about this disease. Yes, you played a role in his alcoholism, but it was not a causative role. Outpatient counseling and Al-anon meetings will help you to work through your grief, give up your guilt, and accept yourself.

Q: For years my mother has complained to me about my father's alcoholism. Although I live in another state, I'm always the middle person. I have given her the phone numbers of counselors, treatment centers and Al-anon. While visiting, I have offered to go with her to Al-anon. I have even suggested that she leave him if he refuses to deal with the problem, but she always has an excuse. Meanwhile, my father never complains about anything as long as he has his bottle.

I am sad for their misery, but I am now unsympathetic because they won't do anything. When I tell this to my mother, she cries and says, "I can't discuss anything with you!" When I am very specific in my advice, she says that's something *they* have to work out themselves. When she cries, I feel guilty because I've run out of patience. Is there anything I can do?

A: Your father will not do anything as long as his co-alcoholic (your mother) enables him to stay the way he is; and your mother will not do anything as long as her co-alcoholic (namely, *you*) enables her to stay the way she is. He has his bottle, and she has you, and you have your pain.

Here is what you can do: (1) Tell your mother "I love you, but I won't talk to you anymore about Dad's drinking unless a concrete change has been made." (2) Go to Al-anon yourself because you are suffering the consequences of your father's alcoholism and you need the support and growth.

Q: My boyfriend doesn't drink. He has been in Alcoholics Anonymous for five years. Living with him used to bug me because he is a perfectionist. Sometimes I couldn't understand why I loved him. Much of the time I was nervous because I had a fear that he might drink again. I finally decided that maybe my fear had to do with my father's drinking. My father was an alcoholic who never did stop drinking.

I read a number of your columns and gave this matter a great deal of thought. I finally decided to go to Al-anon, hoping that maybe I could live with more peace of mind. (Actually, my primary reason for going to Al-anon was that I felt that my boyfriend was just "too special" for me to let him slip away.)

Al-anon has helped me a lot and I now live more comfortably. I now understand that my problem of being nervous around my boyfriend really had to do with my family drinking background (my father's drinking had all of us scared and worrying) and not with the fact that my boyfriend is a perfectionist. I thought this information might help other people whose letters I read in your column all the time.

A: It is quite common for a person from an alcoholic family to become emotionally attached to another alcoholic later in life. I'm glad that you found Al-anon helpful. You may find additional help and education by looking into a relatively new self-help fellowship, groups of which are springing up all over the country. It is called "Adult Children of Alcoholics" and is very helpful for people who, although they are not alcoholic or living with an actively drinking alcoholic, nevertheless continue to have problems with the whole idea of other people's drinking.

Many such people find it difficult to get along comfortably in a society where drinking is the norm for many people. For information on this group, call the Al-anon office or the National Council on Alcoholism in your area.

Q: My boyfriend is attending a drunk-driving educational program. He takes Antabuse, which is supposed to make him unable to drink. For some time now I have been suspicious that he was drinking alcohol again even though I watch him take the Antabuse pill. Yesterday I caught him sneaking a drink. I challenged him about it, and he admitted it. How could he be drinking without getting sick? Anyway, what good are these pills if they don't cure his alcoholism?

A: A person who drinks on top of Antabuse will only get sick if there is enough Antabuse in his system. Your boyfriend could be skipping every other dose. He may have substituted aspirin pills to fool you, he could have gotten some pills which will counteract Antabuse effects, or he could be drinking just barely enough to be able to endure the unpleasant reaction, especially if he has very little Antabuse in his system.

Although Antabuse is an excellent drug, it doesn't "cure" alcoholism. If your boyfriend has not made up his mind to want to stop drinking, then he won't benefit from Antabuse because he will continue to find ways of fooling himself and those who are watching him.

In any case, your boyfriend is a very sick alcoholic because he is willing to endure the discomfort which comes from having some Antabuse in his system, or he is willing to cheat himself and lie to you in order to be able to keep on drinking. It is therefore clear that he needs intensive inpatient treatment.

You need to re-evaluate whether you want to keep this boyfriend. He might be an immature character who enjoys playing "catch me if you can."

Q: I am 14 years old. My big brother takes Antabuse because he had a drinking problem. Twice now I have seen him drink beer during Little League games. His face gets as red as a beet, then he goes behind the stands and throws up. When I told him I saw it, he said he can do it because he is a tough man with a strong constitution. Should I tell my father?

A: You sound as though you love your big brother and you are worried about him. The best way for you to show your love would be to tell your father in the presence of your brother. Your brother has emotional addiction to alcohol and also has false ideas about what a real man is. You might just be the one who can help your parents get your brother into a treatment program.

Q: My wife is a professional person. She is very smart but she's also an alcoholic. She has quit drinking more than a dozen times for periods lasting from a week to months, but she has always relapsed. The problem is that she will not accept help. She says she can only quit on her own.

Can I give her Antabuse without her knowing that she is taking it? For example, could I mix it into her food or slip it into her drinks? I would only do it when she is on a dry spell, anyway. In that way maybe I could gradually extend her periods of sobriety.

A: Slipping somebody Antabuse without their knowledge is technically not feasible because Antabuse is not available in liquid form, and the pill could not possibly be mixed into a drink without it being detectable. More importantly, it would not lead to recovery. Your wife would be intermittently throwing up without knowing what's happening to her. Also, Antabuse is a prescription drug and no physician would prescribe it for you under those circumstances.

Q: Our 23-year-old son is a heroin addict. After much heartbreak and shame, we have finally accepted it. He has done well in a methadone clinic for the last three months. Now he wants to drop out of the clinic because in addition to the methadone, the doctors want him to take Antabuse. That would deprive him of drinking any kind of alcohol.

We are an upper middle class family. Drinking has always been important in our lives because it is a nice social custom. We don't even think our son is an alcoholic. We have not seen him drunk very often, and he says he has no drinking problem. However, my husband points out that our son lives alone. Also, even though our son is a nice boy, he has many times in the past played on our sympathies by being less than truthful. He thinks our son should take the Antabuse and stay in the program. What's the right course of action?

A: Go with your husband's intuition. Since your son lives alone and has played on your sympathies by being "less than truthful many times," you don't really know your son's present drinking habits. On the other hand, the doctors at the methadone clinic see him regularly. They have also probably done some chemical testing that would show that his drinking is out of control. Also, more and more methadone programs prescribe Antabuse to their clients because they are learning that up to 35 percent of their clients—while on methadone—become severe alcoholics. Hence, the need for Antabuse.

The tone of your letter suggests that you are very much ashamed that your son is an addict and that you don't want to "deprive" him of the "nice social custom of drinking." For addicts, drinking is not a nice social custom—it is a potentially fatal behavior. Because you are fine, loving parents, you should go to Al-anon and learn more about this fatal illness so that you can stop killing your son with kindness.

Q: Exactly what drugs are made effective by Naltrexone? Does it include pot, speed, and cocaine?

A: Naltrexone is an opioid antagonist. It blocks only morphine–like (opioid) drugs. Among them are morphine, Demerol, heroin, Dilaudid, Hycodan, Percodan, codeine, Darvon and Talwin. It has no effect on speed (amphetamines), barbiturates, marijuana, cocaine, or alcohol.

I can imagine no greater satisfaction for a person, in looking back on his life and work, than to have been able to give some people, however few, a feeling of genuine pride in belonging to the human species and, beyond that, a zestful yen to justify that pride.

Human Options
Norman Cousins

7

Where Do We Go from Here?

Where do we go from here? Let's go back to the beginnings—
the very beginnings. Genes, endorphins, and enzymes as possible
causes of chemical dependency are beyond us for the moment,
but we can take a look at what's possible for us to do in our
personal lives to prevent drinking and drug abuse in the future.
For long-term prevention we have to address the fundamental
question—what do we teach our children?

Whatever Happened to Baby Jane?

Many of my patients, I found as I got to know them, experienced
getting high even before they were born because alcohol and
drugs flow easily through the placenta. Every time Pregnant Jane
takes a fix—so does Baby Jane in her uterus; whenever Lady Jane
is loaded, so is Fetus Jane. In that sense a pregnant woman never
drinks alone.

Nobody knows for sure what happens to the future baby
when, in the first trimester, drugs flow into the embryo's intra-
cranial mass of fatty jelly, that glob of stuff which is slowly
evolving and convoluting and blossoming and flowering into what
will soon become the infant's brain. What neural pathways,
memory codes, storage capacities, predispositions, and neurochemical idiosyncracies are being programmed? It's awesome!

Well, we do not know what happens in the first trimester, but we do know what happens from the fourth month on: every time momma gets loaded—the baby is zonked. Fetus Jane gets slowly addicted because every day she has a high drug concentration in her blood which she gets from her turned-on mom. Lady Jane and Fetus Jane are drinking buddies, served by the same bartender. And when Lady Jane enters the hospital for labor and delivery, they both get their fix from the same bartender, namely the good doctor. The needles, pills, and anesthetics that momma gets are shared with Fetus Jane.

When the cord is cut, Mother Jane is still okay because she continues to get capsules for sleep, pills for nerves, and shots for pain. (Unbelievably, in certain "modern" hospitals she even gets red wine with her meals to "build up her blood," and her health insurance pays for it to boot!)

Meanwhile back in the nursery, Infant Jane goes "cold turkey," because when the cord was cut, so was her drug supply. That's why she has withdrawal symptoms: irritability, shivers, cramps, or even convulsions. Depending on how alert, well-trained, or hung-over the nurse is, Infant Jane may be diagnosed as nervous, irritable, colicky, or normal. (It may not be evident for months that Infant Jane has Fetal Alcohol Syndrome; and it may be a couple of years before Little Jane is diagnosed as hyperactive, a slow learner, troubled by right-left confusion, handicapped with subnormal intelligence, etc.)

In any case, when Baby Jane gets home from the hospital, she has in effect been "dried out" and goes on the wagon.

More Data on Pregnant Women and Drinking

A recent statement by the surgeon general of the United States recommends that pregnant women should drink no alcoholic beverages because there is increasing evidence that women who drink heavily during pregnancy tend to have babies that manifest Fetal Alcohol Syndrome.

According to a very comprehensive review in the *Journal of the American Medical Association,* such problems range from miscarriage, premature labor and bleeding complications during pregnancy to infants who have low birth weight, small size, structural defects such as facial abnormalities and malformations of various organ systems, including cardiac, urogenital, and skeletal.

The most common central nervous system dysfunctions are mental retardation, irritability, poor motor coordination, learning disability, behavior problems, and hyperactivity in childhood.

When I've said on past occasions that for pregnant women "no drinking is the only safe course," I've received a variety of responses. The most disturbing ones came from physicians who felt that such advice "might be well and good, but patients don't generally want that kind of an answer." The physicians cited a variety of patients' responses such as "my husband won't like that at all."

Some angry lay people have responded by pointing out to me that "there is not enough hard evidence" for the kind of alarmist reaction I was manifesting. Lastly, people in the liquor industry cautioned me verbally and in writing that "two drinks a day is a safe limit."

Well, now that we have the surgeon general's report, the issue should be settled, but is it? I think not.

The fact that people still react with controversy at all is indicative of our national preoccupation with drinking. We seem to think that drinking alcohol is not only a custom, or even a social norm, but that it is actually a necessity, like health care or television. This was shown graphically several years ago in a press conference when Fetal Alcohol Syndrome was first announced to the nation.

A panel of experts from the field of addiction was answering questions for the media. A number of good questions were asked, but one reporter in the press gallery repeatedly asked the same question in different ways: "Just how much can a pregnant woman drink without harming the fetus?"

The panelists answered his question several times. When the same reporter asked his question again, one of the panelists, slightly irritated, said: "Asking the same question over and over won't change the facts. Until further scientific research proves otherwise—the only absolutely safe amount is zero drinking during pregnancy."

Apparently the finality of the answer really angered the reporter. "Now you listen to me!" he practically shouted. "I know you are scientists, but you are not exact enough for me. My point is this: My wife is four months pregnant. Today is our wedding anniversary. In the trunk of my car I have a bottle of vintage wine. I was on my way home to celebrate our anniversary and drink that wine.

"And unless you 'scientists,'" he added with a sneer, "come up with some real evidence that makes sense, my wife and I are going to drink that wine tonight!" With this, he hastily gathered his notes and stormed out of the room.

The audience and the panel were stunned. Was this reporter's outburst an indication of a national attitudinal norm? Was he really saying, "Alcohol is so important in our lives that you can't expect a woman to go on the wagon for nine months on the mere chance that if she didn't it *might* harm her baby!"

Regardless of how we feel about the reporter's remarks, the surgeon general's statement is clear, and the AMA *Journal* article backs it up: drinking when you're pregnant is not worth the risk. Also, if you want your baby to have the right to make his own choice about drinking, then abstaining is the only choice for you, because everything you drink goes through the placenta. Remember, as I said earlier, a pregnant woman never drinks alone.

One last importatnt point must be made. Heavy drinking for any woman of child-bearing age is not a good idea because the most vulnerable time for fetal damage is in the first two months of pregnancy. By the time a woman is sure that she is pregnant (sometimes six weeks), the damage may already be done.

Baby Jane Becomes Teenage Jane

If you'll remember, we left Baby Jane as she was dried out and just home from the hospital. Let's say that for fifteen years she stays on the wagon. Then one day—maybe after a high school football game—Baby Jane (now Teenage Jane) tastes booze and gets drunk for the first time in her life.

Actually, Teenage Jane is not drunk for the first time in her life; she was drunk every day for nine intrauterine months fifteen years ago. Neurochemically speaking, she may be a dry alcoholic who after fifteen years of abstinence, fell off the wagon. For example, she may drink a whole six-pack (indicative of her tolerance), enjoy it, drive the others home, and want to go drinking again as soon as possible. Then, perhaps, she becomes one of those "instant alcoholics" who, at age 30—after fifteen years of unsuccessful social drinking—tells her AA group that she is a "born alcoholic."

Let's make another speculation. Let's assume that Teenage Jane got drunk and made a fool of herself. Therefore, she makes the reasonable decision that "if alcohol does this to me, I will just never drink again." Well, that's easier said than done if Teenage Jane lives in a world where drinking and drugging are portrayed on stage, screen, and billboard as something all winners do, part of the beautiful life, as a sign that you are making it. One nationally run magazine ad says, "Of course it's possible to live without Chivas Regal. The question is, How well?" In a society with that attitude toward alcohol, it will be extremely difficult for her to do anything other than fulfill her biochemical prenatal destiny.

Teenagers Today on a Chemical Treadmill

Regardless of a legacy to drink—or not to drink—inherited from parents, growing up today is rough, not because of the stresses of modern society, but because it is acceptable for adolescents to use alcohol or other drugs to modify or escape those stresses. The danger is that what begins as a temporary cure for a temporary problem eventually becomes a disease that destroys the person's chances for a successful life. It happens because doping the brain interferes with learning, which in the adolescent happens precisely during the time when he is trying to learn how to live.

Here is a clinical example. One night at a party, 14-year-old Susie is practicing her living skills. That means that she is learning how to flirt, how to talk teenage talk and how to look casual, while at the same time keeping her better profile turned in the right direction. (While this description is a bit tongue-in-cheek, don't get me wrong. These are necessary exercises in socialization skills.)

All of a sudden Susie sees Tom, the broad-shouldered, senior class football hero, flashing a smile from across the room.

Susie is frightened by her reaction. She feels a tingle in her groin, and her heart is pounding in her throat. And now, she thinks, "Oh my God—it looks like he is actually starting to walk over toward me!"

Just then, the friend she's been talking to says, "Here, lemme pour some bourbon in your coke and put out that cancer stick! Try some pot." And Susie does.

So, later when Tom actually does talk to her, Susie's panic is gone because her brain is different now. It's drugged, and therefore everything else is easier to handle.

With repeated use, she learns that alcohol, pot, and similar drugs give her psychological protection. Like a brain barrier, they screen out the hassles of parents, teachers, and coaches; they soften the pressures of homework, boredom, and sexual tension; and they take the sting out of mothers who nag about your messy room, fathers who ignore you—or yell at you—and boys who want to go all the way.

During the next few years, Susie tunes out stresses. But stress is also a stimulus for emotional growth, which means that whenever she tunes out stress, she also tunes out opportunities for becoming a mature adult. She is, in effect, taking a look at life and saying, "You want me to keep my room clean, be in school on time, keep my promises most of the time, balance my checkbook, shine my shoes, have a haircut occasionally and keep a part-time job? Too much. I'll drop out. I'll smoke a joint or get loaded somehow. My friends will help me do it."

Her drug and alcohol use increase until she sees the world through drug-colored glasses. When she finally comes to treatment at age 25, she is actually 25 going on 15 because she stopped learning about life when she began living behind the drug-brain barrier. Rehabilitation for her will be an intensive crash course on learning how to live. How to get up in the morning; how to tolerate the frustrations of a mediocre boss; how to handle rush-hour traffic; how to flirt and make small talk at a social function that evening; how to move tactfully away from a bore and how to encourage the interest of someone who is more her type.

Killing with Kindness

In earlier chapters there were many letters from wives and some from husbands who clearly were killing their mates with misguided kindness, that is, they were making excuses for them, ignoring or denying obvious signs of trouble. The same is true for parents and children. In other words, there's a big difference between preventing your children from being drunks or drug users and protecting them from the consequences of their own actions—which probably will only promote substance abuse.

Let's look at a couple of examples. If there's a drug bust at school and your daughter is expelled for possession of pot, then coercing the principal to let her back in school may show your daughter a kind of support, but it also promotes her drug use, because she hasn't had to suffer the consequences of her actions. You took the responsibility for her.

Or maybe your son is hauled into jail for being passed out drunk in his car after a beer bash. So you go to pick him up, call the officers "pigs," and your son a victim of police brutality. That makes a handy rationalization for him—he wasn't responsible for the unpleasantnesss—they were.

One of the challenges and necessities of parenting is allowing the child to become responsible for himself or herself, but it's often difficult to walk that fine line between guiding your child versus harmful tampering. This dilemma of all parents brings another case history to mind. One day a man came to my office with his son. The father said, "Doctor, we need your help. I told my son Johnny here that he's going to have to grow up—I won't be around for the rest of his life to continue to help him."

The father was 68, and Johnny was a 49-year-old alcoholic.

Telling Children about the Risks

Of course, admonishing parents not to overprotect their children does not mean that children shouldn't be taught. John and Sylvia express the concerns of many people. "Dear Dr. Pursch," they write, "My wife and I have three children under 15. We are moderate drinkers; we've had no problems with alcohol. How can we advise our children regarding alcohol?''

Dear John and Sylvia: Alcohol is an intoxicating drug and, for some, can lead to the disease alcoholism. As parents you have an obligation to teach your children about risks involved in alcohol use and the potential they have for developing alcoholism.

Drinking is glamorized as sophisticated and macho. That's why your children need correct information from you so that they can develop proper attitudes. They need to learn that every time a person gets drunk, his or her brain is temporarily damaged (just like when you get an anesthetic); and that this impaired mental state often leads to embarrassing, costly, or potentially fatal situations.

For example, being tipsy or drunk makes them overconfident and therefore puts them at high risk for serious sports injuries while they're trying to have fun swimming, hunting, skiing, or even while playing touch football or picnic softball. And the impaired judgment of being drunk exposes them more easily to pregnancy, venereal disease, arrests, fights, and other socially embarrassing or crimial behaviors, all of which can damage their reputations and future careers.

Finally, they need to know that the number one cause of death for 15- to 24-year-olds is auto accidents involving alcohol. The numbers two and three causes of death are homicide and suicide, most of which also involve alcohol.

Teaching the facts is important. But your children's drinking style will be shaped mostly by the example you set—the manner in which you, as parents, use alcohol.

Your children need to see that you always treat alcohol cautiously, that you don't overuse it; that you and your friends can have fun with or without using alcohol. Most importantly, your children need to see that alcohol is not necessary for calming your nerves; that in times of stress you and your wife know how to comfort each other without using alcohol.

As for the disease alcoholism, your children need to learn that genes, at least to some extent, determine who is susceptible. Equally important, your children need to learn that excellent physical health, high innate intelligence or a pleasing personality style don't protect anyone from losing control over his or her drinking or drug using, and thereby becoming addicted.

You have to be up-front with them about how alcohol has affected members of your family—past and present—in the same way you teach them about other familial diseases, such as diabetes, heart disease, or cancer. If there is alcoholism in your family, your children should be encouraged not to drink alcohol, because the child of an alcoholic has a 30 percent chance of developing the disease himself.

Since millions of advertising dollars are spent annually to persuade people to drink, your children will have to be prepared for the negative reactions they will get from other people if they make the decision not to drink. Your children's ability to live by that decision, at least in the beginning, will be influenced by the manner in which they see you treat non-drinking guests in your home.

In the final analysis, example is still the best teacher. Nature drops the apple close to the tree—but nurture shapes the sapling's growth.

A Final Word

Before we set out to teach our children anything, we must necessarily examine our own attitudes. For example, what do I, as a person, really think and feel about abstainers? What is my personal attitude toward drunks? How do I feel about recovering alcoholics? Should they be trusted back on their old jobs? How many recovering addicts do I know? None? How come I don't know any if there are almost two million of them in this country alone?

"Come to think of it," I'm saying to my wife, "we *do* know one. Larry in our personnel division. He started going to AA a few years ago . . . but now I wonder . . . why don't we see Larry and his wife any more? Could it be that we are avoiding him because we are hard drinkers ourselves?"

All of a sudden prevention begins to look very important. Maybe we should teach our children that drinking and other drug use, although socially acceptable, is a high-risk behavior because of the mind-altering and addictive potential of the drugs. Maybe we should teach our children that if they are uncomfortable in the company of abstainers or at a party where there is no booze, then they have a problem. And if, on the other hand, they are comfortable around toxic people or even seek out their company—then both our children *and* their friends have a problem.

You see, if a woman slurs her words or staggers from too much Seconal, she has overdosed; and if a man slurs his words or stumbles from too much alcohol, he also has overdosed. These people need help and treatment because they have lost their freedom.

Lost their freedom? Yes, because true freedom from chemicals is the ability to make a choice—on every occasion—about using or not using. For example, is drinking appropriate for me tonight? And to what extent, in view of what I am planning to do tomorrow morning? The chemically dependent person is not free because he or she can no longer make that choice consistently. Drinking or drug use, at first casual, may soon become unpredictable, then more and more compulsive until eventually a person *has* to use or drink regardless of the dictates òf good sense or reality. The loaded comedian who falls from the stage, the tipsy matron who trips at her son's wedding, and the pregnant woman who "turns on" her captive fetus—they all have lost their freedom of choice. And none of them really wanted this to happen.

So, where do we go from here? We take the first step forward by understanding the following:

Who has chemical dependency?

Millions of us.

Who suffers as a result of chemical dependency?

Most of us.

Who will it take to change it?

All of us.

About the Author

Joseph A. Pursch, M.D., was born in Chicago and raised in
Yugoslavia. He returned to the U.S., where he worked his way
through college as a window washer, graduated from the Indiana
University School of Medicine, and specialized in psychiatry. As a
Navy flight surgeon he served aboard the carrier USS *Forrestal,*
then became director of the Alcohol Rehabilitation Service at the
Navy's Regional Medical Center in Long Beach, California. Dr.
Pursch holds the President's Distinguished Service Award and has
served on both President Carter's Commission on Alcoholism
and President Reagan's Presidential Commission on Drunk Driving. A well-known media personality, Pursch is also a popular
public speaker.

Index

Absent reflexes, 194.

Abstainers, 312.

Abstinence, 6, 20, 73, 78, 88, 118, 200, 201, 204, 222, 275, 288, 295.

Abstinent, 60, 113.

Abstinent drinkers, 211.

Abused child, 142.

Abusive drinking, 19.

Accept reality, 231.

Acetaldehyde, 270.

Acne rosacea, 290.

Addicted athletes, 25, 27.

Addicted doctors, 243.

Addicted to alcohol, 200.

Addiction Research Foundation *Journal*, 240.

Adult Children of Alcoholics, 124, 256, 298.

After care, 284.

After-care followups, 181.

"Age of anxiety", 195.

Al-anon, 3, 34, 60, 99, 105, 109, 110, 111, 124, 131, 155, 157, 158, 159, 163, 164, 165, 171, 175, 180, 194, 215, 246, 252, 255, 256, 257, 283, 284, 285, 290, 291, 294, 297, 298, 301.

Alcohol abuse, 118, 284.

Alcohol dependency, 170.

Alcohol/drug problem, 25.

Alcohol/Drug Rehab Service, 187.

Alcoholic/addict, 98.

Alcoholic daughter, 148.

Alcoholic dependence, 57.

Alcoholic families, 111.

Alcoholic family, 298.

Alcoholic family dynamics, 138.

Alcoholic home, 142.

Alcoholic husband, 161, 288.

Alcoholic lifestyle, 202.

Alcoholic physicians, 259.

Alcoholic rationalization, 45.

Alcoholic rehabilitation, 138, 216, 293, 294.

Alcoholic rehabilitation centers, 293.

Alcoholic treatment farms, 276.

Alcoholic way of life, 283.

Alcoholic wife, 150.

Alcoholic women, 142.

Alcoholics Anonymous (AA), 3, 21, 34, 52, 60, 66, 67, 68, 71, 88, 89, 107, 115, 117, 120, 133, 139, 154, 161, 163, 170, 173, 174, 175, 176, 180, 181, 185, 191, 194, 221, 237, 242, 243, 246, 247, 249, 252, 256, 257, 258, 266, 267, 271, 273, 283, 284, 285, 288, 289, 290, 291, 294, 295, 296, 297, 307, 313.

Alcoholics Anonymous Comes of Age, 242.

Alcoholics' spouses, 163.

Alcoholism as a family disease, 165.

Alcoholism hospital, 295.

Alcoholism recovery hospital, 147.

Alcoholism test, 247.

Alcoholism treatment, 173.

Alcoholism treatment unit, 131.

Alcohol liver test, 191.

Alcohol rehab center, 296.

Alcohol rehabilitation facility, 112.

Alcohol treatment center, 34, 162.

Alcohol treatment facility, 156, 174.

Alcohol withdrawal, 200.

Aldehydes, 221.

Aldomet, 219.

Allopurinal, 206.

Altered blood, 201.

American Medical Association Center for Health Policy Research, 186, 188.

American Medical News, 186.

Amitriptyline, 210.

Analgesia, 222.

Angina pectoris, 212.

Anorexia, 275.

Another Chance, Hope and Health for the Alcoholic Family, 175.

Antabuse, 181, 218, 220, 221, 269, 270, 271, 273, 274, 289, 298, 299.

Antibiotics, 219, 220.

Anti-convulsant drugs, 174.

Anti-depressant medication, 244.

Phenobarbital elixir, 218.
Physically addicted to alcohol, 200,
207.
Physician-addicts, 241.
Placebo, 197.
Placenta, 303, 306.
Polyneuropathy, 210.
Poor blood, 232.
PPD (poor problem drinker), 129,
130.
Pre-dinner drinks, 206.
Pregnancy, 307.
Pregnant, 303, 304.
Pregnant women, 304, 305, 306.
Pre-intervention meeting, 20.
Premature ejaculation, 140.
Prescription drug abuse, 159.
Prescription-narcotic addiction
(among doctors), 241.
President's Commission on Drunk
Driving, 8, 21, 62, 63.
Prevention, 149.
Primary biliary disease, 203.
Problem drinker, 34, 58, 77, 91.
Process of recovery, 287.
Production-line drunks, 2.
Professional intervention, 61.
Prolixin, 210.
Psychoanalytic thinking, 288.
Psychodynamics, 110.
Psychological addiction, 94, 107.
Psychological and physical
dependence, 108.
Psychological dependence, 57, 167,
170.
Psychological disease, 190.
Psychological impairment, 36.
Psychologically addicted, 106, 229.
Psychopath, 95.
Psychopathology, 111.
Psychopaths, 103.
Psychosomatically ill, 124, 291.
Psychosomatic patient, 275.
Psychotherapy, 170.
"Pure alcoholics", 218.

Quaalude, 249, 250, 286.
Quality of sobriety, 158.

Quotes and terms on drinking and
drugs

A pregnant woman never drinks
alone, 305.
attitude change, 140.
beer roulette, 34.
beeraholic, 246.
beyond will power, 128.
big shot, 45.
"big shot airs", 3.
binge-drinker, 67.
"bitter living through chemistry",
30.
"can take it or leave it", 58.
chain of misery, 111.
chemical gourmands, 168, 198.
chemical lover, 140.
chemical turning point, 46.
"choose no booze", 53.
"clean and serene", 53.
"cold turkey", 196, 200, 285, 304.
"cutting down", 33, 40, 79.
deny your limitations, 47.
"detach", 296.
"do it sober", 53.
drinking buddies, 8, 15, 16, 74, 304.
"drinking to relax", 57.
early stage drinking problems, 32.
"easy does it", 53.
"empty nest syndrome", 76.
eye opener, 9, 239.
"falling out of love", 183.
fear of the stigma, 89.
"feeling no feeling", 230.
"feeling no pain", 194, 230.
fired or retired, 75.
first step, 40.
friendly joint, 7.
garbage cans, 168.
"growing up", 31.
"hair of the dog", 211.
"help to help myself", 112.
"here and now", 276.
"hit bottom", 296.
"instant alcoholics", 19.
"it's not okay to use", 53.
killing with kindness, 309.
learn how to deal with feelings, 231.